# UTICA BEER

# UTICA BEER

## A History of Brewing in the Mohawk Valley

Daniel Shumway

Published by American Palate
A Division of The History Press
Charleston, SC 29403
www.historypress.net



*Back cover, lower: Courtesy Kelly Flatebo.*

First published 2014

Manufactured in the United States

ISBN 978.1.62619.338.3

Library of Congress CIP data applied for.

# CONTENTS

# ACKNOWLEDGEMENTS

There are many people who helped me with the research for this book over the years. First of all, I would like to thank my wife, Barb, for encouraging me to pursue my interest in local brewery history and for correcting my English when necessary. Other people that provided help were the librarians of the Utica library, the curators at the Oneida County Historical Society and the curators at Herkimer County Historical Society. They helped me find old city directories and old newspapers on microfilm.

A fellow breweriana collector, Randy Carlson, of Carlson's Brewery Research provided information from his collection of old brewery trade magazines. Another person I must thank is Thomas M. Tryniski, who has created a website called fultonhistory.com that contains over 23,580,000 New York State newspaper pages that he scanned into a pdf format. These files can be searched using key words, which makes finding information about breweries much easier to do. Prior to finding this site, I had to review microfilm page by page and day by day to see if I could find any mention of the local breweries. This was very time-consuming and tiring on the eyes. The Fulton history website allowed me to complete this book quickly and to fill in holes in the stories of the breweries.

I would like to thank the members of the Brewery Collectibles Club of America (BCCA) and the Eastern Coast Breweriana Association (ECBA) who I have met over the last forty years. They have instilled in me a love of brewing and brewery history.

# INTRODUCTION

This book contains the brewing history of Utica, New York, from 1801 to present. Over this period, Utica had forty-four different breweries. During the 1890s, Utica had a peak of ten operating breweries.

In the first chapter, I cover all the very small breweries that started in Utica from 1801 to 1927. These breweries only lasted a very short time or never progressed past the planning stage. They served their products in saloons connected to their breweries and only served the neighborhoods they were located in.

Chapters 2 through 18 cover small to mid-size breweries. Most of these breweries produced lager beer, which had become popular after the 1850s. Ale was still produced by several breweries, but its popularity was on the decline.

Chapters 19 through 23 cover the larger breweries in Utica that took up brewing after Prohibition was repealed. By this time, all the breweries produced both ale and lager.

Top-fermenting yeast is used to produce ale, porter, Weiss beer and common beer. This yeast has been used since early history. Bottom-fermenting yeast is used to produce lager beer. This yeast was discovered and began to be regularly used starting in the 1850s. Lager beer required an extended rest period at cold temperatures, which required breweries to build storage cellars and stock them with ice that was collected from local rivers and lakes during the winter. In the 1870s, artificial refrigeration was made possible by the invention of refrigeration equipment. This eliminated the need for cutting ice in the winter months and extended the brewing season for lager beer.

Utica, New York, is located halfway between Albany and Syracuse in the center of the state. It is located in Oneida County and has a population of approximately sixty-two thousand people. The area was first settled by Europeans around 1773 because the shallowest spot on the Mohawk River was located there. The Iroquois Indians maintained a settlement at the ford for trading purposes.

In 1794, the first road was constructed from Albany, and in 1797, it was continued to the Genesee River to the west. Utica was incorporated as a village in 1798 and became incorporated as a city in 1832. By 1817, Utica had a population of 2,860. Utica, which was on the western frontier, lay on a direct path from Albany through Montgomery County's Noses. This geologic feature is the only break in the Appalachian Mountain chain from New Hampshire to Georgia. This feature made the building of the Erie and Chenango Canals through Utica a logical choice, which in turn increased the traffic through Utica. Following construction of the waterways, railroads were built along the canals, which greatly aided in the shipping of raw materials and the finished beer. Most of the breweries were located either near the canal or a railroad. This aided in shipping the product and acquiring raw materials for the breweries.

As you read the book, you will notice that just about all the breweries suffered from fires over the years. Some were small and put out with not much damage. Others were major events that destroyed most—if not all—of the breweries. In the early years, most breweries were built from wood. As time went on and breweries continued to burn, more and more of them were made of stone and brick. There were three main causes for brewery fires. Early processes required open flames, which were usually left unattended during the night. The fire was kept low but occasionally flared up and jumped from its containment area, and the fire would spread from there. The second cause of fires was embers coming from the smokestack of a passing train. Trains burned wood or coal at the time, and fires along the train routes were fairly common. The final major cause of fires at breweries was arsonists. Some people thought brewing was bad, and they sought to destroy the source. Other arsonists were disgruntled workers who wanted revenge.

From 1910 until the start of national Prohibition in 1920, only five breweries were still in Utica. They were doing well, and most had just built new additions to their breweries. The West End Brewery was the only brewery in Utica to successfully operate during the entire run of Prohibition. It made sodas, sparkling waters, malt syrups and near beers during this time. The other four breweries operated for short periods of time making cider and had some minor troubles with the authorities over the Prohibition law.

With the end of Prohibition in 1933, the West End Brewing Company became the first brewery in the country to obtain its permit to brew full-strength beer. The West End Brewing Company had been making near beer all along, the brewery had properly aged beer all set to go on 12:01 a.m. on April 7, 1933. Near beer was made as full-strength beer and then had the alcohol removed afterward.

With the end of Prohibition, the large national brewers embarked on an expansion program to increase their market share. This was accomplished by buying up failing breweries or ones that did not reopen after Prohibition. Seven years later, World War II began, which rationed much of the raw materials needed to make and package beer. The largest brewers got the largest share of the materials, and many smaller breweries went out of business. Globe, Eagle and Oneida breweries closed, leaving Utica with only two breweries. After the war, the national brewers continued their expansions, and more regional brewers closed. The Utica Brewing Company lasted until 1959, when it merged with West End.

West End continued to fight against the national brewers, and while it was a struggle, the brewery managed to survive through reinvesting in its business, something it had always done. In the 1990s, laws were being changed in many states making it easier for small microbreweries to start up. Compared to many areas, Utica is behind in the microbrewery craze. Utica has only one brewpub at this writing. More and more brewpubs/microbreweries are being created every day.

The Matt Brewery (West End Brewing Company) celebrated its 125th anniversary in 2013, making it the longest-operating brewery in Utica. The Matt Brewery is continuing its long history of investing back into its business, and in 2014, it plans on adding a beer garden and a building for fermenting and aging tanks. The only other brewery in Utica to last over one hundred years was the Oneida Brewing Company, which operated from 1832 to 1942, a period of 110 years. The brewing history of Utica has been interesting over the years and shows how a well-run business can last through all types of adversity.

# CHAPTER 1
# VERY SMALL UTICA BREWERIES
## 1801–1927

Most early brewers ran their breweries from their residences. These were small affairs that produced ale mainly for sale at the saloons run by the brewer. They bought their supplies from local farmers and their barrels, horses and wagons from local craftsmen.

The earliest mention of a person in the brewing profession was in 1801. Aylmer Johnson was listed as a brewer in the 1801 *Oneida County Gazetteer*. There is no indication of where he brewed his beer, but it was probably in his home.

Deacon Joseph Howard was one of the earliest pioneers in the brewing industry in Oneida County. Around 1802, Deacon Howard erected a brewery at Franklin Furnace near Clayville and engaged a Frenchman named John Turongo as the brewmaster.

James Ure built a brewery near where Nail Creek crossed Varick Street in 1803. He was a Methodist minister and regularly held religious meetings at the brewery. In 1804, he sold the brewery to E. Smith and Captain Aylmer Johnson but remained as a partner. Smith and Johnson named the new company E. Smith & Co., Brewers. The new partnership lasted until April 1805, when Smith decided to run off with all of the company's money. As a result, Ure retook control of the business and brought William Alverson in as a partner. Things went well for a few years, but in 1811, the brewery and four and a half acres of land were sold.

In 1804, William Inman built a brewery in Utica at the corner of Broadway and Whitesboro Streets. Inman, the father of Henry Inman, a noted early American painter, was an aristocratic, well-to-do Englishman who possessed a strong temper. His beer was English ale, brewed in the traditional manner of the British. His product was of such quality that it beat Schenectady beer, which, at the time, was rated the best around and sold for the staggering sum of five dollars a barrel—a fortune in those days.

About 1813, Inman decided to leave Utica for New York City. His brewery seems to have been temporarily without a business successor, for in August 1813, the local newspaper carried an announcement of the presentation of a few "Moral Plays" by Mr. Barnard at Utica's new Temporary Theatre, which was housed in Inman's brewery. During this time, Inman's brewery was also called the Utica Brewery.

The earliest directory of the village of Utica was published in 1817. That directory listed Utica as having two breweries: the Utica Brewery mentioned above and Thomas Harden's brewery, which was also located on the corner of Broadway and Whitesboro Streets. The date when Harden built his brewery is unknown. Thomas Harden died, and the brewery was passed on to his son, John. On February 20, 1827, around 12:30 a.m., it was discovered that the brewery was on fire. The brewery and John Harden's house burned to the ground

Joseph Goodliff purchased a lot, commonly known as the brewery lot, from Jeremiah Van Resselaer on September 30, 1818. He paid $1,500 for the lot, which was 150 feet wide by 144.5 feet deep. It was located in the northwest corner of Varick and what would later become Edwards Street. On this lot, he operated a brewery and malt house producing common beer exclusively. In March 1823, a fire swept through the brewery and malt house, destroying must of the building. He only had a small insurance policy on his stock, but he managed to rebuild the brewery and malt house.

Goodliff sold the brewery lot to his son, Joseph B. Goodliff, for $1,500 on October 2, 1830. Joseph B. was thirty years old at the time and had been working with his father for years. Around this time, the Goodliffs stopped brewing to concentrate on the malting business. By 1832, they were malting five thousand bushels per year. By 1850, the value of the property was listed at $4,000. Around 1843, Joseph B. Goodliff was listed as a brewer again, with his father still listed as a maltster. This endeavor as a brewer lasted until 1849, when Joseph B. returned to being a maltster like his father.

In 1853, Joseph B.'s interest in the brewery lot was sold at a sheriff's sale to his son Allen A. Goodliff for $375. It may be that Joseph B. was having some sort of financial difficulties. Joseph Goodliff Sr. died on July 19, 1853, at the age of eighty-two years and eleven months. Joseph B. continued with the business in the same location. Allen A. Goodliff and his wife sold the brewery lot to Ellen E. Goodliff for $300 in 1855. She was probably the daughter or sister of Allen. Joseph B. remained a maltster for the rest of his life, working until his death in 1881 at the age of eighty-one.

In 1828, Edward Bright operated a brewery on Varick Street near Hamilton. He brewed common beer, porter and Burton ale, producing 1,500 barrels annually. In 1831, Bright offered to lease his brewery on Nail Creek with a dwelling house and attached yard. He stated that the brew and malt house were well constructed and came with equipment capable of brewing fifty barrels of beer per week. He also said that the cellar was spacious, the water excellent and there was no brewery in Utica or its vicinity that had been in operation for years besides this one. Bright was apparently unsuccessful in leasing his brewery and converted it to a tannery in 1832. By 1834, Bright was no longer listed as living in Utica.

J. Bedbury was listed as a brewer in 1829. He resided at Lafayette and Seneca Streets. By 1832, he is listed as a grocer. The Gulf Brewery was the only other brewery operating at the time, and its history is told in a chapter of its own.

New York State had a prohibition law from 1855 to 1856 that prevented the sale of beer in the state. It could still be manufactured, which kept the established brewers in the state in business, as they could export their beer. Once Prohibition ended in 1857, a few new breweries were started in the area with varying degrees of success.

William V. Collins operated a brewery at 62 Broad Street from 1857 to 1858. He produced porter and ale. In 1859, he gave up brewing and opened a saloon at 39 Bleecker Street.

The French Brewery, located at 118 Columbia Street, was built and operated by George Richards in 1858. This brewery produced lager beer exclusively and lasted until 1868.

In 1860, Michael Remmer started a brewery and saloon at 58 Court Street. He produced lager beer, which was sold at his saloon. Prior to opening his brewery, Mr. Remmer was listed as a carpenter and grocer. The brewery and saloon remained in business until 1865. That year, he sold the saloon and moved to a house at the corner of Court and Fay Streets. The new owners of the saloon did not maintain the brewery. Mr. Remmer went back to carpentry and died the following year.

In 1861, Joseph Denk operated a small brewery at 17 Erie Street. The brewery produced lager beer and remained in operation until 1865. Unable to make a living brewing beer, Mr. Denk became a whitewasher.

WILLIAM V. COLLINS,
MANUFACTURER OF
PORTER, ALE AND SUMMER BEVERAGES.
NO. 62 BROAD STREET.
FAMILIES SUPPLIED AT SHORT NOTICE.

Ad from the 1857–58 *Utica City Directory*.

John M. Hahn, who ran a grocery and provision store at 234 Whitesboro Street, started brewing lager beer at his establishment in 1862. This endeavor only lasted one year before he went back to being just a grocer.

Henry H. Haworth, the proprietor of the Corn Hill House, located at 34 South Street since 1861, operated an ale brewery on the premises from 1862 to 1864, after which he opened a grocery store at the site.

In early 1879, Charles Gammel started a Weiss Bier brewery at the corner of Chenango Avenue and Newell Street, between locks 6 and 7 on the Chenango canal. At 9:30 p.m. on Saturday, July 31, 1879, a fire was discovered in the brewery. The fire department arrived at 10:05 p.m. and laid 1,400 feet of hose from the nearest fire hydrant. By that time, the fire was beyond control, and the buildings, with the exception of a barn, were totally destroyed. The fire was thought to be set by an arsonist.

Gammel had closed the brewery at 6:30 p.m. and left it in charge of George Landvogt, his brewer, who slept in the building. Landvogt went to town and did not return until around 10:00 p.m. Robbers entered the brewery through a window, took some money and set the building on fire. The building was constructed in 1877 but was not used as a brewery until 1879. The brewery had a capacity of three thousand bottles daily but was not run to its full capacity. Gammel's loss was estimated to be $8,500. He had only $2,500 of insurance.

The next small brewery in Utica didn't come about until 1889. Frank Schwab started Schwab's Hall and Lager Beer Brewery, Saloon, and Restaurant at 46 Varick Street. The enterprise only lasted one year, and nothing else is known about it.

Three small breweries started up during the 1890s. Christian F. Frey operated a brewery at the corner of Grand and Avery Avenues but was out of business by 1897. Chas. W. Sharp & Co. started a brewery in 1893 and also bottled beer at this time. In May 1897, a number of Uticans were considering the advisability of forming a new brewery. They chose the name "The American Brewing Co." and planned on incorporating with a capital stock of $100,000. A site for the brewery was also said to have been chosen, but the plans never came to pass.

The final mention of a new brewery in Utica before Prohibition came in March 1911. Anselm Mlynarczyk, the editor of the *Spiritual Hammer*, a religious newspaper, proposed building a new brewery in Utica called the Polish Brewery. He was a stockholder in several breweries in Pennsylvania and declared that breweries were good investments. He indicated that there were large Polish communities in all the major cities in central New York. He believed that building a brewery in Utica, which was centrally located, would be a great investment, as shipping would be minimized. He felt that a capital investment of $48,000 would be required and that there would be enough interest to give it a good start. This never got out of the planning stages.

# CHAPTER 2
# BIERBAUER BREWERY

## 1850–1852

Charles Bierbauer was born in Einselthum, Rhenish, Bavaria, on February 18, 1818, and learned the art of brewing in Munich, Vienna and other large cities. He came to this country in 1848 and settled in Lyons, New York.

In 1850, he married Barbara Strohm and moved to Utica. He purchased a tract of land on Third Street in the "Gulf" (at the point where Mary Street crossed Third Street) from Michael Devereux. Bierbauer erected a brewery on this property with capital of less than $3,000, the greater part of which was furnished by his father-in-law, Michael Strohm.

Around Christmastime in 1850, he offered for sale the first glass of lager beer ever brewed in Utica. Prior to this time, all the breweries in Utica had brewed ale exclusively. When he began brewing in Utica, lager beer was looked at as exclusively a German drink and wasn't very popular. For a long time, he furnished nearly all the lager that was drank in Utica. The quality of his product did much to make this drink popular. Bierbauer was very civic minded. He was one of the oldest members of the German Literary Society and took an active interest in the German Free School while it existed. Although Bierbauer understood English, he rarely spoke anything but German. He had a German's love of his mother tongue, of his home and of sociality, and he made many friends. He was always ready to aid the afflicted and distressed, particularly those of his own nationality. He was frank and openhearted and detested all kinds of con artists.

He operated this brewery at 93 Third Street for two years before selling it to Peter Vidvard in 1852 and starting another brewery on the other side of town. Charles Hutten purchased this property in 1855 from Vidvard and operated the brewery at 93 Third Street until the 1890s.

# CHAPTER 3
# WEST SIDE BREWERY
## 1853–1885

In 1852, Charles Bierbauer sold his brewery on Third Street and briefly operated a brewery in a house he rented on South Hamilton Street in west Utica. Next, he purchased six lots on Edward Street from Alrick Hubbell in 1853 and erected what was called the West Utica Brewery. He also conducted a very popular inn and biergarten on the premises. It was at this inn that the Utica Maennerchor was supposed to have been organized in 1866, as Bierbauer was one of the founders. The brewery made around two thousand barrels of lager annually, which found a ready market in Utica.

On July 19, 1860, a suit was brought against Charles Bierbauer by the Commissioners of Excise accusing him of producing a very intoxicating beverage and therefore encouraging drunkenness. After hearing the evidence, the jury could not reach a decision, so the charges were dismissed. The evidence was conflicting, and a great deal was sworn to on both sides. Some of the witnesses had drank lager beer for years and said it did not intoxicate them. Others swore that the alcohol in lager beer was just as intoxicating as brandy. The matter was dropped for the moment. A commentary in the newspaper said, "We must henceforth believe that the brawls, and shouting and reveling, which nightly take place in lager bier saloons, and shock the ear of the passer by with their Babel din, are all the work of sober men, who have only been swilling lager bier."

By 1870, the value of the brewery was $13,000. Bierbauer had extensive cellars that were completely underground, which enabled him to keep his lager at peak condition.

**West Utica Lager Beer Brewery,**
No. 5 EDWARD STREET,
By CHARLES BIERBAUR,
CITY AND COUNTRY TRADE SUPPLIED TO ORDER.
Orders by letter promptly attended to.
TERMS CASH.

Ad from 1864 *Utica City Directory*.

Bierbauer did not brew at all during the summer months, believing that the beer manufactured in warm weather could not meet the high standard he established for his beer.

On December 20, 1873, a beer cask exploded, severely injuring two men at the brewery. Large casks were used to hold beer while it was stored in the cooling vaults. These casks held from four to twenty barrels each. They were pitched on the inside by experienced coopers to prevent the beer from coming in contact with the wood. Bierbauer had hired William Dormer, a cooper, a few days before. Dormer and Buege (a laborer) were at work at the time of the accident, while Bierbauer stood nearby. They had poured the pitch through a boiler-iron funnel, inserted in the bunghole of the cask, and were just rolling the cask to spread the pitch evenly when the head of the cask blew out, causing a loud report. Fire and smoke issued from the cask. Bierbauer extinguished the flames with wood ashes and turned to enter the house when he saw that the explosion had knocked over the two men, who were lying on the ground, unable to move. They were carried into the house, and doctors were called.

The head of the cask was over two inches thick and made of oak plank. Dormer's right arm was badly torn, and his head and limbs were severely injured. Buege's foot was mangled with oak splinters and would probably need to be amputated. Dormer was taken to Syracuse that afternoon on a litter. Bierbauer ordered that the best medical assistance be given them.

The explosion occurred in the yard, which was bounded by wooden buildings, an embankment and picket fence. The cask head was torn to pieces. Several windows were broken, bricks were shaken from chimneys and glass was rattled about in all directions. The iron funnel was thrown to the top of one of the buildings, where it was found bent like a dilapidated old hat.

Bierbauer's forty years of experience as a brewer could not explain why the accident happened. He said the cask was dry, having stood for months with others in a barn. The only possible explanation seems to be that snow may have been accidentally dropped into the barrel against the hot pitch. This would have caused the explosion, or ice may have formed in the cask by condensation or from the dripping of water into the cask.

The brewery produced 735 barrels of lager in 1874 and 848 barrels in 1875. By 1877, the brewery increased production to 1,740 barrels of lager beer. Bierbauer was definitely making a good product. As word spread, his production steadily increased.

An 1874 article stated that though Germans love lager beer, you rarely see a German drunk. Bierbauer said he kept track of the number of glasses he drank one day, and it totaled forty-eight. He indicated that he hadn't felt very thirsty that day either. Most Germans contended that lager was not intoxicating.

In 1878, F.X. Matt I came to work for Bierbauer in Utica. The following year, he went to Canajoharie, New York, to work for Charles Bierbauer's brother Louis, who had greater need for his services at this time. This was great training for young Matt, as he got to work under two experienced master brewers.

Charles Bierbauer went to Herkimer to visit friends on December 25, 1879. As he got off the train and was crossing the street, he was knocked down and run over by a horse and sleigh. Bierbauer sustained severe injuries about the face. A doctor was summoned who treated Bierbauer for his injuries, after which he returned to Utica. He recovered completely after a week.

In 1884, the brewery, which was located between Edward Street and Nail Creek, consisted of various two-story buildings, including a brew house wood kiln, icehouse and a wagon shed, many of which had underground storage cellars. The brewery equipment was powered by horses, and the brew kettle was wood fired. Mathias Wangler, an employee at the brewery, slipped and fell into a tub of boiling water on April 20, 1884. Severely scalded, he died two days later.

While she was married to Charles, Barbara Bierbauer spent most of her life in a brewery and saloon. She never drank beer or any other intoxicant unless it was prescribed by a physician. Through her influence, nothing

Utica, N.Y., July 28. 1874.

M Utica Männerchor

To CHARLES BIERBAUER, Dr.

Manufacturer of

LAGER BEER,

Terms: No. 5 EDWARD STREET, UTICA, N.Y.

July 22. 1874. 79 Keg Bier a $275 $217.25

Obigen Betrag erhalten zu haben bescheinigt

C. Bierbauer

A letterhead from the Bierbauer's West Side Brewery from 1874. *Author's collection.*

West Side Brewery photo taken in 1876. *Author's collection.*

stronger than lager was ever sold in her husband's saloon. Charles Bierbauer developed lung troubles in October 1883. His health got steadily worse over the next several years.

On August 17, 1885, Charles Bierbauer died at his home in Utica at the age of sixty-eight. His wife, Barbara, and adopted son George were unable to continue managing the brewery and consequently put it up for sale a few months later. The brewery was purchased and run as the Columbia Brewing Company briefly before becoming the West End Brewing Company in 1888.

# CHAPTER 4
# HUTTEN'S LAFAYETTE BREWERY
## 1855–1891

One of the earliest lager beer breweries in the Utica area was started by Charles Hutten in the 1850s. Charles Hutten was born on July 31, 1829, in Friedichshafen, Wittenburg, Germany. When he was old enough, he was apprenticed to the brewing trade and became very knowledgeable in the business. He came to America in 1853 and was employed as a foreman in a Brooklyn brewery. Two years later, his father, John G. Hutten, followed him to this country and bought a farm at North Bay on Oneida Lake. Charles joined his father on the farm until 1855, when he came to Utica and got a job at the old Third Avenue brewery, then owned by Peter Vidvard and originally owned by Charles Bierbauer.

In late 1855, John and Charles Hutten moved to Utica and purchased the brewery. Father and son ran the brewery together until John Hutten died in the late 1860s. Charles then took over the brewery himself. The brewery, which was officially located at 93 Third Avenue, changed its name to the Lafayette Brewery sometime after Charles Hutten took over.

In 1874, Utica possessed two lager beer breweries: Hutten's and Bierbauer's. The Hutten brewery employed a large force of men in the manipulation of the brewery apparatus and was able to produce large quantities of lager beer. Production at the brewery in 1874 was 2,158 barrels. This dropped to 1,500 barrels in 1875 before steadily increasing to 2,034 barrels of lager in 1877.

He produced three varieties of bier (beer) known as old stock, bock bier and present use. The stock bier was milder and more pleasant to the

HUTTEN'S
BOCK
BEER!
CAN BE HAD OF HIS CUSTOMERS
FOR THE NEXT TWO WEEKS.

*Left*: Ad from *Utica Daily Press*, April 1889.

*Below*: Ad from the *Utica Daily Press*, July 1891.

HUTTEN'S
Lafayette Brewery.
93 THIRD STREET,
UTICA, N. Y.

taste than the present use variety. Bock bier used a larger proportion of malt and resulted in a beverage that was much more intoxicating than the regular lager.

The brewery sold 2,393 barrels of lager beer in 1879, making it the fourth-largest brewery in the Utica area. Hutten's lager was famous for its strong hop flavor.

In 1884, the brewery consisted of a two-story brew house, three icehouses and several other buildings. Power was generated by coal-fired steam, with heat provided by coal stoves and light by candles. Six people were employed at this time. During the 1880s, the brewery sold about three thousand barrels each year. A large subcellar, 130 feet long by 32 feet wide, was built for storage purposes and became one of the attractions of the brewery.

One small building was added to the brewery by 1888, and some improvements were made to the interior of the brewery. Kerosene oil lamps replaced the previous candlelight.

Charles Hutten died on Wednesday, August 20, 1890, at the age of sixty-one. He had been sick for about one year. Hutten's wife ran the brewery for another year until it was sold at public auction on August 25, 1891. The sale was conducted on the steps of the courthouse by court-appointed referee R.O. Jones. The high bid was $1,000 from John C. Metzger of Ilion.

Hutten's brewery became the Lafayette Brewing Company (1891–96) and then became the Consumer's Brewing Company of Utica (1896–1902).

# CHAPTER 5
# UTICA STAR ALE BREWING COMPANY

## 1873–1901

In 1873, J. Myres & Co.'s Utica Brewery was formed by John J. Myres, James O'Toole, John Quinn and Thomas Quinn. Prior to forming the new company, Myres (alternately spelled "Myers") had been the brewmaster for the Gulf Brewery for forty years. The other members of the firm were experienced brewers who had worked for various other breweries in the city. The brewery was opened on July 4, 1874, on the corner of Mohawk and Jay Streets in Utica. John Myres was the brother-in-law of the Quinns and served as the brewmaster. In 1875, the brewery produced 3,811 barrels of ale, which was quite good for its first full year of operation.

The brewery turned out ale, old stock and porter. All work was done by hand. In 1879, the brewery sold 8,331 barrels of ale and porter, making it the largest brewery in the Utica area. By 1881, it had increased its sales to 12,870 barrels a year, remaining the leader in the city. The brewery was proving to be very profitable.

In 1884, the brewery was renamed the Utica Star Ale Brewery. The old wood framed brew house was razed to make room for a new three-story brick building. Other buildings included a two-story icehouse, a one-story shed/cooperage and one other two-story building. Power and heat were provided by steam and stoves. Lighting consisted of kerosene oil lamps, which were seldom used, with most of the work being done during the daylight hours. The fermenting tanks were located in the cellar, storage tanks and offices on the first floor, malt mill and mash tubs on the second floor and water tanks and boiling kettle on the third floor. Annual capacity at the brewery was ten thousand barrels a year. During 1885, the brewery added a two-and-a-half-story frame barn, eighty by sixty feet, with a twelve- by sixteen-foot wing. The barn faced Jay Street and cost $1,800.

A two-year-old girl was run over and killed by a wagon from the Utica Star Brewery on August 20, 1895. The little girl was playing in the street near her house. When the brewery delivery wagon, heavily loaded, came along, another wagon stood in the roadway, and the driver of the brewery was obliged to rein his horses close to the little girl's house in order to pass. In doing so, he did not notice the child, who was knocked down by the horses, and the front wheels passed over her head and neck. A jury found that the girl's death was accidental and that the driver did not do anything wrong.

In 1886, the brewery commissioned Thomas C. Vein & Co. to do some remodeling. A second story was added to the brew house, and other improvements were made, costing $2,000. The same firm built two houses for Mrs. Myres for $2,000 each. A new barley mill was installed in March 1886. The mill was made by Parsons & Co. of Philadelphia, and it removed the core and other foreign substances from the malt, in addition to grinding, dusting and screening.

By 1888, the brewery consisted of a four-story building, eighty feet square. In addition to this, there were barns, sheds and cooper shops. The complex was operated by steam power generated from a twelve-horsepower engine. The brewery employed fifteen men and had four delivery wagons for making city deliveries. With a capacity of seventy-five barrels daily, the brewery distributed its product throughout Central New York by canal and rail. A one-story addition to the brew house was made in the 1890s.

In September 1888, the four owners of the Utica Star Ale Brewery formed the Eagle Brewing Company to make use of modern methods of brewing rather than revamp the Utica Star Ale Brewing Company. The Utica Star Ale Brewing Company continued to make ale, and the new Eagle Brewing Company made lager beer.

John Myres died on April 20, 1891, after a long illness. Thomas Quinn died the following year. The Utica Star Ale Brewing Company continued to be operated by J. Myres & Co. under the leadership of John Myres widow, Mary; John O'Toole; John Quinn; and Thomas Quinn's widow.

In 1897 and 1898, the brewery produced between eight thousand and ten thousand barrels of ale and porter. Edward E. Taylor was brewmaster and remained in that position until the brewery closed in 1901.

In December 1899, the local papers ran an article about a price war between Utica and Syracuse brewers who were selling beer in Utica. John

Quinn responded on behalf of the brewery, stating, "There is nothing in the story of a war between brewers, and I cannot account for the circulation of such a yarn. Every barrel of beer the Star brewery sends out is worth $6, and that's what we get for it. Bartel has sold beer in Utica for several years. His agency is not a new one." Bartel was a major Syracuse brewer.

On February 8, 1900, Edward Taylor died at his home from Bright's disease. He had worked at the brewery for the previous thirty-three years, twenty-seven of them as a brewmaster. He was born in Utica and was married with eight small children.

James O'Toole, the brewery manager, died on March 28, 1900, at his home. He was born in County Tipperary, Ireland, and came to America when he was twenty-one. He worked in Utica at Hopkins & Lane grocers for many years before he became one of the incorporators of the Utica Star Ale Brewing Company. He was then one of the incorporators of the Eagle Brewing Company.

After his death, the brewery building was utilized as a storehouse by a paper box company. In September 1909, the R.J. Evans Company, real estate agents, sold the Star brewery for Miss Quinn, Mrs. Myres, Miss McGrath and Mrs. Mary Quinn to Anton Tomaino and his wife. Tomaino wanted to erect a three-story apartment house with stores on the ground floor. The brewery buildings were torn down in April 1910, and the brewery passed in history.

## CHAPTER 6

# MOHAWK VALLEY BREWING COMPANY

## 1880–1882

In early 1880, local Utica-area businesses began canvassing capitalists for encouragement in carrying out a project establishing a lager brewing company in Utica. The success of similar enterprises in Rochester, Syracuse and Albany was the motivating force behind the endeavor. It was felt that Utica had the required population base along with the pure water and abundance of ice necessary for a lager brewery. At the time, Utica was also the headquarters for distributing the hops used for brewing in all parts of the world.

Utica already contained several breweries that produced lager, most notably the brewery of Charles Bierbauer and the brewery of Charles Hutten. They were producing lager in moderate quantities and were steadily building up a profitable business.

The local businessmen were proposing to establish a first-class lager brewing company with capital stock of $100,000. Among the people who expressed interest in the project were General James McQuade, W. Jermone Green, A.D. Barber, Thomas R. Thomas, Nicholas G. Kernan, Thomas J. Griffiths, Jacob Faass, John Carton, Daniel N. Crouse, Joseph R. Swan and Jacob Schwab.

By early June 1880, $50,000 of the capital stock was subscribed for. The manufacturing boom in Utica was in full swing, and the project was rapidly being pursued.

On June 6, articles of incorporation were filed in the county clerk's office for the formation of the Mohawk Valley Brewing Company. The documents indicated that the brewery would continue in business for fifty years and would brew lager beer. The capital stock would be $100,000 divided into one hundred shares at $1,000 each.

The trustees for the first year were W. Jermone Green, James McQuade, Amaziah D. Barber, Milton H. Thomson, Robert Middleton, John Carton and Jacob Schwab. The incorporators of the company included T. Jay Griffiths, Thomas R. Thomas, Miles C. Comstock, Joseph R. Swan Jr., Joseph Faass, Theodore P. Ballou and T.O. Grannis, in addition to the previously mentioned trustees. On June 7, the following people were elected as officers of the company: John Carton, president; Jacob Schwab, secretary; and W. Jermone Green, treasurer. The remaining stock was offered to the public at the office of Green & Son, Bankers starting on June 8.

The firm authorized Daniel N. Crouse, who was traveling in Europe, to secure the services of a first-class lager beer brewer for the company. The success of the project so far was attributed to the efforts of Nicholas G. Kernan, who was the leading force of the movement. He had secured the backing of many of Utica's leading businessmen.

All of the capital stock of the company was subscribed for by noon on June 23. George Ralph Jr. of the Oneida Brewery took $5,000 worth, and Hugh Glenn, of Glenn & Manning, closed out the last shares at $4,500. It was felt that there would be no problem securing another $50,000 worth of shares if needed.

The directors of the company now had to find a location for the brewery and hire an architect to build it. F.W. Wolf of Chicago, a well-known brewery architect, was chosen to design the brewery. He arrived in Utica on July 1 to begin searching for a site.

A meeting was held at Bagg's Hotel on July 24 with the architect and prominent members of the company. They had visited various sites in East and West Utica, one north of the Erie Canal and near the Central Railroad tracks, another south of the canal, and one near the Chenango Canal and Asylum. It was claimed that the supply of spring water in the western location was a great advantage, but many of the stockholders preferred the eastern portion of the city. Architect Wolf did not favor the western site. A decision was made to explore additional sites before a final decision was made. The site for the new brewery was selected during the third week of August.

The brewery was to be located between the Erie Canal and the Central Railroad, on the north side of the canal, nearly opposite Wild & Devereux's Knitting Mill and a few hundred feet west of the site of the Mohawk Valley Cotton Mills. The area of the site encompassed three acres, along with an eighty-foot strip of frontage on the south side of the canal. The canal would be crossed by a bridge that would be used for transporting materials and beer between the brewery and the city. The Central Railroad Company agreed to connect the brewery to its tracks with a branch. This gave the brewery first-class railroad and canal facilities for handling its coal, grain, beer and barrels.

The land was purchased from Thomas and James Morehead, Elia Pelleteri and A.B. Johnson for $4,850. The site was approximately 540 feet by 250 feet. F.J. Wolf made his fourth trip to Utica on August 26 to review the site purchased by the company. He was pleased with it and stated that he could have the plans finished within ten days of receiving the order. The brewery could be built and operating in three months.

In early September, the company decided it was too late to begin construction and that it would wait until spring. During the winter, the company would make contracts for materials and machinery.

On September 29, Architect Wolf forwarded a sketch of the ground plan for the new brewery to W. Jermone Green. The plan showed a building shaped like a capital letter E, except that the centerpiece (the boiler house) was not connected to the main building. The long side of the E faced the towpath and canal. Starting at the west end of the building, the plan included the following: a grain elevator 50 by 36 feet in the northwest corner, a steep tank room about the same size and a 100- by 50-foot malt room in the northeast corner. The upper floors were strengthened by a double row of columns. Adjoining the malt house and facing the canal were two malt storage apartments, 24.5 by 20 feet; a 20.5-foot wash house with an engine room in the rear; a 30.5-foot brew house; a 20-foot driveway; an office; and a spare icehouse. In the rear of the brew house and forming the eastern end of the building were the two main icehouses, 35 by 96 feet, with double walls. The 50- by 36-foot boiler house and main chimney were located within the two ends of the main building. A branch track from the Central Railroad was to be built next to the grain elevator and icehouses.

A space of six feet was left between the main front and the towpath. Opposite the driveway, an eighty-foot swing bridge with a windlass and pivot was to be constructed. A statue of Gambrinus was to be placed on one of the archways going over the driveway.

The finalized brewery plans arrived in early December and were on display in the offices of Charles Green & Son. At the annual stockholders meeting held on January 13, 1881, some of the stockholders expressed concern with continuing the project. Apparently, quite a few of them were ready to back out of the project for one reason or another. Another meeting was called for April 2 to act on the question of reducing the capital stock from $100,000 to $80,000.

On April 20, it was announced that no brewery would be built in 1881. No reasons were given for that decision. By August, the brewery was placed in receivership. W.P. Carpenter was placed in charge of closing the company. On August 27, he filed a bond in the county clerk's office.

Several of the original investors still wanted to build a brewery and decided that Binghamton offered a good location. The John Ehresman & Co. Brewery was thus started, lasting until Prohibition.

A meeting of the creditors was held at the office of W.P. Carpenter on November 3 to settle all accounts against the brewery. Carpenter had about $2,000 cash on hand belonging to the company. The real estate owned by the company was to be sold at auction later that month.

The land was sold by the end of the year. Carpenter rendered his final account on March 13, 1882, and the company was legally and officially history.

# CHAPTER 7
# UTICA BREWING COMPANY
## 1880–1893

In 1879, Charles Winslow, Frank Moore, Edward Callahan and Martin McGarvey erected a brewery under the firm name of Winslow, Moore & Co. Other partners in the firm were John Coyne, Michael Hand and Patrick McNierney. The brewery was located on the corner of South and St. Vincent Streets. At that time, St. Vincent Street ended at South Street and did not continue on as it does today.

The brewery was a large three-story wooden building. The first floor contained an office in the front with a storage room in the back. The brew kettles were located on the first floor next to the storage area. The second floor contained the malt room and a storage area. The third floor was largely used for storage. There were several detached buildings that held the cooper shop and the stables, located at the rear of the property.

On April 13, 1881, Callahan, McGarvey and Moore left the brewery to start their own in Syracuse. The Utica Brewing Company sold 7,481 barrels of beer in 1881, making it the third-largest brewery in the area. Only the Oneida and J. Myres breweries sold more beer that year.

On April 18, 1882, articles of incorporation for the Utica Brewing Company were filed in the county clerk's office. The capital stock was set at $16,000. The incorporators were Charles Winslow, John Coyne, Patrick McNierney, Michael Hand and Martin F. McNierney. Charles Winslow was elected president, with Michael Hand serving as manager.

An 1884 map shows that two one-story additions had been made to the brewery. The company's business had increased significantly, and as a result, it was necessary to enlarge the brewery. A wing was built on the east side and the building extended in the rear. The capacity of the brewery was doubled. The new additions contained the engine and boiler rooms and additional storage. By 1884, the brewery employed twelve men. Heat was supplied by coal stoves, and the lights were either gas or oil. There were four large water tanks on the third floor and three on the second floor. On April 9, 1884, the stockholders of the brewery voted to increase the capital stock from $16,000 to $40,000.

On April 23, 1886, the annual meeting of the brewery was held. Michael Hand had left the firm to start his own brewery in another state. He was replaced as vice-president by Patrick McNierney. McNierney continued in his capacity as brewery manager. The annual report for 1886 showed the brewery with $41,338.62 of capital stock paid in and $150.00 of debt. This was a good indication of how well the brewery was doing.

In 1888, the liabilities of the brewery had increased to $326. A map of the brewery property shows that several of the outbuildings, such as the cooper shop and barn, were changed significantly. A fence was added around the perimeter of the brewery, which was now powered by steam. On November 8, 1888, Martin F. McNierney died of pneumonia. He had been the brewery's bookkeeper since 1880.

By 1890, the brewery had debts of $3,500, which was still well below most of its competitors. On May 23, a wheel came off one of the brewery's delivery wagons as it traveled down Eagle Street. The contents were spilled and impeded traffic for a short time.

During the summer of 1890, when representatives of an English brewing syndicate were in the city for the purpose of buying up the Utica breweries, the entire plant of the Utica Brewing Company was offered to them for $100,000. The price was finally brought down to $90,000, but the figure was still considered too high. The representatives declined the offer and left without buying any of the breweries.

Business continued to increase, and in the spring of 1891, it became necessary to make further improvements to the plant. New and modern equipment was installed by the summer. The first floor of the building and wing were used as an office, storeroom and fermenting room. On the second floor were the malt room and more storage rooms. The third floor contained the hop storeroom and the cold- and hot-water vats. The plant was considered the most complete in the city at that time. The company usually brewed three times a week and sold about 850 barrels of beer a month.

Just prior to this expansion, Charles Winslow had become ill. On Friday, May 8, he died at the age of fifty-three. Shortly after his death, people living near the Utica and National Brewing Companies complained to the health department about the stench coming from the nearby gulf. They claimed that the breweries were draining wastes directly into it. This was not the first time the complaint was made. The breweries had claimed in the past that there was no sewer that they could tie into, and as a result, they had to dump into the gulf. A sewer line had been constructed in the area earlier that year, but neither brewery had bothered to hook into it.

On May 6, the health officer directed Sanitary Inspector Casey to go to the breweries and notify the proprietors that legal proceedings would be instituted unless they corrected the problem. At the Board of Health meeting on May 7, Inspector Casey reported that the Utica Brewing Company had connected to the sewer but was still allowing wastewater to run into the gulf. The National Brewing Company was still running all its waste and foul water directly into the gulf. The Board of Health gave both breweries until May 21 to correct the problems. The National Brewing Company was the first to comply. The Utica Brewing Company plans were interrupted by the death of its president, Charles Winslow, on May 8, but it was in compliance by June 4, to everyone's satisfaction.

On July 21, 1891, shortly after 4:30 p.m. while employees of the brewery were at work in the three-story frame building, one of them, Frank Winslow, noticed smoke issuing from the eaves on the south side of the main structure. He immediately notified the rest of the employees of the fire, and a bucket brigade was formed to fight the flames. Charles Winslow Jr., his brother, who was working at the malt press, ran immediately to the city hospital and sent in the alarm.

In the meantime, the employees of the National Brewing Company, located across the street, attached a hose to their engine and soon had a large stream of water pouring on the flames. When the fire chief arrived, he immediately sent in a second alarm. The fire was a hot one that burned rapidly. The flames surrounded the structure, and it was soon clear that it would be impossible to save the burning building. Five streams of water were directed on the flames. By 5:30 p.m., the effect of the great volume of water poured into the building was apparent, and the fire was finally brought under control. Ladders could then be placed against the building, and the fire was completely extinguished by 6:30 p.m.

At one time, it was feared that the boiler would explode, but the fire was pulled out from under it in time, and the valves were opened to allow the steam to escape without danger. During the progress of the fire, one of the large cold-water tanks on the third floor of the building fell through to the first floor, badly damaging the machinery and engine.

The fire was caused by sparks from a defective chimney getting under the eaves and setting the woodwork ablaze. The fire was confined mostly to the main building, with the one-story wing being damaged chiefly by water. The upper flooring was nearly all destroyed, as was a portion of the second floor. The fire damage to the first floor was minimal, with the principal loss caused by water damage. The company books, which were in the office on the first floor, were removed by the employees to a place of safety, and valuable papers were locked in a large safe.

The fire was discovered directly over the malt room in the main building, where the men were engaged in making preparations to brew. There was no beer in the tanks, the last brewing having been completed on July 20. Back on July 18, the last carload of malt, valued at about $800, was drawn to the building and stored. This was all destroyed, along with twenty bales of hops valued at $1,500. There were also stored in the cellar about eight hundred barrels of beer, valued at $3,000. These were not damaged to any extent, as all were sealed in a safe manner to prevent water or air to enter. A large barrel of cylinder oil was moved out of the building to a place of safety. It was estimated that the loss would be about $30,000 on the building and stock. The firm was insured with M.H. & M.G. Thomson for $5,300 and with other insurers for about half of the total loss.

Around 9:30 p.m. that evening, the fire department was again called to the scene to extinguish flames that had made a second appearance. These were brought quickly under control.

An announcement was made on September 9 that the brewery would be rebuilt. On September 25, the owners stated that they expected the work of rebuilding the brewery to be completed in about three weeks. The capacity of the brewery was to remain at one hundred barrels a day.

Rebuilding the brewery proved to be hazardous work. Frank J. Winslow was hurt in early November, dislocating his hip, and his brother Charles Jr. was hurt on November 17 while engaged in work near a vat containing some hot water. He was badly scalded about the neck and face. They both recovered from their injuries and rebuilding of the brewery was completed.

The rebuilt brewery operated by itself for the next couple years, but a vigorous warfare existed among the local brewers, with beer being sold at cost for a while. To combat this fierce competition, the stockholders of the Utica Brewing Company and the National Brewing Company decided to consolidate.

By October 1892, William C. Willcox had purchased the stock of the late John Coyne and the stock belonging to the heirs of the late Charles Winslow. By virtue of these purchases, he now had a controlling interest in the brewery. Patrick McNierney was the only remaining original owner who retained his stock.

Although it was understood that Willcox furnished the capital for the purchase of the Coyne stock, it was controlled in name by Dr. MacOwen. On October 26, a new company was formed with Willcox as president, Dr. MacOwen as vice-president and treasurer and Patrick McNierney as secretary and business manager. Willcox also owned the National Brewing Company across the street. It was also said that Willcox was looking into the purchase of the Fort Schuyler Brewery if he could secure control.

In May 1893, the two breweries joined forces and became known as the Utica National Brewing Company. See the chapter on the Utica National Brewing Company for the continuation of this brewery's story.

Dr. Michael MacOwen was one of the executors of the estate of Charles Winslow. As such, in September 1892, he sold $10,000 worth of stock in the Utica Brewing Company that was owned by Winslow to William C. Willcox. In 1894, the heirs of Charles Winslow objected to what Dr. MacOwen had done. The Surrogate Court ruled in favor of the heirs on December 24, 1894. Dr. MacOwen appealed the decision.

On January 11, 1895, Dr. MacOwen was arrested in New York City by Utica police and returned to Utica. At the police station, MacOwen gave his name and said that he was somewhere between sixty-eight and seventy years old. During these proceedings, he was served papers with an order of attachment for a certified check for $11,500 that he had from the Utica City National Bank, which he then turned over to the police. He was confined on the second floor of the police station for the remainder of the night.

Back in December, Dr. MacOwen was ordered to pay to the credit of the estate the discrepancy of $2,000. In the meantime, however, the Utica Brewing Company and the National Brewing Company, both of which were under the control of William C. Willcox, were consolidated in the fall of 1892, with a nominal capital of $100,000. Dr. MacOwen was made treasurer of the new company, with an annual salary of $1,000.

Dr. MacOwen's objections to the accounting in accordance with the desires of the Winslow heirs were based on his belief that a "freeze out" was in progress among certain stockholders in the Utica Brewing Company, which made one-third of the stock practically valueless. Dr. MacOwen, along with William C. Willcox and Patrick McNierney, was a heavy endorser on notes. Along with the rate war among the city brewers, Mr. Willcox's death and the decision of the surrogate, this caused a crisis in MacOwen's financial affairs.

Earlier in the week, Dr. MacOwen sold ninety-five shares of stock he owned in the Gulf Brewing Company to Moses Barney and William Welch for $10,000. Several days afterward, he sold sixteen of his lots on Nichols Street to J.B. Kennedy and James T. Carahar for $6,500. He then boarded a train for New York City.

A warrant for Dr. MacOwen's arrest was issued that night on the charge of grand larceny in the first degree. It was felt that Dr. MacOwen was going to return to his native Ireland to avoid any further legal complications.

Dr. MacOwen and John J. Clark left Utica at 2:05 p.m. on January 9, 1895, and went to Albany. They switched trains in Albany and took another to New York City. Upon their arrival, they went to Jersey City and registered at Taylor's Hotel. The next day, Dr. MacOwen went to the Franklin National Bank of New York to see the bank president, who was from Utica, for an introduction to the president of the Drexel, Morgan & Co. bank, where he wanted to exchange his check from the Utica City National Bank for $11,500.

The Franklin National president said he needed to communicate with the bank in Utica first before he endorsed the check. He indicated that he should hear back from the bank in the next morning's mail. John Clark came to the bank the next morning for Dr. MacOwen, but nothing was received from the Utica bank. The next time that mail was delivered, Dr. MacOwen came himself, at which time he was arrested by the Utica police.

The doctor's son, Francis P. MacOwen, treasurer for the National Brewing Company, went to New York on January 10 with his father's baggage. He did not meet his father in New York City, as he was already under arrest. He and John Clark then returned to Utica with the baggage.

The First National Bank in Utica also wanted Dr. MacOwen arrested as the bank held a note against the doctor for $13,000 and wanted to make sure it would get its money.

Back in Utica, when interviewed, Dr. MacOwen said he did not intend to leave the country and was simply in New York City for a visit. He also indicated that his son was also in New York City for a visit. The doctor's lawyer said his client had always acted honestly, and he did not think he went to New York City to flee the country. He went for the purpose of securing his bonds—but if Dr. MacOwen intended to leave the country, it was because he had been hounded to death by certain Uticans.

On July 13, 1895, lightning entered the brewery's office via the telephone wires. The batteries in the phone were destroyed, but no other damage occurred.

Dr. Michael A. MacOwen died on January 20, 1896, after an illness of three months. He had suffered from rheumatism for many years and had been confined to his home since October. In November, he was taken to the hospital, where he eventually died. He was born in Newtown Hamilton, County Armagh, Ireland, in 1821. He became a doctor and came to America in 1861. He did not get involved in the brewery until after he retired.

# CHAPTER 8
# EMPIRE BREWING COMPANY
## 1882–1884

The failure of the proposed Mohawk Valley Brewing Company in late 1882 stimulated others to take up the work where it was dropped and give Utica another lager beer brewery. Utica had six breweries in operation in 1882 making beer and ale. From sixteen thousand to twenty thousand barrels of lager beer were consumed in the city, mostly in the summer. Of this quantity, it was estimated that ten thousand to fourteen thousand barrels were supplied by outside sources. Oscar Guelich, who had recently returned to Utica from Germany, where he was engaged in brewing in Berlin, decided that Utica had room for another brewery.

Guelich had recently purchased the Osborne estate in East Utica. Part of this property would be used for his new brewery. The property was bounded by East, Ontario, Mary and Blandina Streets. The recently constructed West Shore Railroad ran by the property.

In early September 1882, construction on the new brewery was begun. Guelich acted as his own builder and drew up his own plans. The main building was forty by one hundred feet and was three stories high. The exterior walls were made of 300,000 bricks, with the interior constructed of wood. The roof of the brewery was made of wood shingles. The first and second floors were twelve feet high, with the third floor being sixteen feet high. The top floor was used for fermenting, with the lower floors being used for storage. The bottom floor was under ground level. The brewery was being set up to produce thirty thousand barrels of lager beer annually.

A brick engine and boiler house, eighteen by eighteen feet, and two frame barns completed the other buildings on the property in the spring of 1883.

The brewery was being built according to a new design. It was to be the first of its kind in the state. Edward W. Voight, a well-known brewer in Detroit, had the only such brewery in the country at that time. The design was founded on patents of David W. Davis, a Detroit inventor. Instead of the normal upper story filled with ice to keep the cellar beneath cool, this new design provided an upper floor with supporters of galvanized iron, so set that they form two arches running across the building. Over these, a limited quantity of ice would be put each day. The ice's melting and consequently its ability to cool the surroundings was stimulated by salt. A circulation of air was maintained through all the floors of the building, the cold air falling and forcing the warmer air up until it struck the iron arches. There it was reduced to the freezing point. A barrel of salt a day was used. The main benefits of this system of cooling and arranging a brewery were economy of ice, cleanliness, no swimmers used and the dryness of the air by storing less ice.

When hops, malt, rice or whatever else was used in making beer is in the process of fermentation, the mass is very sensitive to contamination. When dirt or decomposing matter of any kind is in the building, the beer gets a dirty taste, which can always be detected. The dryness of the air prevents decaying of wood and other matter. Guelich believed that with this style of brewery, he could keep the temperature at a steady thirty-four to thirty-six degrees Fahrenheit in all parts of the building. Water was supplied by driven wells, which provided soft, pure and exceptionally cold water.

When asked why he chose Utica to build his brewery, he responded, "I would no more have thought of starting such an enterprise as this in Utica when I was here twelve years ago than I would of cutting off one of my fingers. At that time I do not believe there was 5,000 barrels of lager beer used in the city a year. But the demand has so increased, here and everywhere, that I now think there is a favorable chance."

Guelich still considered the Utica market to be small and expected that most of his product would be sold elsewhere.

At that time, Rochester was the most prominent brewing center in the state, except for New York City. Syracuse had many breweries but no beer breweries of prominence, and it was believed that a trade in first-class lager beer might be extended in that direction. Albany had one very large beer brewery but concentrated on downriver trade. It was felt that the recently completed West Shore Railroad could give Utica a good method of shipping beer to many locations.

On July 5, 1883, a stock company was formed under the name of the Empire Brewing Company to carry on the business. The capital stock of the company was $40,000, of which $30,000 had been subscribed for. The stock was divided into eight hundred shares.

The directors chosen at the meeting were the Honorable James Miller, S.W. Wetzel, D.T. Everts, James C. Greenman, Oscar W. Guelich and Otto E.C. Guelich. Temporary officers for the company were also chosen. James C. Greenman was elected president; D.T. Everts, secretary; and Oscar W. Guelich, treasurer.

The new company expected that its product would be on the market by September 1, 1883.

A second meeting of the directors was held on July 17. At this meeting, the permanent company officers for the first year were chosen. Several changes were made. D.T. Everts was elected as president; James C. Greenman, vice-president; Samuel W. Wetzel, secretary and treasurer; and Oscar W. Guelich, superintendent. Articles of incorporation were sent to the office of the secretary of state and filed at the county clerk's office several days later.

The deed to the brewery property was transferred from Johanna and Oscar Guelich to the Empire Brewing Company on July 19 for $40,000.

The work of installing all the brewing apparatus went much slower than expected. It was finally completed about a week before Christmas. On Christmas day, brewer Franz Kranz left for New York City to obtain yeast so that the brewing could begin the following week.

At 8:45 p.m. on December 26, 1883, a train on the West Shore Railroad passed by the brewery on its normal run. Burning embers came out of the train's smoke stack and landed on the brewery's roof. At 9:05 p.m., Officer Baxter was on duty on Mohawk Street. He happened to glance westward when he discovered that the roof of a large building at quite a distance was on fire. Officer Baxter went to the nearest fire alarm box and turned in the alarm.

At about the same time, George Dumont, who resided at No. 3 East Street, only a few hundred feet from the fire, was informed by his wife that there was a bright light outside the house. He said it was nothing of importance and paid no more attention to it. A short time later, his wife came back and said that the brewery was on fire.

Mrs. Dumont went to the home of Oscar Guelich, two doors away, and notified Guelich. Guelich, in company with Mr. Dumont, ran to the brewery and was able to save the desk in the office, along with the most valuable books and papers in the office. They then attempted to put out the fire, but it had too much of a head start. The brewery was supplied with city water, but because the building was on high ground, the water pressure was very low.

Two alarms were sent in from different boxes, and this caused some confusion among the firemen. The firemen east of Genesee Street, however, were guided by the light from the fire. The roof, being constructed of shingles, made for a very bright fire. The interior of the building was also made of wood and burned rapidly, aided by the design of the building, which allowed for easy air flow. The exterior brick walls alone prevented the flames from spreading to the barns located nearby. The building was far from the center of the city, and the huge snowdrifts made it hard to get the steamers to the fire. Fire company No. 2's men got to the hydrant at the corner of East and Bleecker Streets and laid about one thousand feet of hose. The hose stream did little good, and it was not until No. 2's steamer arrived and was put into service that effective service could be given. By this time, the roof had burned off, and the interior of the building was a mass of flames. The firemen worked long and diligently in preventing the spread of the fire and wetting down the ruins.

The interior of the building contained all the requisites for the manufacture of lager beer according to the most improved methods. There was a large stock of ice in the icehouse. The building also contained two large copper tanks, a large copper patent cooler, about six hundred barrels and kegs, eighteen bales of hops and a quantity of malt, tubs and hogheads, among other supplies. All of these were destroyed. The roof was also burned off the engine house, but the boiler was filled with water and so was not a total loss.

The cost of the building was about $17,000; the machinery, fixtures and barrels were valued at over $18,000; and the stock was valued at $2,500. The total loss was estimated at $40,000. The insurance amounted to about $23,000. J.B. and J.M. Turnbull had coverage of $6,000 on the building and $6,000 on the contents. The rest of the insurance was spread with various agencies but was mainly with Hoyt & Butler.

At the time of the fire, Guelich, Kranz and three other men were employed at the brewery. The fire was a severe blow, but on February 4, 1884, the stockholders of the brewery decided to rebuild. Work was slated to begin that month.

Guelich, however, had some disagreement with the other members of the company, and as a result, the rebuilding never got under way. After several months, Guelich moved to Worchester, Massachusetts, to start a new brewery. He took with him brewer Kranz and several of the other employees.

This move sapped the will of the company. On July 21, a petition by the remaining directors of the brewery for a voluntary dissolution of the company was presented to Referee J.D. Stone.

The company was dissolved shortly thereafter. A lien on the brewery property was issued on October 15 in favor of the Oneida County Bank for the sum of $2,750 and costs.

On April 9, 1885, the Empire Brewery property, owned by Oscar Guelich, was sold at a sheriff's sale to Charles and Joshua Mather for $2,575. The sale was disputed by Simon and Almira Sayles and ended up in the courts. It took until September 1886 to finally settle the case, with the judgment favoring the Mather brothers. They ended up paying $1,650 for the property. This marked the end of the Empire Brewing Company.

An interesting side note to this story is the continuing troubles of Guelich. On December 27, 1884, almost precisely one year from the last fire, Guelich's new brewery and barn in Massachusetts burned to the ground. The loss was $18,000, with insurance covering $14,600. A portion of the stock was all that was saved. Although Guelich stated that it was his intention to rebuild the brewery, this time with brick, he never did. This ended Guelich's attempts at being a brewer. He moved back to Utica and started a meat market on Liberty Street. Sometime around 1890, he moved to Rochester. He passed away on October 4, 1904, at the Soldier's Home in Bath, New York, at the age of sixty-four. He left his wife, four sons and two daughters.

# CHAPTER 9
# COLUMBIA BREWING COMPANY
## 1885–1888

On October 28, 1885, a meeting of prominent Germans was held at Bierbauer's saloon to discuss the prospects for forming a brewing company after the death of Charles Bierbauer on August 17. After much discussion, the group decided to form a lager beer brewing company with a capital stock of $10,000.

Even though this was only the first meeting to discuss the possibility of a brewery, sixteen of the gentlemen present subscribed for $15,000 worth of stock. John Kohler (Mrs. Bierbauer's brother-in-law) was chosen as the president. Dr. Theodore Deecke was chosen as vice-president, with August Maine serving as secretary and August Bockmann serving as treasurer. A committee was appointed to consult with an architect and examine the Bierbauer brewery to see if it would be advisable to purchase it.

On November 11, a second meeting was held at the Bierbauer saloon. After some discussion, it was decided to name the company the "Columbia Brewing Company" and to increase its capital stock to $50,000. Nearly half of the stock had already been sold, and a committee was appointed to receive subscriptions for more stock. The company announced that it had purchased the old established West Side Brewery and the site for $12,000. A German brewer, with experience in managing breweries in Syracuse, expressed interest in the company.

On December 21, the company filed articles of incorporation at the County clerk's office. The corporation was to last for fifty years with capital stock divided into five hundred shares of $100 each. The trustees for the first year were John Kohler, Henry Roemer, Melnotte M. Brunner, Frank Schaub and George Fretscher. P.F. Bulger was listed as one of the incorporators but not a trustee. The certificate of incorporation was filed in the office of the secretary of state on December 22.

The new company planned to expend $7,000 to $10,000 in putting in a new boiler and engine, along with making other material improvements. The brewery's icehouse would store about two hundred cords of ice. The ice was obtained from nearby Nail Creek, a few hundred feet away. The brewery would make ale at the beginning and lager as soon as practicable.

The Columbia Brewing Company, on 11–17 Edward Street, was formally opened for business on May 6, 1886. The proprietors furnished refreshments for over five hundred visitors. On October 1 of that year, the brewery purchased, through Frank Schaub, the Cornelios property on Varick Street for $11,000 with plans to expand operations.

In a July 1886 report on the Nail Creek nuisance, the city surveyor blamed the Columbia Brewing Company for dumping its refuse into the creek. He indicated that the company should be required to connect the brewery to the Seventh Ward sewer and not empty anything into the creek for public safety. The brewery complied with this request.

On January 6, 1887, the annual meeting of the brewery was held at its office on Edward Street. John Kohler, M.M. Brunner, Frank Schaub, Robert Cromie and J.J. Simon were elected trustees for the following year. At a subsequent meeting of the trustees later that day, John Kohler was chosen as president, Frank Schaub was chosen vice-president and M.M. Brunner was chosen secretary/treasurer.

During the previous year, the company erected several new buildings worth $4,000. In its annual report, the brewery stated that of the $50,000 of capital stock, $15,600 had been paid in and $12,000 had been issued for brewery property. Liabilities of the company did not exceed $21,000.

At the annual meeting of the stockholders in January 1888, the old directors were reelected. Things were not going well for the brewery, however. The annual report filed on January 19 showed that the debt had risen to $30,000, a 43 percent increase from the previous year.

In early February, the company defaulted on its $10,000 mortgage held by Barbara Bierbauer. The sheriff seized the property and the contents. On March 7, Sheriff Batchelor sold the property to a group of gentlemen who would form the West End Brewing Company.

On March 24, a judgment was filed against the Columbia Brewing Company in favor of Robert Cromie for the amount of $13,082.23. Then on March 31, the personal property of the brewery that was not sold to the original group of gentlemen was sold to Cromie for $2,000.00.

This was the end of the Columbia Brewing Company and marked the birth of the West End Brewing Company.

# CHAPTER 10

# HOLYOKE BREWING COMPANY

## 1886–1891

This brewery was never built in Utica, but the principal owners were from Utica, and the brewery was incorporated here. The articles of incorporation of the Holyoke Brewing Company were filed in the Oneida County clerk's office on Saturday, December 4, 1886. The company was formed for the purpose of conducting the manufacture and brewing of ale, beer and porter. Capital stock was $75,000, divided into 750 shares of $100 each.

The trustees for the first year were John Coyne, Thomas McNierney, Lewis F. Lux and Charles A. Lux. A part of the business was to be carried out in Chicopee, Massachusetts, and the other part in Utica. John Coyne was the president of the new company, and Thomas McNierney was the treasurer. The new five-story brick brewery was erected in Willimansett, Massachusetts, instead of in Chicopee.

A certificate was filed in the Oneida County clerk's office on December 19, 1888, showing that the capital stock of the brewery amounted to $60,000 all paid in. The 1888 annual report for the brewery stated that it had debts amounting to $3,797.

Any connection to Utica ended in 1891 when Coyne sold his interest in the brewery due to his health. In April 1891, he caught a severe case of German measles, which confined him to his house until he died on February 27, 1892, at the age of forty-five. The brewery continued under the Holyoke name until 1890. In 1890, the name was changed to the Hampden Brewing Company, which eventually became the Hampden-Harvard Brewing Company and lasted until 1975.

# CHAPTER 11
# LAFAYETTE BREWING COMPANY
## 1891–1896

Charles Hutten was one of the first lager beer brewers located in Utica (see chapter 4). After he died in August 1890, his wife kept the brewery running until his estate could be sold. She did not have any desire to continue to run the brewery on her own.

Many legal questions had to be answered before the brewery could be sold. It was not until August 25, 1891, that the brewery was sold at public auction, a little over a year from Hutten's death.

The sale of the brewery was conducted by referee R.O. Jones on the steps of the courthouse. The first bid was for $800. The property was eventually sold to John C. Metzger of Ilion for $1,000, subject to a mortgage of $4,000 and interest of 5 percent. Other bidders for the brewery included Fred Haak, Fred D. Haak, John E. Jacquemin and Gottlieb Zitzner.

On September 24, H. Ray Barnes, Michael Doll and John C. Metzger formed a co-partnership to run the brewery recently purchased by Metzger. The brewery was known after this as the Lafayette Brewing Company. New and modern equipment was ordered and installed in the following months. The new owners felt that they could begin brewing sometime in December. Barnes was chosen to act as business manager of the new firm. Fred Hoeschele was maintained as the head brewmaster.

A May 1892 ad in the *Utica Morning Herald* announced that Charles Mayer would bottle lager from the Lafayette Brewing Company at his new bottling house at the corner of Mohawk and Mary Streets.

Fred W. Hoeschele resigned in July 1892 after having served for the previous twenty years as a brewmaster. He was replaced by Karl Schurer, who came to Utica from Meridan, Connecticut. In his youth, he attended the Brew School in Wurtemburg, Bavaria, and afterward worked at the D. Schorr Brewery in Musches, Bavaria, for eight years. After coming to America, he worked with Charles A. King for eight and a half years. Later, he started a new brewery at Meridan, Connecticut, and ran it for three years. He had built the brewery up from three thousand to forty-seven thousand barrels a year until it was purchased by an English syndicate.

Immediately upon taking possession of the Lafayette brewery, the new Utica firm made general renovations to the entire plant. It increased capacity so that the total output was brought up to thirty thousand barrels a year. A thirty-ton ice machine was purchased, new fermenting rooms with asphalt floors were constructed and the wooden cellar bottoms were removed and replaced with concrete.

New mash tubs, fermenting tubs, storage casks and kegs were added to the equipment. A new boiler was added. A large brick addition was built next to the old brewery, while the work of filling in the gulf in the rear of the plant was expedited. On October 1, a new flag was flying from the new staff at the brewery in honor of Schurer's first brew of lager, which was tried and commended at scores of places.

The brewery never developed the way the firm had hoped, and by 1895, it was in financial trouble. It managed to obtain the money it needed by added a new partner to the firm. William F. Doll, a saloon owner, became a part owner of the brewery.

On March 10, 1896, Sheriff Weaver sold the Lafayette brewery property at auction. The sale took place in the office of the brewery. A dispute arose over what happened to some of the personal property of the brewery. Barnes, who had previously owned the brewery, said that some of it was sold when the business failed. An attorney for Michael Doll, who was one of the bidders, asked that the whole property be sold together, which the sheriff did. Barrows started with a $2,000 bid. The price rose in bidding between Barrows and Doll until it reached $6,500, when Doll quit. It halted at $6,500 and jumped to $11,000 with a bid from Barnes. Barrows added $100 to the bid but after awhile withdrew his bid. Barnes was the highest bidder and announced that the purchaser was Mrs. Rosilla Shorer.

The sale was left open until March 21 without advertising in case of default of payment by the purchaser. It was reported that Mrs. Shorer had purchased the brewery on behalf of certain capitalists in Utica who intended to form a stock company and carry on the business. Mrs. Shorer was the mother-in-law of H. Ray Barnes. The capacity of the brewery was listed at 20,000 barrels per year. Mrs. Sarah Winston held the mortgage and had instructed her attorney to foreclose. The claims against the property, including mortgage and sheriff's fees, amounted to $11,475. Shorer was given until March 21 to complete the sale. She failed to complete the sale, and the sheriff resold the property to Michael Doll for $11,100 on April 6, 1896. Doll did not keep possession of the brewery for long. He sold the brewery to Matthew Hart of New York City on September 14, 1896, and it became the Consumers' Brewing Company of Utica.

# CHAPTER 12
# GULF BREWERY (GULF BREWING COMPANY)

## 1820–1918

The Gulf Brewery was built in the early 1820s and was located on Jay Street at the Public Basin in Utica. Matthew Codd was the proprietor as early as 1824. In the summer of 1825, he advertised his summer beer, which was ready for delivery and was equal to the quality of what he sold the previous year. Any orders left at the post office would be immediately attended to.

In an April 1827 ad, Codd stated, "Although he [Codd himself] cannot state that he was the first person to supply the inhabitants of this village with good beer or that his beer is not surpassed by any—he can state that he was the first brewer in America who made beer, that would without injury to its flavor or strength bear transportation in the warmest weather. Codd felt grateful for the support given to his establishment and the increasing demand for his summer beer, induces him to request his friends and the Public order early to prevent disappointment. Orders will be personally and promptly attended to." He also sold Irish whiskey, hops, malt and good seed barley.

Early in its history, the brewery burned to the ground and had to be rebuilt. In 1828, the brewery was enlarged and was turning out two hundred barrels of ale weekly when at full production. This made Gulf a very large brewery in those days, as most breweries were producing only a few hundred barrels yearly. Gulf shipped its products to New York City and southern markets in addition to supplying the local consumers.

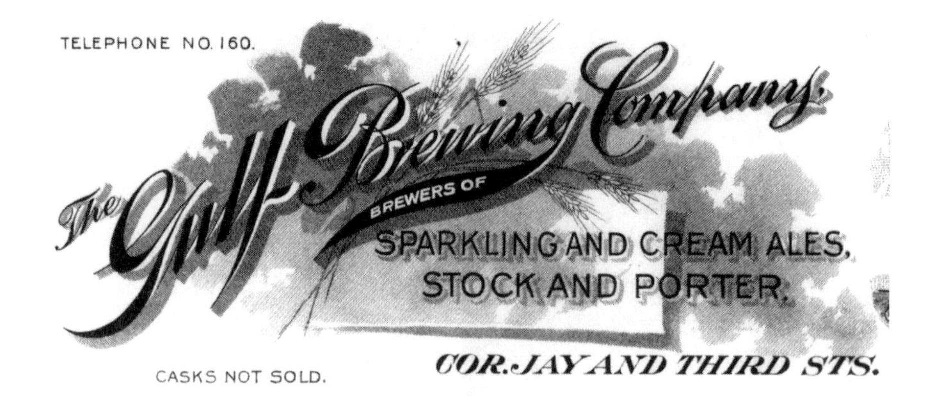


A 1905 sales receipt from the Gulf Brewing Company. *Author's collection.*

Around 1829, Codd sold his interest in the brewery to John C. Devereux, who ran the brewery until the mid-1830s. The brewery was sold to John C. Tynan, who formed J.C. Tynan & Co. Tynan must have decided he needed more capital to operate the brewery, so he took Michael McQuade in as a partner, forming McQuade, Tynan & Co. on August 30, 1836. McQuade and his partners formed a stock company to raise the money for the purchase. Roscoe Conkling, a famous figure in Utica history, was one of the major stockholders. In those years, the brewery produced both ales and malt whiskey. The neighborhood was on the fringe of the country at the time. The Erie Canal basin was near the brewery, and the canalboats backed up to the rear of the plant to wait out winter each year.

In 1840, James McIntosh was listed as a brewer. John Myres (Myers) was a maltster for the firm, and Thomas Mann was an agent. Myres had joined the brewery around 1833 and eventually became head brewmaster around 1850. He left the company in 1873 to start the Utica Star Ale Brewery with several other gentlemen.

Louis Brosemer commenced to learn the art of brewing at the Gulf Brewery under the instruction of Michael McQuade in 1845. He stayed at the brewery until 1848, when he left to form the L. Brosemer Brewing Company in Oswego, New York.

In the summer of 1848, Michael McQuade and Hubbard C. Pond, who together now owned the brewery, erected a new brewery on the site of the old one that they had previously torn down. The brewery was now listed as being at the corner of Jay Street and Third Avenue. Pond had joined the

GULF BREWERY,
Capital Stock, $50,000.
☞ Manufacturers of BEER, and dealers in BARLEY, MALT, HOPS, STAVES and WOOD. The
STOCK ALE
Manufactured at this establishment is confidently recommended as being superior to any in market. Office cor. Jay and Third Street, Utica.
M. McQUADE, Prest. and Agent.

"The Gulf Brewery."

M. McQUADE,
PRESIDENT AND AGENT,
MANUFACTURERS OF
BEER AND MALT,
AND DEALERS IN
BARLEY, HOPS, STAVES AND WOOD.

Their "INVIGORATOR OLD ALE," has maintained a reputation for the past TWENTY-FIVE YEARS, as being
SUPERIOR TO ANY ALE IN MARKET.
ORDERS LEFT AT THE OFFICE,
CORNER OF JAY AND THIRD STREETS,
or at the Counting Room of the Evening Telegraph Office, No. 47 Genesee St. will receive prompt attention.

*Above*: Ad from the 1857–58 *Utica City Directory*.

*Left*: Ad from the 1861–62 *Utica City Directory*.

brewery around 1845. Before becoming involved with the brewery, he was a machinist by trade.

In 1852, the Gulf Brewery was incorporated with capital stock of $50,000. T.J. Harding was listed as an agent and manager of the brewery during this time.

On March 14, 1859, an attempt was made to rob the brewery, but it failed because the robbers could not find the keys to the safe. The brewery had, however, been robbed two days earlier, with the crooks successfully getting away with twenty-five dollars in change. In the earlier robbery, the crooks found the keys to two safes. As a result, the keys were relocated and hidden. The police finally caught the three men who committed the robberies on March 16. They were sent to jail awaiting action of the grand jury in their cases.

Frederick J. Harding joined the brewery in 1862 as a bookkeeper. Thomas Quinn was the brewery engineer from 1862 to 1874, when he left with Myers to form the Utica Star Ale Brewery.

The office of the brewery was entered by burglars on January 15, 1863, and the safe was robbed. The robbers entered the office through a window and opened the safe using a cold chisel. They took thirty dollars in good money and fifteen dollars in counterfeit money. This was the third time the brewery had been robbed in five days.

Two burglars broke into the brewery on the night of March 30, 1866, but were discovered by several men who had been placed on watch by the owners. They captured the thieves quickly, but as they were taking them out of the building, one of them escaped briefly before being recaptured. They were then taken to jail. The bail was set at $1,000 each, which they could not obtain, so they remained in jail until their trial before a grand jury. On September 22, 1866, the safe was again broken into, and three dollars was taken. The thieves also robbed two stores but were later caught.

An eight-year-old boy had both hands badly injured at the brewery on September 2, 1872. The employees of the brewery were hoisting ice with blocks and tackle. The boy was playing in the yard and got the fingers of his right hand into one of the blocks. In an effort to free his hand, he then got the left hand caught as well. Two fingers of his right hand were taken off, and the flesh on that hand was badly lacerated. The left hand received flesh wounds. It was thought that the right hand might have to be amputated.

Production at the brewery was 7,323 barrels in 1874 and 7,821 barrels in 1875.

In March 1874, five young men were charged with breaking into the brewery one night and stealing all the beer they could drink. They then left, leaving the faucets open and causing a large quantity of beer to spill out onto the floor.

The employees of the Gulf Brewery raised a centennial liberty pole and hung a twenty-foot flag on July 1876.

Hubbard C. Pond, who was McQuade's partner in the brewery from 1848 to 1852, died on February 24, 1878 after an illness of seven weeks.

When the Old Fort Schuyler Distillery was built on Catharine Street in Utica in 1878, the manufacture of malt whiskey was no longer necessary at the Gulf Brewery. Both concerns were run by the same people. In 1879, the brewery sold 6,918 barrels of ale, making it the second-largest brewery in the Utica area that year.

On April 5, 1879, Michael McQuade died in his home after a long illness at the age of seventy-eight. He was born on September 29, 1801, in the county of Tyrone, parish of Clogher, Ireland. Following his brother Thomas, he came to Utica in 1822, where he became a cooper. McQuade became partners with John Tynan in the brewery in 1836. He was very active in politics in Utica, was a very generous man and had a love of music.

Colonel James McQuade severed his connection to the brewery on May 4, 1880, and returned to New York City to pursue other employment. The employees of the brewery presented him with a valuable locket as a going-away gift.

A severe wind and rainstorm hit Utica on February 12, 1881, and caused much damage. The cupola of the Gulf Brewery was blown off during the storm. C.E. Tapping, of the Gulf Brewery, and Martin H. Neejer, formerly of the Utica Brewing Company, became connected to McGarvey and Quinn's new brewery in Syracuse on June 19, 1881. The new brewery became known as the Moore & Quinn Brewing Company.

On July 14, 1881, the Gulf Brewery and a Syracuse brewery announced that they were exchanging brewers. Charles E. Topping, who had been at the Gulf Brewery for several years, was joining the Syracuse brewery, and William Draper was leaving the Syracuse brewery to work at the Gulf Brewery.

On the night of November 28, 1881, the brewing department of the brewery burned to the ground. The malting and stock departments were saved by a brick partition and the quick work of the firemen. The Gulf Brewery, at this time, was a large wooden structure. The north half of the building contained the engine, boiler, cooler and all the machinery and apparatus for the manufacture of ale and the office of the company. The south half contained the malting floor, stock and storage rooms. The two sections were separated by a brick wall with iron doors. After business hours,

Eddie Harding, the brewer and son of superintendent, Frederick Harding, visited the premises one last time before calling it quits for the day. After touring the premises and finding nothing unusual, he went home.

The fire started slightly after 9:00 p.m. The alarm was given about 9:20 p.m. from a fire box located at Mrs. Matthew Quinn's store at the corner of Bleecker and Third Streets. There was a fierce east wind blowing, and the temperature hovered around fifteen degrees. The wind forced heavy volumes of dense smoke over to West Utica, and for a time, no one could locate the fire. Considerable excitement was caused on Genesee Street and in the vicinity of the Opera House, with many fearing that the fire was close by.

Chemical engine No.1 was the first to arrive. The firemen who entered the brewery found that the fire was located in the hop slide at the northwest corner of the building. Steamers No. 2 and 4 arrived shortly after to help. It was so cold that the water froze as soon as it touched the building. Within fifteen minutes, the roof, ladders and garments of the firemen were coated with ice, which greatly hindered their work.

The fire had progressed to a point that it was impossible to save the brewing department. The firemen concentrated on preventing the flames from passing beyond the brick wall into the malting room and the property west of the brewery. The smoke and steam were blinding and stifling, but the firemen held their own. Occupants of the buildings west of the brewery got out on their roofs and kept them wet with pails of water. Steamer No. 1, which had been kept in reserve, was called in. The fire was finally put out long after midnight.

Because Superintendent Harding's son had just finished inspecting the brewery a few hours earlier and found nothing amiss, it was believed the fire had been purposely set. The estimated loss was between $10,000 and $20,000. The brewery was covered for the loss by various insurance policies. In addition to losing the brew house and machinery, one hundred barrels of ale were lost valued at $500. The fire also put the ten men employed by the brewery out of work until the brewery could be rebuilt. Rival brewers Coyne, O'Toole, Finn, McNierney and Hand were present at the fire and offered what assistance they could. The *Daily Observer* stated the next day that it "never saw ale turned out of a brewery faster than it was last night. The 'Star' gazers and the 'Ralphites' never equaled it." The last comment referring to two Utica breweries; "Star" gazers referred to the Utica Star Ale Brewery, and "Ralphites" referred to the Oneida Brewery.

General James McQuade, the president of Gulf Brewery, was in New York City at the time of the fire and was notified by telegraph. He replied that the business of the moment made it desirable that he should remain in the city but that he would come if absolutely necessary. General McQuade was heavily involved in politics at the time.

Horatio S. VanValkenburgh, who was employed at the brewery, went to bed at 9:00 p.m. on the night of the fire. The next morning, he started to work around 7:00 a.m. as usual. As he walked down the street, a man shouted from across the street, "Hello! How many barrels of ale have you sold this morning?" Another yelled, "Out of a job, I see!" When he reached Chancellor Square, he was being hailed with cries of: "I'll come over and help you drink up what's left!" "Got some dry clothes on!" "You needn't hurry down to light the fire this morning!" Finally halting a passing friend, he asked, "Say, what's the matter anyway? I haven't met anything but crazy or drunken men since I left home." His friend replied, "Haven't you heard?" "Heard what?" was his reply. "The brewery's burned!" exclaimed his friend. Upon hearing this, VanValkenburg ran the rest of the way to the brewery.

On December 15, 1881, a decision was made to rebuild the brewery. Daniel J. Cone was hired to remove the ruins of the fire so that construction could begin. Demolition proceeded smoothly except for one incident. On December 31, Superintendent Harding was assisting in the removal of a burnt timber. As the timber was being lifted, it broke, and part of it struck a glancing blow to Harding's head. Harding received a bad cut and narrowly escaped being crushed as the timber that struck him was very heavy.

The brewery produced 7,463 barrels of ale in 1881, making it the fourth-largest brewery in the city. If the fire had not disrupted production, it would have been third largest. Reconstruction of the brewery took place during the first three months of 1882. As a result, production in 1882 was down from the previous year. A total of 5,234 barrels were produced. The brewery reopened on Tuesday, April 25, 1882.

P.J. McQuade was elected president and treasurer for the brewery in 1882. At this time, he was also city clerk for Utica. Frederick J. Harding became the manager and agent for the brewery.

Times were changing for the Gulf Brewery. General James McQuade was more interested in his political career than in running the family business. On July 19, he sold the brewery to Moses Barney, James F. Roe and Dr. M.A. MacOwen for $35,000. These gentlemen made a $10,000 down payment. The next day, they filed articles of incorporation in the county clerk's office. The newly formed corporation was called the Gulf Brewing Company and had capital stock of $36,000. The trustees for the first year were Moses Barney, James F. Roe and Dr. M.A. MacOwen.

On August 2, Amaziah D. Barber, through his attorneys, began the foreclosure of two mortgages on the Gulf Brewery. One was for $10,000 given in 1848, on which $2,000 remained unpaid. The second mortgage was given in 1869 for $80,000. No mention is made how much was left to repay. The new brewery owners promised to pay off the mortgages, and Barber dropped his foreclosure procedures.

The following year, during a meeting held on July 24, Dr. MacOwen was elected as president, with James Roe serving as treasurer and Moses Barney serving as secretary.

The brewery in 1884 consisted of a four-story brew house with washing and packing facilities in the basement. The fermenting tanks were on the first floor, while the mash tub and offices were located on the second floor. The third floor contained storage. The malt mill was located on the fourth floor. A second group of buildings contained a wagon and barrel shed and a cooper shop. Heat was provided by coal stoves, and light was provided by kerosene lamps. Ten people were employed at the time. The annual report of the brewery for 1884 showed that its capital stock was all paid in and that its debts were $24,784.33.

Moses Barney took on the job of treasurer, in addition to secretary, in 1885. On March 24, General James McQuade died at the age of fifty-five. Debts had decreased to $23,012.12 in 1885.

William A. Palmer, a worker at the brewery, died after being severely scalded in an accident at the brewery around 4:00 p.m. on July 9, 1885. Lawrence Baker, the brewery engineer, testified at the inquest held on July 14 that he had been working on the boiler. He left the boiler and started the engine. He then heard that Palmer had been burned by the water and steam from the exhaust pipe of the engine. He stopped the engine at once, but it was too late. The pipe was two feet outside the building and about fifteen feet from the ground. The wagon Palmer had been sitting on was thirteen feet high, bringing him near the exhaust pipe.

Michael F. Clark, a cooper at the brewery, saw the accident. He saw Palmer drive up to the grain house. He had just stopped his horses when Clark saw some water come out of the pipe. Palmer jumped out of the wagon and walked into the brewery with Charles Winslow. Winslow removed Palmer's clothing and applied yeast to the burns. He was burned from the shoulders to near the hips. Clark went for sweet oil, limo water (a mixture of quicklime and water impervious to air that was used in the 1880s to protect cuts and burns) and cotton batting, which he applied to Palmer's back at the direction of Dr. MacOwen. Palmer complained of a pain in his stomach both before and after he was burned. The exhaust pipe had been in its present place for at least thirty years, and Clark indicated that it had never injured anyone before.

Charles B. Winslow, another brewery worker, did not see the accident but helped apply yeast to Palmer's burns. He also gave him two doses of whiskey, and someone else gave him a third. He indicated that Palmer complained more about his stomach hurting than his burns.

Dr. Michael A. MacOwen, who was in the brewery office at the time of the accident, testified that he found the two men applying yeast to Palmer's burns and ordered linseed oil for him. He told the men to give Palmer whiskey for the pain in his stomach. Palmer indicated that he had drunk some ale in the brewery and thought he would be sick if he had the whiskey. He was convinced to drink the whiskey.

After he was all bandaged up, MacOwen wanted to send him to the hospital, but Palmer wanted to go home so his mother would not worry. He left the brewery two hours after the accident. After he got home, he became delirious, and the family doctor was called. Palmer did not become conscious again. His condition did not improve, and he died on July 12.

A jury indicated that the exhaust pipe was in a dangerous place and should be replaced, moved, boxed or in some manner made safe to avoid a repeat of the accident. The jury also found that, to a certain extent, the Gulf Brewery was indirectly responsible for the death of William A. Palmer.

On July 20, 1886, at a meeting of the board of trustees, the following officers were chosen for the ensuing year; as president, Moses Barney replaced Dr. MacOwen; secretary and treasurer, William F. Welch; and superintendent, William F. Barney. The brewery's debts continued to drop. They were $20,958.52 for 1886.

Throughout its existence, the Gulf Brewing Company was strictly an ale brewery, producing sparkling and cream ales, stock and porter. Through the late 1800s, the brewery had a capacity of ten thousand barrels a year. In 1888, the brewery sold some land across the street that held its icehouse to a group that was forming the Eagle Brewing Company.

In 1888, the brewery covered an area of 250 by 260 feet. On the land was a five-story frame brew house building, 60 by 150 feet, with a four-story annex and numerous minor structures. The capacity of the brewery allowed for the production of seventy-five barrels of ale and porter daily. Power was supplied by a twelve-horsepower engine. The brewery employed twelve to fifteen workers and five teams of horses for delivery.

William F. Barney took over the duties of secretary that year, with William Welch retaining the office of treasurer.

On April 12, 1889, burglars broke into the brewery by smashing an outer door. The brewery safe was untouched, and only an old coat was stolen.

The annual report for 1891 indicated a debt of $448.69 with a capital stock of $36,000 all paid in. The brewery was in very good financial shape.

With the opening of Jay Street in the 1890s (previously it was a dead end because of a stream and pond), the brewery had to move its offices and washroom. A seventy- by thirty-foot brick addition was made to the brewery in the summer of 1896. This contained the new offices and a powerhouse. The lighting was converted from kerosene to gas.

In July 1898, the brewery refused to discharge a nonunion cooper to give his job to an unemployed union worker. The local union withdrew its union stamps from the brewery and declared its product unfair.

A Utica paper wrote an article in December 1899 about a beer price war between brewers in Utica and about Syracuse breweries selling beer in Utica. William F. Welch, of the Gulf Brewing Company and treasurer of the Brewers Association, said in response, "There has been no cut in the price of beer. It is selling for the same price as always and there is no kick coming on the business with the exception of the war tax. Syracuse has always sold beer here, so you see there is nothing very startling in that. Our organization is a guarantee that there is no war between East and West Utica."

William Lafferty became brewmaster by 1901. He would remain in that position until Prohibition. Officers for the brewery remained unchanged until 1903, when William F. Welch assumed the duties of manager along with that of treasurer. During this time, he was also secretary and treasurer for the Eagle Brewing Company.

In early 1905, Moses Barney died, and Welch assumed the leadership of the brewery. His wife, Mary A. Barney, became secretary for the brewery.

The pitch kettle at the brewery caught fire at 11:30 a.m. on May 4, 1905. The fire department was called, but brewery employees successfully put the fire out using ashes before the fire company got there.

A new four-story iron-and-brick stock house was built in early 1906. Its dimensions were fifty by one hundred feet. The Gulf Brewing Company was trying to sell the Utica Brewing Company buildings on the corner of South and St. Vincent Streets in January 1907. It is unclear how they acquired the property.

Construction of a new four-story brew and mill house began in late 1907. This was being built to modernize the brewery and meet increased demand. In February 1908, the following equipment was ordered from Kaestner & Co., Chicago: a Kaestner-patented hydraulic mashing machine, an all-steel non-explosive malt mill and an improved rice rake.

A 1905 Gulf Brewing Company letterhead. *Author's collection.*

By 1912, Welch had become president of both the Gulf Brewing Company and Eagle Brewing Company. The brewery continued under his guidance until Prohibition, during which time the brewery remained inactive. Edwin B. Welch became secretary in 1920, succeeding his mother.

The fire alarm went off at the brewery on September 21, 1916. When the firemen got there, no fire was discovered. It was determined that escaping steam set off the alarm.

On June 11, 1917, a major storm came through the area. Both the Gulf and Eagle breweries were surrounded by water, which rapidly filled the cellars. Despite the inconvenience, business went on at the breweries. The horses used to pull the delivery wagons had to swim at times to reach the buildings.

As Prohibition began, the local breweries were looking for way to stay in business with varying degrees of success. They leased the buildings to a baking company and a butter manufacturer.

Sometime in 1923, the Utica Baking Company leased space in the rear part of the brewery. A fire of unknown causes occurred on April

A 1910 Gulf Brewing Company envelope. *Author's collection.*

26, 1923. The brick building itself was not damaged to any great extent, with the exception of the roof, but the entire interior was gutted. The baker was taken to the hospital after a skylight had fallen on him while he was fighting the flames. An explosion was heard in the baking plant shortly after the fire started, probably when the blaze reached some supplies stored there.

The loss was estimated to be $12,000 for proprietor Fred Reynolds. Tons of water was poured into the bakery through the mass of smoke and flames as large quantities of lard and other supplies sizzled and sputtered.

In May 1923, the Charles A. Weinant & Co., Inc. took over the building and remodeled it to fit the company's purposes. It transformed the building from a somewhat dilapidated structure into an office, creamery and warehouse. Thousands of dollars' worth of new equipment was installed, and the daily capacity of the plant was two tons. The company produced only one product: "Mohawk Valley Brand Butter."

The Gulf Brewing Company formed the Mohawk Valley Beverages Company in late 1923. This company would produce various kinds of soft drinks. It sold brewers' grains to farmers at ten cents a bushel.

On August 25, 1926, federal agents made a tour of inspection of the brewery. At that time, they claimed to have found thirteen half barrels of beer allegedly containing more than the lawful percentage of alcohol.

A revocation action brought by the federal government to deprive the Mohawk Valley Beverage Company of its license to operate was held on October 16 in front of Mrs. Edna Lee of Buffalo, who was the revocation referee.

The brewery claimed that a break in the ice machinery used to lower the temperature of the beverage resulted in fermentation that had not been intended. It further claimed that it had not been the intention or plan of the company to sell or distribute the beer.

The government maintained that the beer contained an unlawful amount of alcohol and that it was stored in violation of the regulations of the license permitting the concern to manufacture near beer and other cereal beverages. On November 1, Mrs. Edna Lee ruled that the brewery could keep its license to operate.

Making soft drinks could be a dangerous business. Raymond Luebbert, thirty, was killed instantly on March 1, 1930, when the gauge head of a carbonating machine blew off and struck him in the forehead. Luebbert was employed as brewmaster at the time of the accident and had been in that position for four years. He was alone in the basement, where he was engaged in carbonating beverages. He was believed to have put the pressure on a dual compressed air tank, and in some manner, double pressure developed.

Myron Cramer was in the office alone at the time and, upon hearing the sound of an explosion, went to the basement to investigate. He found Luebbert lying on the floor and went next door to summon help. By the time the doctor arrived, Luebbert was dead.

After Luebbert's death, the old brewery was inactive until after Prohibition, when it briefly became the Globe Brewing Company.

# CHAPTER 13
# CONSUMERS' BREWING COMPANY OF UTICA

## 1896–1902

On April 10, 1896, the old Lafayette brewery on the corner of Third and Mary Streets was sold at auction under foreclosure of a mortgage. Mrs. Rosilla Shorer, mother-in-law to one of the previous owners (Barnes), bought the plant and property for $11,000. This did not last long, as she failed to make good on her bid. On May 6, Michael Doll purchased the brewery for the same amount. Doll, in turn, sold the brewery on September 14 to Leo Levy of New York City.

Levy then began renovating the old brewery. Michael Doll was contracted to put the brewery into working condition to manufacture ale and lager. New equipment worth $20,000 was purchased and was expected to be installed in about five weeks. A Buffalo Refrigerating Machine was one of the new pieces of equipment. When fully operational, the brewery was expected to employ fifteen men.

On October 10, the Consumers' Brewery Company of Utica was incorporated. The name of the brewery was chosen to show people that its products would be made with the customer in mind. The company's capital stock was set at $50,000. Max Hart, Herman Elkan and Leo Levy were named directors of the firm. The deed for the brewery property was transferred from Levy to the new company for the sum of one dollar on October 17.

On October 14, 1896, the Hines brothers, who had for the last six months conducted a laundry in the building formerly used for office purposes by the defunct Lafayette brewery, gave a dancing party for a large number of their

CONSUMERS'
BREWING COMPANY,
Corner Third Avenue and Mary Street.
FIRST BREWING OF
REAL GERMAN LAGER BEER
WILL BE READY FOR THE MARKET
XMAS DAY.

Ad from the *Utica Daily Press*, December 1896.

friends. The night's festivities were a farewell, as the building would now be occupied by the new Consumers' Brewing Company of Utica.

As soon as the property was in the brewery's possession, work in renovating, refitting and remodeling the entire plant was immediately begun. New machinery for the making of the best beer, a new ice machine, new tubs and vats were put in, and no expense was spared to place the brewery on a level with the best in the country. The brewery started operations on Monday, November 2, 1896.

The brewery was conducted on the co-operative plan. Beside the present officers and stockholders, no one could be received into the corporation except saloonkeepers. A great many saloonkeepers were interviewed, and they expressed a belief that a brewery conducted on these lines would be a great success. Twenty-five union men were employed by the brewery.

Max Hart, who was secretary and treasurer for the new firm, was given entire charge of the brewery. August Mueller, a brewer, was hired to run the day-to-day activities of the brewery.

August Mueller was an expert brewer in New York City and was about to enter a partnership with a Connecticut capitalist when the latter died. For the previous ten years, Mueller had been brewmaster and superintendent at the H&F Haffen Brewery and Jacob Rupert Brewery in New York City. As his experience was to be his share of the partnership without money, he had to look for employment. He met a man named McLaughlin, a noted Buffalo maltster, who held a claim of $3,500 against the old LaFayette brewery in Utica. McLaughlin said the place up in Utica was just the one for Mueller and that he could arrange for his going there to run the brewery. About the same time, Mueller met Max Hart, a whiskey agent in New York, and told him of the Utica brewery. Ten days after the conversation, Hart came to Utica and bought the brewery with several others.

The old Lafayette brewery was groaning under a mortgage of $13,000 held by Mrs. D.D. Winston of Utica. Hart and his partners bought the plant, paying for it with a mortgage of $16,000 given to Mrs. Winston. It was also arranged, probably by a second mortgage, that McLaughlin would have a $3,500 claim on the brewery. Thus, Max Hart paid $19,500 for the brewery without a cent of money apparently passing through his hands.

On December 22, the brewery ran an ad indicating that the first brewing of "Real German Lager Beer" would be ready by Christmas day. After that first brewing, the brewery received innumerable congratulations on the success of its first-class brew of beer. Testimonials were received by at least fifteen prominent saloonkeepers and were run in a December 28 newspaper ad. Despite this great start, problems at the brewery were only beginning.

On December 27, Mueller was stabbed by Martin Seagle. The incident did not prove fatal. Peter Christman was the only witness to the stabbing. Christman recalled the incident, saying, "One morning after Seagle had been discharged he came around, and Mueller told him he could not see him till the next day, and ordered him out. Seagle refused to go and Mueller was about to try to throw him out when I pushed Seagle out the door. He did not resist. I saw he had a knife and I closed the door. Mueller pushed me out of the way, and the next thing I heard Mueller yell, 'I am struck.' I carried Mueller into the house; he was bleeding considerable. Seagle was slightly intoxicated and very excited." Christman said that Seagle was about the brewery a good deal the day of the assault. Mueller got excited when he came there in the evening and tried to throw him out. Mueller punched Seagle once and chased him. At one time, Mueller had Seagle by the throat. In response to Christman's recollection, Mueller gave the following account of the incident:

> *One of the regular brewery workers was sick so I hired Seagle to take his place. On the Tuesday in question he was cleaning tubs or kegs and they*

*were not cleaned satisfactory to me, so I told him he should stop work. That noon he came around and wanted the card for his pay, which I gave him, allowing $2.35 for one and a half days. His pay was $1.50 per day. I did not see him again until that night at 6 o'clock. I was standing in the brewery, talking, when he entered by the back way. I asked him what he wanted. He said he wanted to speak to me. I told him he would have to come around the next day, as I had no time then. He stayed around the engine room and I told him to get out. He went about six or seven feet and stopped. I took him by the arm to the door and pushed him out. Christman (a witness) did not interfere. I did not have him by the throat at any time, neither did I strike him. After he had gone out of the door he started to come back, and I went out and ordered him out of the yard, telling him that as we had no use for him and he had been paid he should get away. He came toward me with a knife and struck me. I grabbed his hand as he did so. In taking hold of his hand I also grabbed the knife blade, which he drew through my hand, cutting it badly.*

Mueller said that Christman saw everything that occurred. He admitted that he was excited and had drunk about fifteen glasses of beer.

Seagle was apprehended in a nearby saloon, standing at the bar drinking a glass of ale. He had been drinking some but was not drunk. Seagle had a wife and four children. He was charged with assault in the first degree and was remanded to jail without bail. The opinion of many at the time was that Seagle had acted in self-defense. The police were unable to find the knife that cut Mueller. Seagle had many people on his side, and in the end, nothing came of the incident. The charges were dropped.

The brewery was closed by the sheriff on Saturday, February 27, 1897, on two executions issued from the Supreme Court. The announcement of the closing came as a surprise to many people, as they thought that all the outstanding judgments, amounting to about $1,500, would be paid.

Since the first brew of lager was put on sale, the product of the brewery had met with general favor. Many people thought the brewery would probably be reorganized, with one of the creditors as a leading member of the firm.

Early in the week, two executions were issued by Justice Rogers in favor of Scheehl & Hayes, one of the creditors, for $76.80 and Michael Doll for $98.66. Twenty bales of hops were attached to cover the amount. The hops were to be sold on March 1. Suits were brought against the brewery by Ogden & Clark, the Quigley Furniture Company, Utica Advocate, N.M. Lawton,

Utica Press Company, Shaughnessy Bros. and Hicks & Kuoll amounting to $600. W. & N.E. Kernan had a bill against Max Hart personally, in favor of Charles Millar & Son for a larger amount.

Hart had been absent from the city for some time, and all summons in suits against the company were served on the bookkeeper, James Strickland.

A brew was underway, and brewer August Mueller was instructed to finish it under the direction of the sheriff. The judgments were issued in favor of C.H. McLaughlin, maltster from Buffalo.

On March 9, 1897, attorney P.C.J. De Angelis appeared in the matter of the voluntary dissolution of the brewery and obtained an injunction stopping a sale of the personal property at auction that was to take place that day. I.J. Evans was appointed receiver to take charge of the property, and his bond was fixed at $10,000. Max Hart left for New York City on March 9, 1897. Attorneys from both sides presented arguments for how the auction should be conducted.

The brewery was sold at public auction on the morning of April 14, 1897. At the opening of the sale, receiver Evans read several typewritten pages that described the brewery and its assets and then asked for bids. The court had set the minimum bid at $6,000. Charles McLaughlin made the first bid for $2,500, but it was not accepted. August Mueller then made a bid for $6,000. The receiver announced that the sale would be open for five more minutes, but no other bids were forthcoming. Mueller was required to pay 20 percent of the purchase price immediately. As the sale was closed, Mueller produced a bulky express money envelope and, with Butler, Evans and attorney De Angelis, retired to the private office, where the first condition of the sale was fulfilled.

Mueller stated that operations at the brewery would begin again as soon as the transfer could be completed. Included in the sale were eight hundred kegs, eight horses and wagons and the equipment used in manufacturing beer. The brewery produced less than five hundred barrels in 1897. An injunction was issued temporarily forbidding the sale of the company by the sheriff because of the attachment papers on the brewery filed by Charles McLaughlin.

Justice Hiscock made the decision that the papers did not sufficiently show proof that the previous owners were trying to defraud creditors. He did, however, invalidate the sale of the brewery on April 24 because of a failure to state that there was a second mortgage on the property. The mortgage was held by the firm of Neidlinger & Sons of New York, a malt firm, for the sum of $1,344. Mueller's money was returned to him, and the resale was held on

April 29. Again, only a minimum bid greater than $6,000 would be accepted. Terms were set that one-fifth of the purchase price must be deposited at the sale and the remainder paid within five days after confirmation of the receiver's report. C.H. McLaughlin of Buffalo submitted the only bid ($5,500), and the sale was postponed until May 5. On May 5, Receiver Evans asked Mueller if he still wished to bid $6,000. Mueller replied yes, and when McLaughlin did not raise his bid, the property was sold to Mueller. For much of the month of June, creditors fought in the courts over their share of the $6,000.

Max Hart, the former proprietor of the brewery, was arrested in New York City on a charge of grand larceny brought by Thomas Bowen in connection with a horse deal. He was brought back to Utica on June 5. In police court on June 29, Bowen's lawyer said that while the matter had not been settled, Bowen had decided to withdraw his complaint. As a result, Hart was discharged and returned to New York City.

On January 17, 1898, he was again arrested in New York City, this time on a charge of grand larceny in the second degree on a complaint of Charles McLaughlin, who furnished the malt used at the brewery. He was brought back to Utica, where bail was set at $500. After posting bail, he returned to New York City. The case was finally settled in June, with Hart ordered to make restitution.

In 1898, G.A. Heckel is listed as manager of the brewery, with August Mueller still listed as proprietor. Things were not going well for Mueller and the brewery. On December 2, the brewery was sold to a group of investors headed by David A. Dischler. The new firm incorporated and issued capital stock worth $15,000. It was decided to retain the same name for the brewery. Dischler was chosen as president, with John P. Day serving as vice-president/secretary and Thomas W. Reinbrecht as treasurer. Mueller remained as brewmaster.

The main buildings of the brewery were two-story structures consisting of a brew house, a wash house, a powerhouse, a cold storage building and an office/apartment building. Power and heat were generated from coal-fired steam, and the lights were powered by gas. Several smaller buildings were also located on the brewery property.

In March 1899, the brewery changed its name to the Consumers' Brewery Inc. On May 19, Michael J. Griffin was elected vice-president/secretary for the company after Day left. Dischler was president, and Reinbrecht was treasurer. In the summer of 1899, the brewery made improvements in its buildings and constructed new stables.

A study done back in 1899 concluded that five to six times as much ale was sold in Utica as lager. Based on the findings, the brewery added an ale department to its plant in 1900. The first ale was produced and on the

TELEPHONE 612. UTICA, N. Y. ......... 189

Received of Consumer's Brewing Co.

......Cask Beer at $......per Cask. Warranted Good. To remain the property of the said Consumers' Brewing Co. until paid for.

$ ......... Casks to be returned in good order or paid for at $2.00 each.

DELIVERED BY

Customers are particularly requested not to receive any Kegs without stamps.

All Orders by letter Promptly Attended to.

Consumer's Brewing Company receipt from 1901. *Author's collection.*

market on January 1, 1900. The annual report for the brewery for the first year ending on December 1, 1899, showed that the business during that period had been more than double that of any similar time. The lager side of the plant was also enlarged. Old casks were being replaced with new and larger ones. Inquiries for Consumers' bottled lager became so frequent that the company awarded the contract to Charles Mayer (located at the corner of Mohawk and Mary Streets) to bottle its products exclusively.

In early 1900, the *American Journal of Health* gave the products made by the brewery high praise for quality and purity. Many brewers at this time used cheaper ingredients to take the place of malt and hops, but Consumers' only used hops and malt, which resulted in their high praise. The directors of the company for 1900 were Dischler, Griffin and Reinbrecht. They also served as officers of the company.

On January 7, 1901, the company filed a certificate of increase of capital stock from $30,000 to $100,000 with the secretary of state. The amount of capital stock paid in was $30,000 and debts and liabilities totaled $50,000. By the middle of 1901, William Casey became president of the company when Dischler left. Casey was also a partner in Casey & Vaughn that owned a saloon at 8 Columbia Street. The brewery was producing ale, porter and lager. It bottled its own products. William Draper was the brewmaster.

In November 1901, Michael H. Sexton was appointed by Justice Merwin as temporary receiver in the voluntary dissolution of the corporation.

The brewery closed its doors for good in 1902.

# CHAPTER 14
# NATIONAL BREWING COMPANY

## 1890–1893

W.C. Willcox purchased the old Eaton Match factory buildings located at 193–203 South Street in Utica in early 1890. A large group of men were employed to convert the buildings into a brewery. An eighty-horsepower boiler and engine was installed to furnish heat for all the buildings, as well as provide power for the operation of machinery. The water supply was obtained from a well that produced sixty barrels an hour. The water was remarkably cold, being within six degrees of freezing year round. Storage vaults were constructed underground to minimize the need for ice. The brewery was located across the street from the Utica Brewing Company owned by Charles Winslow.

On Wednesday, April 23, 1890, articles of incorporation for the National Brewing Company were filed in the county clerk's office. The incorporators were listed as William C. Willcox, William G. Willcox and Frank J. Cronk. Capital stock was $20,000 divided into two hundred shares of $100 each.

William C. Willcox, who also owned a cigar company, was chosen as president, with William G. Willcox serving as treasurer and Frank J. Cronk serving as secretary, a function he also performed at the cigar company.

Mr. Willcox stated that the intention of the brewery was to make ale similar to the style of a Philadelphia pale ale, Ogdensburg ale and other ales in their class. George H. Wallace of New York City was chosen as brewmaster. He had thirty-six years of experience at this time and had been an instructor to the brewing business. The plant had a capacity of twenty-five thousand barrels per year. Operations began at the new brewery on May 1.

The newly formed company purchased the brewery from W.C. Willcox on May 10.

In June, the brewery began drilling another well to ensure that it had enough water to keep up with anticipated demand. During the drilling, a pocket of natural gas was hit. Enough gas was coming out of the hole to warrant further exploration.

A forty-foot derrick was constructed over the well in July to sink the hole deeper with hopes of finding enough gas to make the endeavor profitable. By August, enough gas was being generated that the brewery decided to connect its furnaces to the well. It was thought that there would be sufficient gas to furnish one-half of the fuel needed by the brewery.

A pipe from the well to the engine room of the brewery was laid by the end of August. An ordinary stopcock was used to regulate the flow of gas. The gas was directed to a number of watch-shaped burners that had perforations in the tops and sides. This spread the flames out in all directions, thereby covering a large area.

By October, the natural gas was being used to supply the lighting in the offices and buildings, along with powering the equipment. The supply was increasing, and Willcox planned to drop a torpedo in the well with the hopes of striking a larger vein. This endeavor did not produce any noticeable changes in the amount of gas coming from the well, and no further attempts were made to increase production of the gas.

Things were going well for the new brewery. The public liked its products, and demand was increasing. Not everyone, however, was thrilled at having another brewery in the area.

In December 1890, the brewery developed plans and specifications for the construction of a new brick building. The new building would be eighty feet by sixty feet and would be four stories high with an elevator. One portion of the building would be used for malting, and the cellars would provide additional storage. With these facilities, the company would be able to more readily supply its rapidly increasing trade. James Crandell had the contract for the brick and stonework, and the Jones Bros. had the carpenter work.

In May 1891, people living near the National Brewing Company and the Utica Brewing Company were complaining bitterly of the stench coming from the gulf. They claimed that the breweries were draining wastes directly into it.

This was not the first time a complaint had been entered. Health officials said that in late 1890, the breweries were draining into the gulf because there were no sewers with which to hook up. The matter was dropped because of the lack of a sewer. By 1891, the area had sewers, but neither brewery had bothered to hook up to them. On May 6, Sanitary Inspector Casey was directed by the health officer to go to the breweries and notify the proprietors that unless a remedy was forthcoming, legal proceedings would be instituted against the breweries for polluting the stream and maintaining a public nuisance.

At a May 7 Board of Health meeting, Inspector Casey reported that the Utica Brewing Company was allowing wastewater to run into the gulf. The foul water from rinsing the brewery's barrels, however, was conveyed into the St. Vincent Street sewer. The National Brewing Company, on the other hand, ran all its waste and foul water directly into the gulf, blackening the ground and covering it with slime.

The Board of Health gave both breweries until May 21 to correct the problems. The National Brewing Company was the first to comply and was completely hooked up to the sewer system by May 13.

In the summer of 1891, extensive improvements were made at the brewery. To make room for a new masher and a number of new tanks, the brewery added two stories to its main building. This work was completed by the end of July. The Billings Patent Masher that had been ordered in February was installed in July and weighed twenty-two tons. The masher was made of steel and had a capacity of two hundred barrels per day. It had cost the brewery $10,000.

On July 21, a fire broke out in the Utica Brewing Company across the street. Upon hearing the alarms, employees of the National brewery, headed by John H. Holleran, laid their fire hose and had the first stream on the fire. Had the hose been longer, the workers felt that they could have put out the fire and saved the brewery. Instead, the Utica Brewing Company burned to the ground.

Prior to August 1891, the saloon owners enjoyed the benefits of a price war between the local breweries. Beer was selling for five dollars a barrel. After a good deal of skirmishing in which no one brewery came out ahead financially, the breweries decided that the most profitable way of doing business would be with a uniform price.

On August 29, the Oneida and Herkimer Counties Ale Association was formally organized in the office of William Willcox. He was the president of the National Brewing Company. Willcox was elected the president of the association; Fred Ralph, vice-president; and Theodore B. Davis, secretary and treasurer.

The price of beer was then at six dollars per barrel, and members of the association resolved to sell only at that figure. All the ale breweries in Utica were included, as were the breweries in Oriskany Falls and Ilion. Meetings were held on the first Saturday of the month and were harmonious until the March 1892 meeting. In that meeting, a scheme for consolidating all the Utica breweries was brought up and discussed. It was argued that by placing all under one management and in one corporation, a vast amount would be saved in manufacturing, selling and handling the beer. Some of the present breweries could be shut down and sold for other purposes.

It was reported that the majority were in favor of doing it but wanted to wait and see the workings of a similar plan that had been recently put into effect in Syracuse. From this, a disagreement among the members started. It appears that everyone but Willcox was in agreement. He brought matters to a head by pulling out of the association.

On April 7, agents of the National Brewing Company went out and started selling the company's beer for $4.50 per barrel. This was $1.50 lower than the agreed upon price. Orders for around four thousand barrels were taken that morning. The other breweries did little business that day.

Inquiries were made of Willcox, but he could not be found. The office said he went to Albany. A meeting was held in Moses Barney's office, where the matter was discussed at length. The Oneida and Herkimer Counties Ale Association decided to match the reduction, but no action was taken that day. The next day, they met at Willcox's office. Willcox was still absent. In this meeting, they decided to drop the price to four dollar per barrel. The organization resolved to maintain the lower price to try to drive the National Brewing Company out of business.

There was little or no profit at $4.00 to $4.50 a barrel, and it was now a matter of endurance to the winner. The association blamed the state of affairs completely on Willcox. When the association was first organized, he was very supportive but then violated the agreement when he withdrew without notice. The agreement allowed a withdrawal by giving notice at any regular meeting. Willcox did not do this, however.

The association also claimed that the National Brewing Company had recently installed a new masher and was making cheap inferior ale, using corn instead of barley. National officials responded that the corn was simply converted to sugar and that only the best products were used for its ale. The brewery was confident that it was not in danger of being driven out of business.

Why Willcox suddenly turned against the organization was the topic of much discussion. One prominent brewer said that after the talk of consolidating, Willcox wanted to form a little syndicate of four breweries that were situated along the gulf on the east side of town. The breweries were National, Utica, Gulf and Utica Star. He would leave the others out in the cold and then annihilate them, but failing this, he preferred to take his chances alone. Thus, another beer war began. The National and Willcox would end up being the losers.

In 1892, a large number of shares of the capital stock changed hands. As a result, the stockholders met for reorganization. New officers were chosen: president, Wm. C. Willcox; vice-president and treasurer, Dr. M.A. MacOwen; secretary and general manager, Patrick McNierney.

A vigorous warfare existed among the local brewers at the time. Willcox began to sell his beer at cost in an effort to gain more market share. This made local saloonkeepers very happy and did increase sales, but ultimately, this tactic could not go on. A decision was made to consolidate with the Utica Brewing Company.

In May 1893, the two breweries joined forces and became known as the Utica National Brewing Company. The remainder of the story is told in the Utica National Brewing Company chapter.

In 1911 the old brewery buildings were torn down. A new Kendall Button Factory was built on the site and was finished by March.

# CHAPTER 15
# UTICA NATIONAL BREWING COMPANY
## 1893–1901

In May 1893, the National Brewing Company and the Utica Brewing Company merged in an attempt to combat increasing competition from other brewers. Alterations and improvements were made in the Utica Brewing Company buildings to increase its capacity to 150 barrels a day. The Utica brewery was to be operated at full capacity, while the National brewery plant would only be used as needed.

Things went well for the brewery at the beginning, and business was booming. In 1893, the brewery expanded with capital stock of $160,000. This was a very sizable sum of money in those days. Each company contributed $80,000. The name of the brewery was changed at this time to the Utica National Brewing Company, with John R. Taylor as the head brewer.

The new brewery consisted of several groups of buildings. The first group of buildings contained a four-story structure with offices, fermenting tanks and storage; a two-story building with a wash house and mill; a four-story brew house; a one-story beer vault; and a one-story power house. The second group of buildings contained a well house, a beer cellar and storage houses. There were also several smaller buildings on the premises.

John A. Goodale became president in 1894. By early 1895, the brewery had made an application for a receiver. Business had fallen greatly over the past two years. Josiah Perry was appointed temporary receiver for the company. Liabilities were quoted at $87,000, with assets at $50,000. William F. Barney of the Watertown Brewing Company and William Welch of the

Gulf Brewing Company offered to help in the management of the brewery while it was being reorganized.

James A. Douglass of Oriskany Falls and John C. Metzger of Utica appraised the property of the Utica National Brewing Company for receiver Perry on January 18, 1895. The value of the personal property was estimated at $35,000 and the real estate at $60,000 to $75,000.

A hearing was held on April 20, 1895, before referee C.A. Miller to hear proofs as to whether the brewery should be dissolved. Principal creditors were First National Bank, Dr. MacOwen, Brookhall Malting Company of Mohawk, Oswego Malting Company, Carr Insurance and Mrs. Quigley.

One of the principal questions to be litigated was whether a claim of over $50,000 of the First National Bank of Utica was a claim that the brewery was bound to pay. The Utica National Brewing Company was a consolidation of two breweries. Some of the creditors claimed that the new consolidated company did not assume the payment of this indebtedness, while the First National Bank claimed that the statute itself makes the debt, although originally contracted by the old brewing company, a debt of the new company. Later, the report of C.H. Miller stated that the company did not have sufficient money to pay its debts and that it should be dissolved and a receiver appointed.

At a hearing before Justice Wright on August 10, 1895, some people objected to a confirmation of Miller's report. Judge Wright granted an order confirming the report, dissolving the corporation and appointing Josiah Perry as permanent receiver.

The company was formed by the consolidation of the Utica and the National breweries on South Street, and when that action was taken, William C. Willcox had given notes prior to his death aggregating $38,000 to liquidate the debts of the National brewery so the new company might begin business with a clean ledger. The First National Bank held these notes and, after the death of Willcox, demanded payment from the company on the grounds that renewal of a note does not pay debt and that the brewery was therefore liable for the old debts.

The Supreme Court heard the case again on October 15, 1895. The earlier ruling was upheld, and the corporation could be dissolved. Josiah Perry was made permanent receiver again. Perry advertised the sale of the brewery on January 1896. The brewery's real estate and property would be auctioned on February 12, 1896, to the highest bidder.

The property consisted of two breweries, one located on the north side and the other on the south side of South Street. Attached to the brewery on the south side was a fully equipped barn, and attached to the brewery on the north side were two tenement houses.

Each brewing plant had all the appliances and equipment for making and brewing ales of all kinds, including all tools, tubs, casks, barrels and all other appliances for making, storing and setting ale.

There were about 1,900 barrels for storing ale, 780 half barrels, 490 hogsheads, 300 stock barrels, four horses, several sets of single and double harnesses, two hay cutters, seven delivery wagons, one buggy and one cutter, a large quantity of hops and 400 barrels of ale.

Also included in the sale would be $27,000 worth of accounts receivable due the National Brewing Company from customers who had purchased ale made by them. The brewery would be kept in operation until the completion of the sale. Terms of the sale were 10 percent due the day of the sale and the rest immediately on confirmation of the sale by the Supreme Court.

The property of the brewery was sold by auctioneer James F. Hone for receiver Perry on February 12, 1896. It was sold to William Welch for $30,100, subject to a mortgage of $2,000. Bidding was spirited and started at $20,000 by the Oswego Malting Company. It was understood that Welch bought the property in the interests of several Utica parties who intended to form a company to operate the brewery. The Supreme Court confirmed the sale on March 14, 1896.

Legal problems for the brewery continued. On July 1, 1896, the brewery was sold at public auction for unpaid assessments. The city was the sole bidder. The attorney representing the brewery objected to the sale of the property on the grounds that the assessments were illegal. The assessments were for $1,047.48 and $709.51. The brewery was given fifteen months to redeem the property.

In August 1897, attorneys for Ella Wilcox, executrix of the will of the late William Willcox, served notice of appeal concerning the report of the referee in the affairs of the Utica National Brewing Company. On October 18 and 19, the matter was heard before the Court of Appeals in Albany. The Court of Appeals upheld the original ruling, and the legal battles came to an end.

Upon Willcox's death, Patrick McNierney became manager of the brewery. An effort was made to consolidate the Utica breweries in late 1899. A group of New York City bankers wanted to secure the breweries in a deal similar to the deal that was reached with breweries in the Albany area.

The first attempt to consolidate was before the new revenue tax went into effect. The tax was used to help fund the Spanish-American War. As a base of sale, an offer was made in the amount six and one-half times the average profits of the breweries for three years, or $195,000 for a brewery that could show an annual profit of $10,000. Cash or its equivalent was offered, and 2.5 percent was ready as a deposit to bind the bargain. The offer was made by Bell Bros. of New York City, a banking house.

When the revenue tax went into effect, the tax on beer was increased from one dollar to three dollars per barrel. This cut the profits, and now a brewery that sold forty thousand barrels of beer a year and paid the necessary tax before it left the brewery must hustle. The offer of Bell Bros. was withdrawn, as it was no longer a profitable proposal.

The owners of the breweries could not make a go of it and in March 1900 offered both breweries for sale. Terms and all other information could be obtained by addressing or calling on William F. Welch at the Gulf Brewing Company's office on Jay Street. By 1901 (the brewery's last year in operation), William F. Welch had become president of the brewery. Welch was also connected to the Eagle Brewing Company (treasurer) and the Gulf Brewing Company (secretary and treasurer).

# CHAPTER 16
# FORT SCHUYLER BREWERY (FORT SCHUYLER BREWING COMPANY)

## 1884–1918

In the spring of 1884, William J. Brown, Stephen A. Failey, Robert P. Joyce and Edward H. Harding formed Brown, Failey & Company with the intention of entering the brewing business. They immediately started to search for a location for their brewery. In July, they purchased the Old Fort Schuyler Distillery on Catharine Street from Thomas R. McQuade. The building and property was purchased for $15,000.

This property was a triangular-shaped plot of land where Catharine Street joined the Erie Canal. The building had been vacant for the previous six years. The People's Brewing Company was located across the street.

The new owners planned to spend approximately $25,000 in improvements to the building to convert it to a brewery. They announced September 1 as their projected startup date. They decided to call their brewery the Fort Schuyler Brewery partly because the old building had previously used the Fort Schuyler name and partly out of recognition of an old Revolutionary War–era fort that went by that name in the area. By the middle of August, most of the renovations were complete, and the new equipment was in place. The first brewing of the firm was made on September 20, a couple weeks behind schedule. The brewery was set up to produce ales only.

The firm of Brown, Failey & Company of the Fort Schuyler Brewery was dissolved by mutual consent on March 19, 1886, when William Brown decided to retire. A new firm, Failey, Joyce & Company, was created in its place to run the brewery. The new firm bought the brewery on April 2 from William E. Lewis, who was acting as a receiver for the old company. Stephen

An 1885 trade card from Brown, Failey & Company Fort Schuyler Brewery. *Ron Gavin private collection.*

A. Failey was president of the new firm, with Robert P. Joyce serving as secretary and Daniel F. Shaughnessy serving as treasurer.

By 1888, the brewery consisted of a one-story powerhouse, a three-story brew house and a one-story steaming and cooper shop. There was also a wagon shed on the property. The company office was located on the first floor of the brew house. Power and heat were provided by coal-fired steam, and the lights were gas powered. In 1891, the brewery changed its name to the Fort Schuyler Brewing Company. James P. Sheridan became manager of the brewery in 1896.

On March 14, 1896, William E. Lewis was appointed receiver for the brewery by Justice Hiscock in Syracuse on behalf of Sarah A. Sheridan and Kittie Failey. Together with Jennie A. Joyce, they were partners in the business, which was conducted by J.P. Sheridan, Stephen A. Failey and R.P. Joyce. The lawyer for Mrs. Sheridan and Mrs. Failey asked that Mr. Sheridan and Mr. Failey be appointed receivers, alleging that Mr. Joyce was incompetent to run the business, and affidavits were read to substantiate this fact. One was to the effect that Joyce would take orders for beer but would keep the orders for a week or so. Then another affidavit was read to the effect that a purchaser of beer wanted it delivered a week after the order, but the beer came the next day and the purchaser refused to take it. Other affidavits were read to show that Joyce was not trustworthy and that he injured the business. Joyce's attorneys opposed the appointing of the two receivers and wanted some disinterested party. Mr. Lewis was thus agreed upon. His bond was for $5,000. The assets of the company were between $17,000 and $18,000. After reviewing the case, Lewis sold the property on April 2, 1896, to John Doyle. The brewery continued in operation.

Robert Joyce, one of the founders of the brewery, died on June 10, 1896, of pneumonia at the age of thirty-nine. He was running a grocery at the time and had by then left the brewery.

Peter Kerwin, a longtime brewer at Fort Schuyler, resigned in June 1896 to take a similar position at the People's Brewing Company. His fellow employees presented him with a ring and a going-away gift.

In 1897, the brewery produced between five thousand and six thousand barrels of ale and porter. This increased to between ten thousand and twelve thousand barrels in 1898. J.P. Sheridan was brewmaster in 1898. F.X. Schmelsle was an agent and peddler for the brewery in 1898, bottling its products and selling them locally.

In 1900, the officers for the company were John Doyle, president; Henry B. Moore, vice-president and treasurer; and Frank J. Winslow, secretary and manager. At the annual stockholder meeting, it was decided to make some extensive repairs to the plant and to add a three-story addition on the rear section of the plant. New refrigeration and other equipment were to be purchased. In May, a Case refrigerating machine was subsequently installed, capable of making ten tons of ice a day. A new storage cellar was constructed, with new vats installed so that 1,500 barrels of ale could be kept in refrigerated storage at one time. A new Theurer filter was installed. This filter type had been exclusively used at the Pabst brewery. This was the first one installed in the East. A new eighty-horsepower horizontal boiler, manufactured by Beach & Co. of Hartford, Connecticut, was the last upgrade made by the brewery.

On May 29, 1900, the first brewing of ale was made in the newly renovated brewery. The brewery remained under the same ownership until 1901. That year, it was sold to Edward S. Callahan. Callahan was a graduate of the National Brewers' Academy in New York. He changed the name of the brewery on May 4 to the Callahan Brewery and added extra employees to the workforce. Callahan was a recent graduate from the Institute for Scientific Brewing in New York.

John Wallace was working on the second floor of the brewery, which was dimly lit on October 15, 1901. He accidently fell through an open trapdoor to the floor below. He struck the ground on his side and lay unconscious for some time. He was later discovered and taken to the hospital, where it was determined that he had suffered a broken hip.

The Callahan Brewery was offered for sale in March 1902. Possession could be given at once.

In September 1902, a group of local retail liquor dealers completed plans for the resumption of brewing at the old Fort Schuyler brewery. It was put back in working condition, and the operation of the brewery was to be conducted by a corporation known as the Home Brewing Company. The group never carried out its plans. By early 1903, a different group of investors purchased the old brewery from the estate of Edward Callahan. Callahan had died in late 1902.

The new investors formed the Fort Schuyler Brewing Company and incorporated with capital stock of $20,000.

John Doyle served as president of the new company, with Frank J. Winslow serving as secretary and brewmaster and Henry B. Moore serving as vice-president and treasurer.

One of the first decisions made by the new company was to advertise in the local newspapers in an effort to increase sales and public awareness of its product. This idea seemed to work, and before long, almost all the other breweries in town were following suit. The enormous increase in business prompted the brewery to add new equipment to keep up with the demand. A large Loew filter was installed in April 1904.

Extensive repairs were made to the brewery in the first half of 1905, which was necessitated by the increasing business. A refrigerating plant was installed. Three more stories were added to the rear of the plant, and a large amount of modern machinery was installed.

On March 21, 1905, the cooper shop at the brewery caught fire. It was extinguished after about thirty minutes.

On November 6, 1905, a drunk stole a brewery delivery wagon, which he then crashed. As the two brewery deliverymen were placing a barrel of beer in a cellar of a saloon at the corner of John and Catharine Streets around 11:00 a.m., a drunk named Cooney mounted the wagon. He picked up the reins and started the team down John Street at a lively pace. His condition was such that he was unable to stand still and kept swaying back

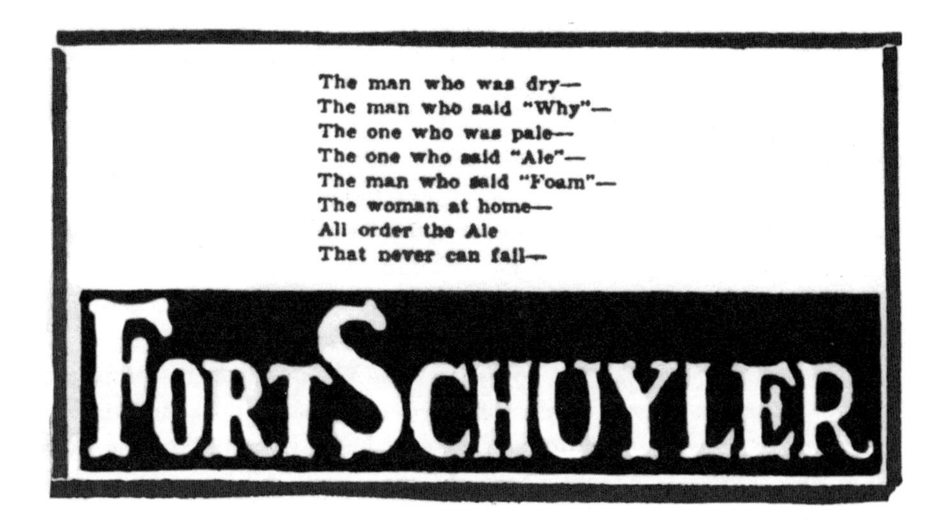


Ad from *Utica Daily Press*, April 1904.

and forth. The brewery wagon finally collided with a heavily loaded farmer's rig, coming to a sudden stop. When the two teams and wagons collided, the horses fell to the ground and were hurt. One of the wheels on the brewery wagon was smashed, and the farmer's rig was badly damaged. Cooney was thrown from the wagon. Someone called for an ambulance. When it arrived, the driver discovered that Cooney was very drunk and not really hurt, and he ended up taking him to the police station.

In early 1906, the brewery opened its newly reconstructed storage house, which would also serve as a bottling plant for the brewery. It was located on the old Peoples Brewing Company site across the street from the main brewery.

In June 1906, the brewery became the distributer for Budweiser in the Utica area. Job Parker & Sons had been the Budweiser distributers in Utica up until this time. Fort Schuyler's advertising in newspapers increased after this, but most of the ads were for Budweiser and only mentioned Fort Schuyler as the distributer.

Fort Schuyler's decision to distribute Budweiser resulted from a need for additional capital, and because its products were ales, the company felt that distributing Budweiser (a lager) would not hurt its sales. The Oneida Brewing Company followed the company's lead and became distributers for Pabst lager.

This idea to distribute for larger breweries may have helped over the next few years, but then the Eagle Brewing Company launched a major campaign in Utica to buy local products. This campaign was a success, and Budweiser/Fort Schuyler sales declined.

John Doyle, brewery president, died of a heart attack on August 21, 1906, while driving around the city in his electric automobile. He was sixty-three years old. He was born in Ireland and came to this country as a small boy with his parents. They came to Utica to settle. Doyle started the Utica Brick Works in 1875 with his partner, Ed Callahan. He ran that business alone after Callahan died in 1902. It was in 1903 that he became interested in the brewery when the widow of Ed Callahan was looking to sell the place.

On September 26, 1906, a two-story frame barn on the west side of Second Street, just north of Catharine Street, belonging to the brewery caught fire. The fire started around 2:30 p.m. in the lower part of the barn but quickly spread to the upper floor, which was filled with straw. The fire department responded promptly and managed to get the fire under control. The roof of the barn was burned off, and the interior was badly scorched. The origin of the fire was unknown. The loss to the brewery was estimated at $1,000 and was covered by insurance. Around 9:30 p.m. that night, the fire department had to return to the brewery to put out a small fire that started in some dust next to the siding of the barn.

The brewery bought an old brick building adjoining its property in 1907 to allow for the erection of an addition. While demolishing the building, workmen found an old city directory containing a number of U.S. gold certificates between the pages. The building's previous owner was a miserly old woman who had died several years before and had apparently hidden the certificates in the book for safekeeping.

The new addition was a steel frame storage house (eighty-five feet by eighty feet). It was two stories high, entirely fireproof and constructed of brick, steel and concrete. The capacity of the building was 3,600 barrels and was connected to the brewery proper by a subway seven feet high and five feet wide. A new power plant was also being constructed. This was also two stories high, thirty-six feet by forty feet and constructed of brick and concrete. It contained two 125-horsepower boilers. This building was also connected to the main brewery by a tunnel. Finally, a new stable was constructed, large enough to accommodate twenty-five horses.

Henry B. Moore had become president of the brewery by 1909, though he still retained his treasurer's position. Frank J. Winslow was still secretary and had also accepted the responsibility of plant manager. In late 1909, the brewery offered preferred 8 percent stock in the company to generate more needed capital. William Chase became brewmaster in 1909, replacing Winslow.

In late 1909, the brewery amended its charter, increasing its capital stock from $20,000 to $100,000. By 1911, William Calre became brewmaster and remained in that position until Prohibition.

On December 19, 1912, the brewery fired one of its union workers because he broke an adding machine and was drunk on the job. The worker claimed that the breaking of the adding machine was an accident and said that he wasn't drunk on the job. He had several witnesses to prove it. All of this was to no avail. The worker remained fired.

On Tuesday, February 22, eight brewery union workers went out on strike against the company, claiming that the fired worker had been unjustly discharged. The brewery declared that the action of discharging the man was taken only after a sufficient cause—the destroying of the company's property.

The manager of the brewery said that the contract between the brewery and the union had been fully recognized by the brewery. The contract existing between the two parties was made the previous April. The union label would not be restored to the brewery's products until it conceded to the demands of the international union headquarters and the Brewery Workmen's Union, Local 64.

The dispute was finally worked out on April 6, 1912, six weeks after it started. The terms under which the union agreed to return to work were not made public, but it was understood that both sides made concessions. It is not known whether the fired employee got his job back.

The wages of brewery workers at the Fort Schuyler Brewing Company at that time were eighteen dollars per week for eight hours per day of inside work and eighteen dollars per week for nine hours a day for work on the wagons.

A sleigh belonging to the brewery and loaded down with heavy barrels of beer became struck on the trolley tracks, blocking both the north- and southbound lines for more than ten minutes on December 29, 1915. Horses from another team were unhitched and attached to the stuck brewery wagon. The sleigh still did not budge. Finally, a 180-horsepower Samson motor truck got behind the wagon and pushed it off the tracks.

The brewery was assessed at $11,800 in 1918 and paid $439 in City and County taxes. It was the smallest brewery operating in Utica at this time.

During the years before Prohibition, the brewery added storage facilities a short distance down the street. With the coming of Prohibition, Fort Schuyler, like many of the other breweries in the area, searched for a way to continue in business. The company's first endeavor occurred in 1919 when it formed the New England Cider Company. This seemed to be one of the first ideas to which many of the local breweries turned. They were advertising pure sweet apple cider in any quantity for forty-five cents per gallon.

Fort Schuyler Brewing Company letterhead from 1914. *Ron Gavin private collection.*

Frank J. Winslow leased the brewery property from the company and applied for a cereal beverage permit on August 28, 1926. He was granted the permit on December 31, 1926. However, by September 1927, the government was looking to revoke the beverage permit owned by Frank J. Winslow. Following a hearing before Judge Edna Lee, the revocation was made on the contention that an underground tunnel adjoined the brewery premises with others at the brewery. Agents reported that a plank was thrown across the mouth of the tunnel and that the partition could be moved on concealed hinges.

An application for reinstatement of the Fort Schuyler Brewing Company's cereal beverage was made on March 17, 1928, before Judge Frederick Bryant in Syracuse. Lawyers for Winslow contended that the partition had always been a door and that the general conditions affecting its construction were known to the authorities at the time the license was first granted. The passageway had existed since 1904 and was used to carry heating pipes from the boiler building to the brewery proper. Since Prohibition and up to January 11, 1926, the passageway was used for conveying packages and barrels from the cooperage across from the brewery.

On October 17, 1928, federal judge Frederick Bryant decided in favor of the brewery, and its permit was restored. In his decision, Judge Bryant did not decide whether the tunnel had a door or a dead wall but found that the place had been closed as ordered by prohibition officials.

When Prohibition ended, a new group of investors leased the brewery facilities and formed the Utica Brewing Company.

# CHAPTER 17
# HOME BREWING COMPANY

## 1902

In the summer of 1902, the leading saloonkeepers in Utica began exploring the idea of starting a brewery so that they might provide themselves with beer at better rates than they were paying. They entered into negotiations looking to acquire the Fort Schuyler brewery plant, which was idle at the time.

The plant, although old as a brewery, had relatively new equipment. It had the latest improved filters installed two years before, as well as a new ice machine and cold storage plant. A number of meetings were held for those interested. On August 5, Thomas Ryan, who ran the Consumers' Brewery in Syracuse, and his brewer, Mr. Morgan, looked over the old brewery to ascertain what it would cost to put it back in operation. They made a report the next day that was very encouraging.

The new company was to be formed as a result of the refusal of the local brewers to cut the price of their beer when the sixty-dollar revenue tax was taken off. The saloonkeepers had asked for half of the sixty-dollar reduction to be passed along to them, but the brewers refused to do so. There were twenty-five interested parties who represented some of the largest saloons in the area.

They were also in correspondence with some of the largest lager beer brewers in the country and had received their assurances that they could be supplied with the best quality lager at competitive rates. They decided to proceed with the project.

At a meeting held the next week, a decision was made to incorporate with $10,000 capital with $5,000 to be paid in. At the meeting, $1,200 was paid in by various parties with the remainder being due at any time during the next thirty days. The owners of the old Fort Schuyler brewery were notified to get the plant in readiness. The former manager was expected to return from New York City to oversee the work to get the plant ready.

On August 15, another meeting was held in which temporary officers were elected and a name for the brewery was selected. It was resolved to form a company to be known as the Home Brewing Company. The following temporary officers were elected; Julius Wick, president; E.J. Fish, vice-president; Joseph Wurz, secretary; and John P. Murphy, treasurer. A committee was appointed to go to Cincinnati and buy 350 barrels, and the attorney was instructed to file articles of incorporation in Albany. The company also obtained options on the Fort Schuyler brewery property.

By late August, certain people thought the idea had gone far enough. They got together with some of the stockholders of the new company and bought them out. This caused the whole project to fold.

In dropping the project, not all the men interested in the new company were consulted. Nine of them knew nothing of the affair until after the deal was made. The president of the company and the other members who did know about the deal were paid $150 for their $100 interest in the company and would get their beer at a reduced rate. At that time, it was stated that Utica beer was being sold outside the city for $5 per barrel, while in Utica it was being sold for $6 per barrel. The local breweries were accused of being behind the buyout, but all the breweries emphatically denied this.

William F. Welch, president of the Gulf Brewing Company and secretary and treasurer of the Eagle Brewing Company, said, "I can speak for both the companies in which I am interested when I say that neither of them had anything to do with the plans for the Home Brewing project falling through. We have not bought a single share of the stock and we have not made a single concession. The men in the proposed company had nothing to sell and we are not in the habit of paying for something for nothing. The idea that we are selling beer cheaper outside the city than we are in Utica is also wrong. We are not selling it at lower prices, in fact in some places we are getting more than we do here."

G. Fred Ralph, treasurer of the Oneida Brewing Company, said, "The whole story, that the breweries now running bought the saloonkeepers not to start their brewery, is wrong. I can answer for the Oneida Brewery and assure you that it had nothing whatever to with any such scheme."

F.X. Matt, treasurer and superintendent of the West End Brewing Company, said, "The article saying that the breweries of Utica had bought out the stockholders of the Home Brewing Company and that we are selling beer outside the city at $5 a barrel is untrue in every word. In the first place the saloonkeepers were not organized. They had no stock and had nothing to sell. Not one of them was ever approached by any of us in any way. We had absolutely nothing to do with the Home Brewing Company or its stockholders at any time. As to the statement about our selling beer at $5 outside the city, as I said before, it is not true. On the contrary we are getting better prices outside the city than we get here."

The president of the Home Brewing Company, Julius Wick, said in response, "All I know is that Joe Wagner paid me $150 Thursday for my $100 share in the brewery. How or where he got it, I don't know. I know I got it and I don't worry." Who Wagner was working for is unknown, as he does not appear to be a stockholder in any of the local breweries.

The last meeting of the stockholders was held, and only nine out of the twenty-seven original members showed up. Acting on the information they had on hand, they concluded that the project was dead. They knew that at least one of the members had been bought out (Wick) and that others had been approached. They decided to dissolve the company.

Three days later, one of the stockholders of the new company showed a check for $94 and some odd cents and remarked: "This is what they sent me back of my $100 share. It cost me a little over $5."

This concluded the saloonkeeper's attempt at getting better prices by starting their own brewery.

# CHAPTER 18
# PEOPLE'S BREWING COMPANY
## 1882–1899

In early 1882, many beer retailers were dissatisfied with the price they had to pay for beer, as well as the fact that most of it came from out of town. A few of these men got together to explore the possibility of starting a brewery. Each was asked to survey various other retailers in the city to see if there would be enough potential support.

James Baker and Luke Hill were asked to see if the Gulf Brewery (recently devastated by fire) was for sale. On June 6, forty interested retailers met in Firemen's Hall in Utica to consider the brewery project. Alderman James Hayes was called to chair the meeting, and James Hackett was made secretary.

Reports were heard from various gentlemen on how many people were interested in buying shares in the new brewery and the approximate total that might be raised. Luke Hill reported that the Gulf Brewery could be bought for a low figure, which would be revealed later that week.

Alderman Hayes said that when the last new brewery was started in Utica, the price of beer was put down to $5 per barrel. If sixty of the saloon keepers subscribed for one share each, it would make $6,000, or enough to do business with. He believed beer could be made and sold at a profit at $5 per barrel. If all the retailers agreed to take beer from the new brewery, there would be plenty of business.

Hill reported that he had contacted an architect and had been told that a brewery could be built and equipped in good shape for $15,000. John Doyle thought it would require $20,000 to build and equip a new brewery. He believed one hundred saloonkeepers could be found who would subscribe

$200 each. Each stockholder would sign a contract to take all his beer from the new brewery. The capital need not all be paid in at once but could be called for as needed.

Alderman Hayes said he felt that no subscriber should be allowed to take more than five shares, so as to get as many retailers as possible interested. The Utica brewery on South Street was considered a good business of average size that brewed 230 barrels a week. Hayes said that if sixty dealers were interested and sold an average of three barrels a week, the demand would be 180 barrels a week, or just about what an average-sized brewery could produce successfully.

Doyle made a motion that articles of incorporation be drawn up. A committee of three (Doyle, Rowe and Carey) was appointed to accomplish this. Shares in the new brewery were limited to a total of two hundred. Doyle, Lehman and Ballou were appointed to a committee to circulate the stock subscription lists among the retailers. The committee on buildings (Luke and Baker) was authorized to make an estimate of the proposed cost of the new brewery either in East or West Utica, preferably on a paved street.

At a later meeting held on June 23, a decision was made to proceed with the new brewery and not wait until all the stock was subscribed for. Many felt that if they did not get started at this time, they never would.

A committee of ten was formed to make nominations for the places of the five directors at the next meeting. Chairman Hayes said he thought it was important that the committee act with caution, naming some men from the center of the city and some from the eastern part, some to represent the German element, some the Irish and some the American.

At the June 28 follow-up meeting, People's Brewing Company was chosen as the company name. James Hayes, F. Louis Faass, John Carey, Timothy Coakley and John Doyle were nominated and chosen as directors of the new company. During that same meeting, Hayes was chosen to serve as president, Coakley was chosen secretary and Faass was chosen treasurer. The capital stock of the company was fixed at $15,000 and was divided into 150 shares. A call for 25 percent of the subscriptions was made immediately.

On July 25, the new company filed articles of incorporation at the county clerk's office. James Hayes, F. Louis Faass and John Doyle were appointed to select a site for the new brewery. Several pieces of property were under consideration. Among them were the Wilsey lot, at the corner of Second and Catharine Streets; the Wagner lot on Erie Street; five lots on South Street, next to the City Hospital, owned by Michael Hopkins; a lot on Bleecker Street near the House of Good Shephard, owned by O.C. Guelich; and three lots at the corner of South Street and McQuade Avenue owned by T.S. McIncrow.

The Wilsey lot was chosen and purchased on July 31 for $2,500. The lot was one hundred feet square and had a barn on it occupied by J.A. Curry. The lot was located across from the Old Fort Schuyler Distillery and was felt to be in a very good location for shipping by either canal or railroad.

The plans and estimates for the brewery had been prepared by architect Thomas Birt. James Warren was awarded the contract for the excavation and masonry work at the brewery site. By August 15, the excavation work was nearly done. Warren had stated in his contract that all his work would be finished by September. The contract for the carpentry work, trimming and painting of the brewery was awarded to the firm of Riley & Brazille for the sum of $3,200. The remaining work for the brewery was contracted to Joseph Beecher. By December 1882, the building was nearly complete.

The brewery was constructed of wood and was three stories high, with a basement. The dimensions were forty by seventy-five feet. It was constructed with an eye to utilizing all the space to the best advantage. The capacity of the brewery was 135 barrels of ale per day, which was greater than that of any other brewing establishment in the city at that time.

On the first floor was the malt mill, with the attending apparatus. Here the malt was prepared for use, with fifty bushels per hour being ground if necessary. It was then carried by a grain elevator to the third story and placed in a large bin. The malt mill was purchased from A. Dobler in New York City.

When this malt was desired for use, it was carried to the second floor by the grain elevator and placed in a masher. The masher had a capacity of about 275 bushels. Here the malt was mashed and prepared for the boiling tub. It was then carried by this same elevator to the top of the third story. The top story was very high and was divided by staging into three levels. At the highest part of the building was the boiling tub, provided with copper pipes. Into this, the mashed malt and hops were placed and boiled by means of hot steam being forced through the pipes. This tub was ten feet ten inches in diameter and had a capacity of 135 barrels. It was about 45 barrels larger than any similar tub in the city.

Next to this tub stood a smaller tub that had a capacity of about ninety barrels. This was the cooling tub. The contents of the boiling tub were transferred by means of a pipe into this tub. Under these tubs, and on the third floor proper, were two tubs of a capacity of one hundred barrels each. One of these tubs was furnished with a tier of copper pipes in the bottom and was for the purpose of heating and keeping hot water. The other tub was for surplus hot water, and thus warm water was kept constantly on hand. In case anything should happen to the boiling or cooling tubs, these tubs could be used also for those purposes. On this floor, the portion of the building facing Second Street was divided off for a malt room.

On the second floor, besides the masher, were two tubs used for fermenting purposes. The contents of the cooling tub were carried by a pipe to this floor. It ran through a network of copper cooling pipes into the fermenting tubs. These tubs had a capacity of one hundred barrels each. The contents of these tubs were then carried by pipes to the first floor into two tempering tubs. Here the beer was cooled to a certain temperature and was then drawn off into barrels and was ready for the market. There were nine of these tubs made of cedar. They were purchased from Burkhadt's Sons of Philadelphia.

The front portion of the first floor had been partitioned off into an office for the managers. This floor also contained the hopper scales. These had a capacity of two hundred bushels and were purchased from French, Kincaid & Co. The engine for the brewery was located on this floor, and in the rear of the building stood the boiler. The forty-horsepower engine and boiler were purchased from Skinner & Arnold of Albany. The basement was eleven feet high and was constructed on solid rock. It was well lighted and ventilated. The beer was stored here when ready for the market.

Running through the center of the building from the basement to the top story was a six-foot-square elevator. This was used for all purposes of the brewery other than the carrying of grain, which was done in a separate elevator. The elevator was made by J.W. Reedy of New York City. The copper work for the brewery was done by John Trageser's Steam Copper Works in New York City and was very expensive for the times, costing nearly $2,500. The building was heated by steam, and the plumbing was done by Edward Martin.

The brewery was expected to be in operation sometime between January 1 and 10, 1883. Only ale was planned to be brewed for the first year. On Monday, January 29, 1883, the stockholders gave a reception at the brewery to celebrate the opening. A large crowd attended to sample the first brewing and the free lunch. Everyone present had a good time and left with best wishes for the success of the brewery and stockholders. There were fifty-two stockholders when the brewery finally began operating. Every one of them was a retail dealer and had committed to using 825 barrels of ale per month.

On February 8, 1883, William McTiernan was elected as a director of the brewery in place of John Curry who had died. The company had received a number of orders from Syracuse and other cities and villages for its ale but had been unable to fill them, owing to the large demand in this city and immediate vicinity. On December 6, Phillip V. Faass was appointed superintendent. Samuel Finn, an old and well-known brewer, was engaged to take charge of the brewings. At a meeting held in early April 1883, the status of the brewery was reviewed, and everything was found to be in good order.

On September 14, the local papers reported that Superintendent Faass was suspended, pending an examination of the books by Thomas McIncrow. It was claimed that there was a shortage on his accounts. Faass admitted that a shortage occurred but only in a small account. He attributed this to carelessness on his part and posted a $5,000 bond to cover any shortage that might be found. The following day, Superintendent Faass stated that he was not suspended and that he was asked only if he had any objections to having the books inspected. He answered that he did not and, to show good faith, voluntarily offered to give a bond to cover any shortage that they might find. The bond was not required and was never asked for. The problem was resolved to everyone's satisfaction shortly afterward, and business returned to normal.

At the third-annual meeting in 1884, the financial report of treasurer F. Louis Faass showed the brewery to be in good condition. The brewery at this time was producing about eight hundred barrels of ale per month and employed eight people.

The following year, J.A. Curry and M. Welch were elected to the board of directors, replacing J. Carey and J. Doyle. The 1885 annual report showed that the brewery had $15,500 of its $18,000 in capital stock paid in. The existing debts for the company were $10,865.47.

During the early morning hours of June 23, 1886, a fire was discovered in the brewery's barn by Frederick Stark, who had been awakened by the barking of a dog in the brewery. He hastened with another neighbor to the barn and tried to break in the door to free the horses that were penned up within the barn.

The fire was burning along the upper end of the building. It had already burned through most of the lower floor. When the fire was finally put out, the building was a total loss. Three of the brewery's horses were killed in the fire. Horses from several other barns nearby were taken to safer places. The barn was surrounded by other frame buildings, which escaped damage due to a calm night. The brewery's president estimated the loss at $1,500. The building was insured for $500 and the contents for another $500.

In July, the brewery hired Riley & Brazil to construct a new barn. The new barn measured twenty-two by thirty feet and was one and a half stories high. It was built at a cost of $430. A big windstorm hit Utica on October 13, 1886, and the tin roof on the brewery was blown off. At the 1886 annual meeting, Dr. Thomas J. Bergen and George T. Helfert were elected to the board of directors, replacing Curry and Welch. The brewery was a little further in debt than the previous year. All the officers of the brewery were let go and replaced. James Hayes was elected president and superintendent; Dr. Thomas Bergen was made vice-president; Timothy Coakley, secretary; and F. Louis Faass, treasurer.

By 1888, the smaller buildings on the brewery grounds had been connected together with new buildings of various uses. The brewery force had grown to ten people. That same year saw the construction of the Fort Schuyler Brewery across the street, adding to the intense competition already felt among many local breweries.

A dividend of 6 percent was declared and paid to the stockholders at the annual meeting in 1888. The annual report for 1888 showed that the brewery was becoming more profitable. The existing debts had been reduced to $7,526.89. In 1889, a 7 percent dividend was paid.

On January 13, 1890, John J. Finn, the head brewer at the brewery, was arrested and charged with committing assault in the second degree on a fellow employee. Finn had knocked down Daniel McGuire with a club while at the brewery. McGuire's skull was fractured, and his condition was thought to be critical.

Finn waived examination and was held to await action of the grand jury. On January 20, Finn was released on $500 bail. Several weeks later, Finn stated that he had settled the case with McGuire and that the complaint would be withdrawn.

During the 1890s, business was good enough to justify further expansion of the brewery. A large one-story addition was added to the brew house, which became the wash house. All buildings belonging to the brewery were connected together during these years. Capacity at the expanded brewery was four hundred barrels a year, which still made the brewery one of the smallest in Utica. At the 1890 annual meeting, John M. Hayes, Thomas P. Farrell and William Hayes became trustees, replacing Bergen, Coakley and Faass. John Hayes replaced Faass as treasurer, and Farrell replaced Coakley as secretary. The brewery produced between four thousand and five thousand barrels of ale and porter up until 1897. Its output in 1898 dropped to between three thousand and four thousand barrels. The 1891 annual report showed debts of $1,955 versus assets of $37,890. In 1892, this changed to debts of $2,715 versus assets of $32,952.

In August 1897, the brewery was assessed at $10,000. President James Hayes indicated that he thought this total was too high. He said the company paid that much for the property fifteen years ago but that the value of the property had depreciated and was now only worth $8,000. Apparently, he was convincing as the assessment was lowered to $8,000.

The brewmaster for the brewery in 1897–98 was Peter Kervin.

The January 1899 annual report for the brewery listed debts of $1,427 and assets of $40,000. This report was either optimistic or an outright lie. On February 6, 1899, Nicholas Kernan, representing a majority of stockholders of the brewery, made an application for the appointment of a receiver. Charles I. Shumway opposed the motion on behalf of certain creditors. Kernan said that the company was worth about $15,000 and was mortgaged for $2,500. He said actions had been brought by creditors to collect claims amounting to $5,900, and as the company was unable to meet the claims, it had decided to close the business. The major creditor was the Oneida firm of Stewart & Barton. They objected on the grounds that the company was still solvent. The case was argued in court for a few weeks. On March 4, Justice Scripture gave the directors of the company five days to reach an agreement as to the disposition of the brewery, refusing the application for a receiver on the grounds that the business was solvent. A meeting of the stockholders and directors was held in which it was decided to sell the brewery to the firm of Stewart & Barton of Oneida (dealers in malt and brewers' supplies) with the understanding that it would pay the indebtedness of the company in full. The debts amounted to $12,000.

The brewery was reorganized by the proprietors, with R.A. Stewart as president; Avery Barton, vice-president; W.S. Ryan, secretary; and Thomas O'Brien, treasurer. After the completion of some necessary alterations and additions, the brewery was to be put back in operation. This was not to be, however. On April 28, the brewery suffered a major fire. The boiler room in the rear and the stables escaped the fire, but the main building, a three-story structure, was badly damaged.

John Quinn and Stephen Failey, formerly employed by the brewery, were on Third Avenue and Catharine Street around 10:00 p.m. on April 28. They noticed a bright light on the top floor of the brewery, about in the center of the building, and they went to investigate. Suddenly, the flames burst through the roof. An alarm was sent from box 7, which was located in front of the brewery.

The fire succeeded in getting a good start within minutes. At first, it was located entirely on the top floor in the rear part of the building. The third floor contained the malt room in the east end and the brewing room. It was open to the roof, with the exception of platforms about the vats. The flames enveloped a large cupola over the brewing kettle. The fire department arrived quickly but had to fight their way through the gathering crowds of spectators. Ladders were placed on the north and south sides of the building, and hoses were turned on the top floor. Two streams were applied in the rear, but the water seemed to have little effect. The aerial truck stationed in front of the brewery was brought into action. The seventy-five-foot extension ladder was raised to the apex of the building, and another hose was added to the fire. Some of the firemen finally got on the third floor, where they groped around to find the exact location of the fire. Once the source was located, the fire was extinguished in about twenty minutes. The firemen did not leave the scene until 12:30 a.m. the next morning to make sure the fire would not restart.

Mr. Barton, one of the new owners, was on the scene within minutes after the fire started. He said the brewery was insured for $14,000, which he did not think would fully cover the loss. The company had recently allowed $4,000 in insurance to lapse.

The company had just finished a brewing of beer, and four hundred barrels were in the storerooms. A carload of malt had just been placed in the malt bins, and eighteen bales of hops were on one floor. The beer, hops and malt were valued at $6,000. Barton was unable to estimate the loss of the equipment and building. There was a brewing kettle holding two hundred barrels of beer, a steam elevator, malt tubs, fermenting and temporizing tubs and other appliances, which were located where the fire seemed to rage the fiercest.

The origin of the fire was in the chimney in the rear part of the main building. There was a banked fire in the boiler shed, but it was not thought to be the cause. Instead, a defect in the chimney was thought to be the cause of the fire. The brewery was never rebuilt.

On June 7, James Hayes, the ex-president of the brewery and one of the original founders, died at his home. He had been ill with pneumonia for several weeks.

An order was granted by Justice Scripture on July 6, 1901, for the dissolution of the People's Brewing Company. The brewery was sold at auction on August 7, 1902, by James F. Home for the company. It was purchased by Thomas O'Brien of Oneida for $3,000. The lot was one hundred feet square. O'Brien was the last treasurer of the brewery. The bidding for the brewery started at $2,900. The firm's old accounts were then offered and were bought in a lump for $2.50 by J.E. Duross of New York, the brewery's attorney.

The sale was for the purpose of closing up the voluntary dissolution of the company and to perfect the title. The sale price included a mortgage of $2,000 on the property. O'Brien was also a member of the malting company of Stewart, Barton & O'Brien of Oneida. He said that his firm planned to build up the business of the brewery again and indicated that a new plant would be put in shortly.

The remaining brewery buildings were torn down in 1904 and the property sold.

# CHAPTER 19
# GLOBE BREWING COMPANY

## 1933–1936

The Gulf Brewing Company resumed operations in the summer of 1933 as the Globe Brewing Company, Inc., after being idle during Prohibition.

Eli Cramer and his brothers, Myron and Harry, purchased the old Gulf Brewing Company plant in early 1933. They had come to America from their native country of Lithuania to seek a better life. Eli Cramer was the president and manager of the brewery. The new brewmaster at the brewery was John Merkt, who, before Prohibition, worked for the Lemp Brewery in St. Louis. During Prohibition, Merkt was the brewmaster at the Frontenac Brewery in Montreal for five years and Grant's Spring Brewery in Hamilton, Ontario for eight years.

In March 1933, in anticipation of the end of Prohibition, the owners of the brewery commissioned the construction of a new bottling plant to be built on an adjoining property at the southeast corner of Third Avenue and Jay Street. The new bottling works were built by contractors Charles and Frank Alt. The structure, a one-story building of fifty by eighty-five feet, was constructed so that other stories could be added later. The exterior walls were brick, while the inside walls were a glazed tile wainscoting with light gray brick walls above. The building cost $15,000 to construct, with another $45,000 spent on equipment. The bottling works used the best technology of the times.

Empty cases and bottles were received in the basement by means of a chute. Here the empty cases were placed on a conveyor belt that took them to where they could be reused. The bottles were placed on a conveyor leading to the soaker, which was located on the ground floor, at a rate of sixty bottles per minute. The soaker, a large machine built by the Liquid Carbonic Company, gave the bottles a bath in three different solutions, after which they were rinsed.

From the soaker and rinser, the bottles went to the filling machine, capper, pasteurizer, labeling machine and then to the packer. The bottles came to the packer on a separate conveyor from the conveyor carrying the empty cases. Once filled, the cases left the packing area on incline rollers to the storage area.

On June 28, 1933, the brewery obtained a temporary federal license at the Bureau of Internal Revenue in Syracuse, permitting operation until July 1. A new license (U-241) costing $1,000 had to be obtained to continue brewing after July 1. The brewery obtained its state permit (D-40) shortly after. Brewing was started on July 1 and distribution planned to begin on August 1. Globe was the fourth brewery in Utica to get back up and running.

The brewery at first concentrated on making one product, Royal Style Ale. The ale was made with barley malt, jiffimalt cornflakes and domestic and imported hops. This went on sale for the first time on Saturday, July 22, 1933, in kegs only and only in the local area.

As more ale became available, it was also bottled. Royal Style Ale was distributed from Albany to Syracuse and from Binghamton to Watertown. A second product was introduced later in the year called Dictator Beer.

The brewery was running at full capacity by April 1934 and was making various improvements and adjustments in preparation for the increased demand of spring and summer trade. During this time, it purchased many new barrels, beer cases and bottles. They also planned to add a double shift to meet the warm weather demand.

Forty people were working at the brewery at this time, and the plant was operated under strict NRA regulations and had union labor. A fleet of four trucks were used in delivering the beer, which was kept in cold storage rooms after being barreled at a temperature of thirty-four degrees Fahrenheit. It was kept at this temperature when delivered to ensure the best quality.

Royal Style Ale, porter and Dictator Lager were available in both draft and bottles.

*Opposite, top*: Globe Brewing Company letterhead from 1934. *Author's collection.*

*Opposite, bottom*: Ad from *Utica Daily Press*, July 1933.

PHONE 2-2630 JUN 30 1934

UTICA, N. Y., 193

M Chas. Denslow
Forestport N.Y.

To Globe Brewing Co., Inc. Dr.

Brewers of

Royal Style Ale, Porter and Dictator Lager

ALSO BOTTLERS OF THE
FAMOUS ROYAL STYLE ALE AND
DICTATOR LAGER

610 JAY ST.

# TODAY

## YOU CAN HAVE THE PLEASURE OF ENJOYING UTICA'S NEWEST DRINK

# "ROYAL STYLE ALE"

THE PERFECTLY BLENDED AND PROPERLY AGED ALE

## "FIT FOR A KING"

**A Product of the Globe Brewing Company, Inc., Utica, N. Y.**

**Call for It at Your Favorite Restaurant, Hotel or Club -- We Know You'll Like It!**

ROYAL STYLE ALE is a combination of the choicest Barley Malt, Jiffimalt (made from corn) Domestic and Imported Hops, the very finest obtainable. They are skillfully blended and aged to give you an ale that surpasses all other ales. It has a flavor you'll not forget.

ROYAL STYLE ALE is due to be the most popular ale on the market today because it is made right, under the supervision of an expert brewmaster with considerable experience manufacturing ales. It contains only the best of ingredients, is made under the most sanitary conditions, and best of all . . . "IT IS PROPERLY AGED."

Always ask to be served this popular drink, "ROYAL STYLE ALE," then you will know you have received the best.

The Globe Brewing Co., Inc., is the newest and most modern brewery in Central New York. The present building was erected in 1908 and was formerly known as the Gulf Brewing Co. The equipment is the newest and most up-to-date kind procurable. We have the facilities for producing large quantities of beers manufactured and aged as beer should be to make it good. The reason you have had to wait so long for ROYAL STYLE ALE is not because we can't produce it fast enough, but simply because we won't place it on sale until we know it has been properly aged.

**"ROYAL STYLE ALE" IN BOTTLES SOON**

Our modern new bottling plant will soon be in operation with all the latest equipment for handling bottled goods. The building is now completed and the machinery nearly all installed. Just as soon as everything is completed you will be able to have this favorite drink in handy bottles for home use. Watch this paper for annoucements in the very near future.

ORDERS TAKEN TODAY FOR IMMEDIATE DELIVERY
ANOTHER TREAT AWAITS YOU SOON--"LAGER BEER"--WATCH FOR IT!

# GLOBE BREWING CO., INC.

610 JAY STREET UTICA, NEW YORK

In 1936, a major drought hit the country. This greatly increased the cost of raw materials used by brewers. The brewery had never really recovered from Prohibition and could not absorb the increased costs. It closed its doors. The brewery denied a report that it had been sold to the Utica Brewing Company in April 1936.

The following year (1937) saw a national recession, so it was unlikely that the brewery could have survived anyway. The Utica Brewing Company bought the brewery buildings in late 1936 and moved its operations from its Catharine Street facilities. During its short life, the brewery produced Royal Style Ale, Dictator Beer, Royal Style Porter and Globe XXXX India Pale Ale.

It wasn't until June 19, 1939, that the Globe Brewing Company, Inc. was officially dissolved. The secretary of state certified that the corporation had complied with the laws and was now officially dissolved.

After closing the brewery, Eli Cramer went on to open a wholesale beer and wine distributorship, which he ran until 1957. At that time, he opened E. Cramer & Son, Inc., a men's clothing store, in the New Hartford Shopping Center. He died on March 16, 1984, at the age of ninety-three.

# CHAPTER 20
# UTICA BREWING COMPANY

## 1933–1959

The Utica Brewing Company was organized in early 1933, with the anticipation of the end of Prohibition. John H. Lalor served as president and treasurer, Mrs. G.B. Lalor was vice-president and John F. Ryan was secretary and sales manager.

John H. Lalor had previously worked at the Eagle Brewing Company for fifteen years under the guidance of his uncle, William F. Welch, who was Eagle's president and treasurer. John F. Ryan was formerly connected with the Oneida Brewing Company for twenty-five years in the capacity of secretary and manager.

Lalor was not a brewmaster, so to fill that position, he engaged the services of Henry J. Luebbert, an old-time brewmaster, to preside over the exacting operations of the brewer's art. Mr. Luebbert had been brewmaster and superintendent at the Eagle Brewing Company for over forty years, during which he built a well-known reputation for making fine beer.

The company leased the old Fort Schuyler brewery at 434 Catherine Street and adopted the name "Fort Schuyler" for its products. As Prohibition came to an end, the brewery ran into a little trouble securing its state and federal brewing permits. The Utica Brewing Company and the Globe Brewing Company applied for the state permit through the supervisor of permits in New York City and were refused. The two breweries appealed to Congressman Sisson on June 7 for help in securing the licenses, claiming that they were turned down because they had refused to pay a bribe of $102,000.

# FORT SCHUYLER BEER

Manufactured by The Utica Brewing Company, located at 434 Catherine St., and brewed by Utica's best known brewmaster, HENRY J. LUEBBERT.

THE UTICA BREWING COMPANY will strive to establish an unexcelled reputation based upon a thorough knowledge of the manufacture of its product, made from only the choicest materials producing a carefully brewed, carefully *aged* beer, from a formula which for many years produced a beer noted for its very *distinctive* and *mellow* flavor.

JOHN H. LALOR, the President and Treasurer, has had many years experience in the brewery business, having been associated with The Eagle Brewing Company for a period of 15 years.

JOHN F. RYAN, Secretary and Sales Manager, was formerly connected with the Oneida Brewing Company for 25 years in the capacity of Secretary and Manager.

HENRY J. LUEBBERT, the Master Brewer and Superintendent, needs no introduction to Uticans having served in the same capacity for over 40 years for The Eagle Brewing Company, during which time he established his well known reputation for a beer which will speak for itself—and whenever you drink it you'll say, "It was well worth the waiting."

FORT SCHUYLER BEER will be on draught at all first class hotels and restaurants THURSDAY, AUGUST 17th.

# UTICA BREWING CO.

434 Catherine Street Utica, N. Y.

Phone 2-5524

Patronize Fort Schuyler Beer—A local product—Assist Utica labor—Satisfy yourself and keep the money you spend in circulation in Utica.

Ad from *Utica Daily Press*, August 1933.

On June 20, Commissioner of Industrial Alcohol Dr. James Doran said that action on the applications for licenses would be handled by Supervisor of Permits Moss in New York City, and the matter would be looked into. It had been Supervisor Moss who originally turned down the breweries' applications. The cases were settled in July, and both breweries obtained the necessary licenses to brew and sell beer. The Utica Brewing Company received federal permit U-227 and state permit D-47.

A bottling plant was erected on the opposite side of Catharine Street near Park Avenue across from the brewery during the spring of 1933 to enable the brewery to bottle its products when they became available.

Fort Schuyler Lager was available on draft on Thursday, August 17, 1933, at all first-class hotels and restaurants. Bottled Fort Schuyler followed shortly thereafter. In addition, the brewery began producing Fort Schuyler Three Star Ale, Bock, and Stock Ale soon after.

By 1936, the company had outgrown the leased premises on Catharine Street. When the Globe Brewing Company facilities on Jay and Third Street became available, the company purchased the facilities and relocated. An interesting sidelight of the transaction is that the Globe plant, formerly owned by the Gulf Brewing Company, was operated for many years by William F. Welch, who was the uncle of John Lalor.

On July 13, 1937, the five breweries in Utica and Rome created the Utica Brewers Exchange Inc., to help regulate the industry when they filed incorporation papers.

Among the purposes of the exchange were enforcement of fair competition standards, freedom from unjust or unlawful exactions, maintaining friendly labor and employee relations, exchanging information on standings of merchants and observing and supporting all laws pertaining to the brewing industry and to cooperate with governmental authorities in compliance with such laws.

The incorporators were; John H. Lalor of the Utica Brewing Company, John M. Quinn of the Eagle Brewing Company, Wilbur B. Ralph of the Oneida Brewing Company, Walter J. Matt of the West End Brewing Company, and Albert E. Ellinger of the Fort Stanwix Brewing Company in Rome.

The brewery was thoroughly modernized by 1942. It was air-conditioned throughout, with the air changed every thirty minutes. The various steps of brewing were carried on in a labyrinthine atmosphere of narrow passageways, steep stairways, high platforms, towering tanks and vast cellars. A gleaming copper brew kettle of 230-barrel capacity produced

A 1940s ad for Utica Brewing Company. *Author's collection.*

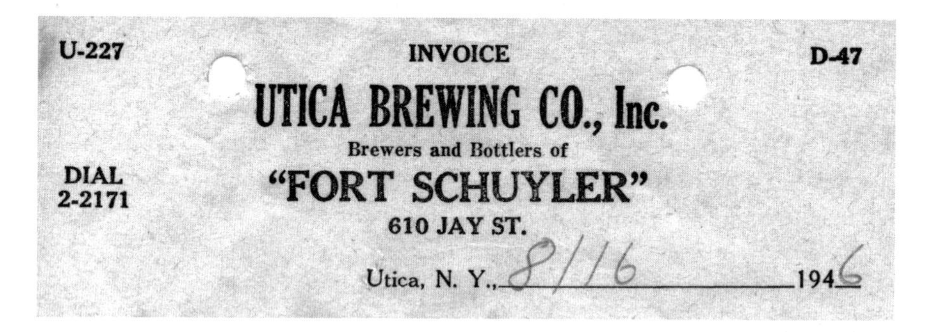
U-227 INVOICE D-47

UTICA BREWING CO., Inc.

Brewers and Bottlers of

"FORT SCHUYLER"

610 JAY ST.

DIAL 2-2171

Utica, N. Y., 8/16 1946

A 1946 Utica Brewing Company invoice. *Author's collection.*

the daily wort from the choicest malt and hops. The latest type of brine cooler cooled the wort, and ten huge tanks stored it during fermentation. Every ounce of beer was thoroughly filtered and then measured by government-sealed meters as it flowed to the racking room to be kegged or to the adjoining bottling plant.

The bottling plant, operating with the latest automatic machines, could bottle forty-five thousand bottles of Fort Schuyler Lager a day.

On June 14, 1941, the State Liquor Authority ordered the brewery's license canceled on the grounds that the licensee rendered services to retail licensees, violating the provisions of Section 103, subdivision 7 of the Alcoholic Beverage Control law relative to invoices. The licensee, having failed to report delinquent retailers, sold on credit to delinquents and did not keep adequate books and records. After much explaining, the brewery retained its license.

In 1942, the brewery employed a workforce of forty. Anthony Ligas was brewmaster, replacing Henry J. Luebbert, who had died a few years earlier. The company's yearly production was approximately fifty thousand barrels, and distribution covered a seventy-five-mile radius.

On the night of July 14, 1943, a fire was discovered in the cupola of the brewery. The fire was confined to the cupola, which contained a malt conveyor. The conveyor belt had been slipping, and fire officials thought that friction ignited dust particles in the cupola. One fireman was severely burned, and the high aerial ladder on which he was working was scorched. It was felt that a backdraft or a possible explosion of dust in the cupola caused the flames to shoot out against the ladder and fireman.

Firemen were handicapped in fighting the blaze because in the vicinity of the blaze, there was little room to stand. There was a low roof on two sides of the cupola but just a cornice on the other two sides. No estimate of the damage costs was available at the time.

After the war, the United States committed to rebuilding Europe. As a result, many items in the United States continued to be rationed, beer included.

In early 1946, a meeting was held by the local Restaurant and Liquor Dealers and Utica's two remaining breweries, West End and Utica Brewing. They discussed the problem of how to get along with 30 percent less beer.

Walter Matt and John Lalor spoke for the breweries, saying that an equal distribution of beer would be made available to their customers and that monthly quotas would be set up. Each establishment would receive 30 percent less than the year before.

In 1947, the brewery's capacity was increased to 75,000 barrels. Through the 1950s, the capacity of the brewery was 100,000 barrels, although the actual production never strayed much above the 50,000-barrel level. In October, the brewery asked for a reduction in its assessment total for 1948 from $87,759 to $29,000 as the property in question was part of the old Eagle brewery and not the whole thing.

In 1950, Three Star Ale was replaced by Fort Schuyler Light Ale. A complete modernization of the brewery was announced at a cost of several hundred thousand dollars. The brewery floor space was expanded to 158,200 square feet. Included in this expansion were new offices, a new copper mash tub, a new bottling line and a canning line. The canning line was added to the bottling department to fill cone-top cans. This was really a modified bottling line as cone-top beer cans were very similar to short beer bottles.

The new bottling line washed, pasteurized, labeled and packaged the bottles in one continuous process. The bottle washing machine washes the bottle four times with cleaning chemicals, a fifth time with fresh water and then gives the bottle three additional rinses. The bottling plant was arranged so that all types of bottles and cans could be efficiently packaged.

A carelessly tossed lit cigarette set fire to a boarded-up window and window frame on May 13, 1950. The fire occurred in the old Eagle brewery building, which the Utica Brewing Company was using as a warehouse. Firemen quickly put out the blaze with minimal damage.

John G. Haeberlein was hired as brewmaster in December 1950. He had previously been at the Stanton Brewery in Troy, New York, and was a graduate of the United States Brewers' Academy in 1937. Peter A. Bollenbacher replaced Haeberlein as brewmaster in December 1952. He was formerly brewmaster at the Miami Valley Brewing Company, in Dayton, Ohio. He had also worked at the American Brewery in Baltimore, the Fort Pitt Brewery in Pittsburgh and Carling's in Cleveland. He represented the fifth generation of his family to be in the brewing business. The company reported that with the appointment of Bollenbacher, the brewery would present a new beer, lighter and dryer, to meet with current tastes. He remained as brewmaster until 1958. Franz Biller, a native of Baden, Germany, was appointed brewmaster in 1957. Biller had previously worked at the James Hanley brewery in Providence, Rhode Island. He learned the brewing trade in Europe and was awarded the title "Master Brewer" at the age of twenty-six. At the Utica brewery, Biller had charge of the processing and brewing facilities. The last brewmaster employed by the brewery was Paul Zoffman, who was hired in 1958.

Around 1953, Farquhar & Co. was employed by the brewery as its advertising agency. This lasted until the consolidation with West End in 1959.

In 1954 and 1955, the brewery won the Safety Award for no disabling injuries in companies employing fewer than one hundred people. In 1956, the brewery added a canning line for the first time. This line filled cone top–style cans made by Continental Can Company. J.F. Ryan, secretary for the brewery, retired and was replaced with F.T. Costello, who had worked as assistant secretary since 1949.

A 1950s ad for Utica Brewing Co. *Author's collection.*

The brewery changed the design of its packaging in 1957 to feature a picture of the fort for which the products are named on one side and a logotype against a background of red for the beer carriers and green for the ale carriers on the other side. This new design was created to be more distinctive on store shelves. The carriers were produced at the Thames River plant of the Gair Boxboard and Folding Carton Division of Continental Can Company. The brewery packaged two styles of bottles as well as cone-top cans in these carriers.

In May 1957, the employees of the brewery received a three-dollar-per-week raise in the new one-year contract signed by the union and management. It was similar to the deal worked out at West End.

A fire almost completely destroyed the brewery's warehouse at 615 Jay Street on June 20, 1958. The flames were noticed around 4:00 p.m. by the company bookkeeping machine operator and by the company engineer. Mary Connors (bookkeeping machine operator) was working in the main office when she glanced out the window and saw flames shooting from the wooden garages in the rear of the brick warehouse. Sanders (the company engineer) happened to walk to the rear of the main office about the same time and saw the flames. They immediately instructed the switchboard operator to call the fire department.

The warehouse faced Third Avenue and ran back behind the main office, which faced Jay Street. Both buildings were part of the old Eagle brewery.

By the time firemen arrived, the flames had almost destroyed the dried-out timber of the garages in the rear of the main part of the brick warehouse. A brisk wind whipped the flames into a soaring inferno. The firemen turned streams of water on the fire from every possible angle. They were hampered by being partly blocked from the main area of the flames by adjoining multiple dwellings.

Hundreds of empty wooden beer cases stored in the warehouse burned, adding to the swiftness with which the flames swept through the building. The blaze was brought under control by 5:00 p.m. Hundreds of spectators surrounded the building. Police had to move them back from the heat and flames several times and finally cordoned off the area.

Lalor (the brewery president) and fire officials believed the fire could have been caused by children in the area. Lalor said, "We have had trouble with children starting fires here in the past, and I think they really got one going this time." He estimated that the damage to the warehouse was more than $5,000 but indicated that it would be completely covered by insurance.

On May 20, 1959, the brewery announced that it was consolidating with the West End Brewing Company. The presidents of both companies, John Lalor of the Utica Brewing Company and Walter Matt of the West End Brewing Company, said that production of Fort Schuyler Beer would be continued at the West End plant through the newly formed Fort Schuyler

*Top*: West End Brewing Company calendar without calendar pad from the 1900s. *Author's collection.*

*Left*: Eagle Brewing Company tray from the 1940s. *Author's collection.*

*Top*: West End Brewing Company metal sign from the 1900s. *Author's collection.*

*Middle*: West End Brewing Company tray from the 1910s. *Author's collection.*

*Bottom*: West End Brewing Company composite sign advertising sodas from the 1920s. *Author's collection.*

*Top*: Gulf Brewing Company tray from the 1910s. *Author's collection.*

*Left*: Globe Brewing Company tray from 1934. *Author's collection.*

Utica Brewing Company cardboard sign from the 1950s. *Author's collection.*

*Left*: A 1961 Schultz bock cloth sign (West End Brewing Company). *Author's collection.*

*Below*: A 1965 photo of the West End Brewing Company. *Author's collection.*

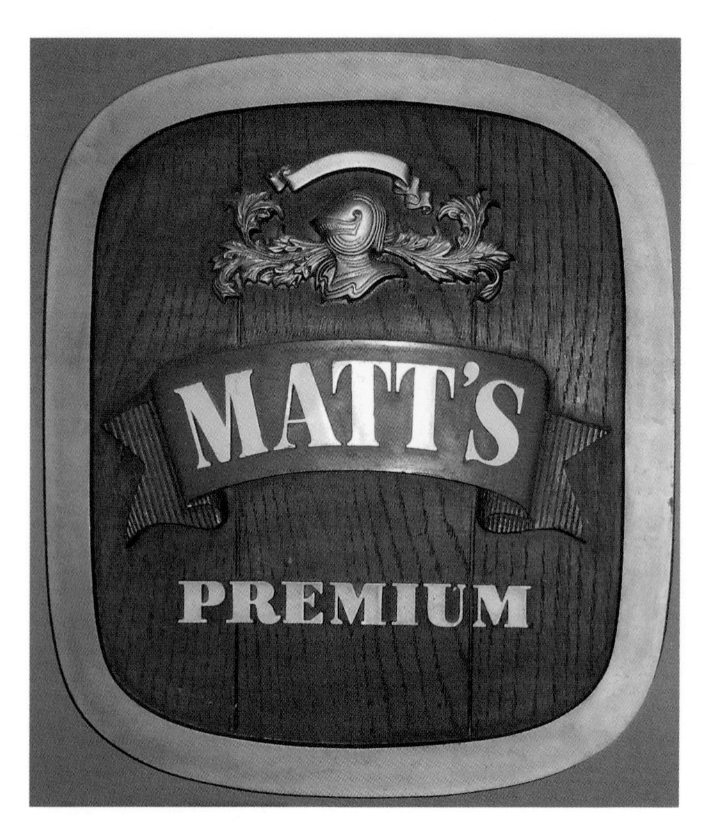


Matt's (West End Brewing Company) molded sign from the 1980s. *Author's collection.*

A 2010 photo of the interior of the brew house at the F.X. Matt Brewing Company. *Author's collection.*

*Left*: A 1938 West End Brewing Company fiftieth anniversary calendar. *Author's collection.*

*Below*: A 1939 West End Brewing Company postcard. *Author's collection.*

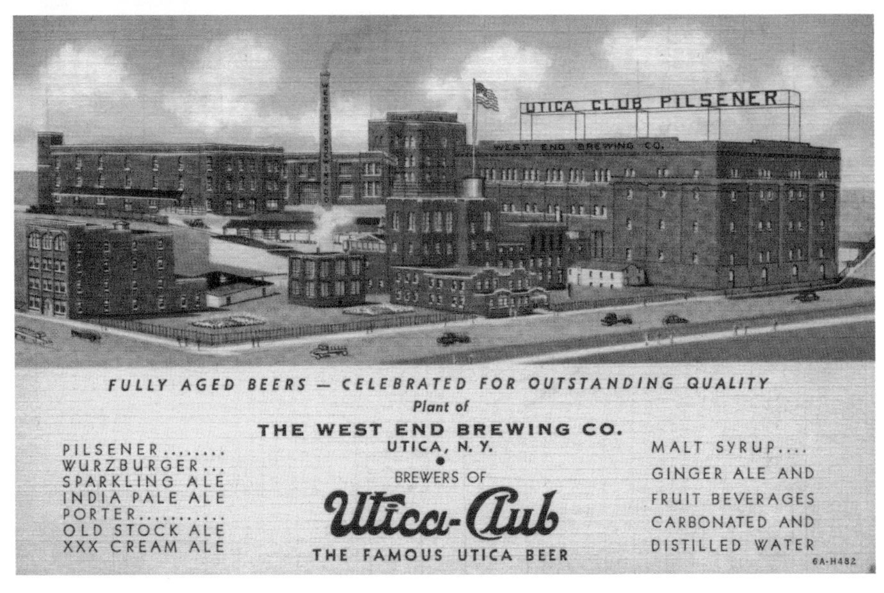

West End Brewing Company molded sign from the 1940s. *Author's collection.*

A 1962 Schultz and Dooley (West End Brewing Company) cardboard sign showing four steins, two bottles and one can. *Author's collection.*

Nick (chairman) and Fred (president) Matt of the F.X. Matt Brewing Company in 2013. *Brewery collection.*

F.X. Matt Brewing Company. *Brewery collection.*

*Above*: A group of early West End Brewing Company bottles. *Author's collection.*

*Left*: Saranac Pomegranate Wheat was the first use of pomegranate in a beer by a large brewer. *Author's collection.*

*Opposite, top*: A group of Utica Club bottles show the label changes over the years. *Author's collection.*

*Opposite, middle*: A group of Saranac bottles made since the 1980s. *Author's collection.*

*Opposite, bottom*: A selection of Utica Club beer cans that were produced from 1959 to 2013. *Author's collection.*

A 2010 photo of the west side of the F.X. Matt Brewing Company. *Author's collection.*

A postcard of F.X. Matt Brewing Company tour center and gift shop from the 1980s. *Author's collection.*

2013 photo of the Nail Creek Brewery sign. *Author's collection.*

The first Saranac Lager label from the 1980s. *Author's collection.*

Saranac's Pale Ale. *Courtesy of Kelly Flatebo.*

Saranac's Adirondack Lager. *Courtesy of Kelly Flatebo.*

Saranac's White IPA. *Courtesy of Kelly Flatebo.*

Utica Club
PILSENER
LAGER BEER
Utica Club
PILSENER LAGER BEER
Utica Club
Utica Club
Pilsener
Utica Club
PILSENER
BEER
Utica Club
XX
PURE
PILSENER
LAGER BEER

SARANAC
1888
SARANAC
PILSENER BEER
GOLDEN
12 FLUID OUNCES
SEASON'S
BEST
F.X. MATT'S TRADITIONAL
SEASON'S
BEST
PREMIUM AMBER BEER
SARANAC
Harvest Ale
HIGH
PEAKS
HIGH PEAKS
Imperial IPA
SARANAC
IPA
SARANAC
DRY HOP LAGE

Utica Club
PILSENER
LAGER BEER
Utica Club
PILSENER
LAGER BEER
Utica Club
PILSENER LAGER BEER
Utica Club
25 YEARS
Schultz & Dooley
Utica Club
Pilsener Beer
40 YEARS
Schultz & Dooley
Utica Club
PILSENER
BEER
12 FL. OZ.
Utica
Club
Utica Club
XX
PURE
PILSENER
LAGER BEER

A 2013 Utica Club beer can from the F.X. Matt Brewing Company. *Author's collection.*

Division. Sales of Fort Schuyler were to be continued with the same sales personnel, and as many of the forty brewery employees as possible were to be absorbed by West End.

The Utica Brewing Company buildings on Jay Street were not part of the consolidation and were later sold.

John Lalor stated, "We are taking great care to keep the individual character of Fort Schuyler Beer; it will continue to be brewed in the same way as it has in the past."

One of the reasons that the Utica Brewing Company joined forces with West End was the feeling that the consolidation would allow more efficient operation, give better service and make available greater resources for advertising and sales promotion.

The final truckload of Fort Schuyler Beer came out of the brewery on Friday, May 22, 1959, and went to Auburn, New York.

The final slate of officers for the brewery were as follows: J.H. Lalor, president, treasurer, purchasing agent and sales manager; G.B Lalor, vice-president; F.T. Costello, secretary; Paul Zoffman, master brewer; W. Sanders, chief engineer; and C. Stuckey, bottling superintendent.

The Utica Brewing Company as a separate entity ended with the consolidation. West End maintained the Fort Schuyler Division for a few years before absorbing it completely.

# CHAPTER 21
# ONEIDA BREWERY (ONEIDA BREWING COMPANY)

## 1832–1942

The city of Utica was incorporated in 1832. That year, T. Van Sice & Co. was formed to start a brewery at the corner of State and Court Streets. The brewery was called the Oneida Brewery. The brewery consisted of a brick building thirty feet wide by one hundred feet long with a stone malt house attached. Mr. Van Sice informed the general public on December 10, 1833, that the brewery was ready to supply them with ale of its manufacture not inferior to any to be found on the market before. He claimed to have one of the most experienced brewers to oversee the establishment, though the brewer remains unknown.

This endeavor did not last, as the company went bankrupt. In October of the next year, the brewery was advertised for sale. The sale was set for November 12 at 10:00 a.m. The assignees in charge of selling the assets were Soab Stafford, J.C. Shippy and Alfred Louis.

The brewery was purchased by J.C. Shippy, one of the assignees. He announced that he had engaged an experienced maltster and brewer and was ready to furnish the public with a superior article. Again, this brewer is unknown. The product of the brewery was available on December 23, 1834. Mr. Shippy also indicated that he would pay market prices for four thousand bushels of first-rate barley.

How long Shippy owned the brewery is uncertain. By 1848, the brewery was owned by Stephen Thorn & Co. Thorn came from England in 1822 to settle in Utica. He ran a provisions store and lent money to people. The brewery was also known as the Sand Bank Brewery for a period of time but eventually became known as the Oneida Brewery permanently.

The brewing process originally used at the brewery was primitive and time consuming. The malt was ground by treadmill with ox-power. The malt was then carried by hand and emptied into the mash tubs containing water of a high temperature. Men used hand rakes to mix the malt and water.

After this, the hot wort was allowed to settle and was then dipped by hand into crude receptacles called fire kettles. These were built of masonry and heated by wood fires. The hot wort was then boiled, and hops were added at various intervals.

After reaching a boil for a while, the hot wort was pumped from the kettle to a surface cooler to start the process of cooling and aerating the hot wort. Once the wort was cooled a number of degrees, it was run down to the hot wort cooler on the floor below. The hot wort flowed into the V-shaped pans on the top of the cooler and continued to run down the outside of this cooler until it reached the pan at the base of it, all the while being cooled by means of cold water flowing through the inside of the cooler. The process required four hours to cool eighty-five barrels of wort.

The cooled wort was then run into a starting tub to which yeast was added. After the fermentation had progressed to a certain extent in the starting tub and had reached a temperature where it was necessary to control the fermentation, the wort was run down and divided equally into two small tubs located directly beneath the starting tub. Here, floats of swimmers (devices containing ice) were floated on the fermenting wort. The object of this process was to control the temperature as much as possible, though generally, this was very unsatisfactory.

After fermentation had advanced to a stage where good heavy yeast was on top of the fermenting wort, the swimmers were removed, while some of the yeast was skimmed off into containers and saved for future brewings. After the yeast was skimmed, the swimmers were again floated in the fermenters and the temperature lowered gradually, with the yeast being periodically skimmed off until the completion of fermentation. At this point, the wort was ready for racking.

The ale was transferred from the fermentation tubs to barrels. At this time, the finished ale wort was racked from the fermenting tubs with about 20 percent of krausen (or fresh ale wort, which at this stage was unfermented and contained a considerable quantity of yeast and was about sixteen hours into fermentation). This fresh ale wort was added to the finished ale mentioned above along with carbonic acid gas. It was necessary to have a pressure of sixty to seventy-five pounds per square inch in the barrels.

After racking, the barrels were rolled and tiered in the cellar. The barrels were taken down and rolled about every other day to thoroughly mix the krausen with the ale. Before sending to customers, the ale was stored in the cellar at a temperature of seventy degrees Fahrenheit for about ten to fourteen days in order to age the ale and secure enormous pressure. The customer could put the barrel in the cellar and the natural pressure in the cask would force the last glass of ale out of the barrel to the tap, as in those days, the air pump was unknown.

The ale was not aged as long as it was later in that century, and the necessity of having such an enormous pressure on the casks by the addition of krausen (which caused the ale to be in a constant state of fermentation) produced ale that was not clear or brilliant. This required the tavern owner to use a large pitcher when pouring the ale and let it set until the foam reduced to an acceptable level. The brewery produced ales and beer and sold barley, malt and hops until around 1870, when it decided to produce ales only.

The brewery was robbed in early October 1848 by William Abbott, who had been hired a few days before. He stole a dress coat, one pair of pantaloons, a razor and sundry other articles. A liberal reward was offered for his apprehension and the return of the stolen articles.

In April 1851, an attempt was made to burn the brewery. Three men with blackened faces and dark lanterns were discovered attempting to set fire to the building. The night watchman attempted to arrest them but was beaten, and the three escaped. In August of this same year, a large addition was added to the brewery that was almost as large as the original building.

A major fire completely destroyed the brewery on March 26, 1853. The fire was the work of an arsonist named John Miller, who had worked for the brewery but had quit about a month before the fire was set. He held a grudge against owner Thorn for not letting him see someone a few weeks before.

Miller was captured quickly and admitted in court that he set the fire. He described how he did it, saying, "Several of the men who worked at the brewery slept there. I went in the front door, went to the stairs and called the men who slept there. I then went down cellar, came up stairs and from there into the mash room, went then into another kiln, took some shavings from the wood shed, and then put into a barrel, took some fire [coals] out of the kiln and put them into this barrel and set the barrel on the stairs which go

ONEIDA BREWERY.

STEPHEN THORN & CO.,

Manufacturers of

BEER AND PORTER,

And dealers in BARLEY, MALT, HOPS, &c., Corner Court & State Sts., Utica.

☞ The ALE and PORTER manufactured at this Establishment is recommended by physicians as the most wholesome and healthful beverage in use.

Ad from the 1858–59 *Utica City Directory*.

into the mash room, the fire kindled immediately. I went out in the backyard and came out on Court Street."

He hung around the area, setting another fire, and then went into a saloon. After a while, he went down to the brewery to watch the fire. Someone there remembered seeing Miller in the area around the time the fire had started. The police were informed, and Miller was apprehended and confessed to setting the fire. He also admitted to setting several other fires. He turned state's evidence in the trial of two other arsonists (who he knew) to save himself from hanging. He was sentenced to prison and escaped the hangman's noose.

Stephen Thorn & Company ran the brewery until 1862, when Francis Midlam purchased it and formed F. Midlam & Co. Thorn retired and lived in Utica until his death on August 16, 1878.

F. Midlam & Co. had largely increased business and maintained a high reputation when a major fire struck. Around 3:30 a.m. on May 22, 1862, a fire was discovered, and by 7:00 a.m., it had largely destroyed the brewery. The flames were first discovered near the brew kettles and were thought to have originated from the fire kept constantly burning under them in the manufacture of ale. The loss of the building, fixtures and stock was estimated at $12,000. The firemen saved about $4,000 worth of ale stored in the cellar. The firm was fully insured for the loss.

F. Midlam & Co. rebuilt the brewery with all the latest improvements and was prepared to furnish pale, cream and amber ales. Half and quarter casks of ale were expressly for family use. The brewers in the city had an agreement at the time to not sell present-use beer for less than seven dollars a barrel. The brewers signing the agreement were J. & G. Greenway & Co. in Syracuse, Kelly & Gaheen in Rome, Swits & Carley

ONEIDA BREWERY,
Corner of Court & State Streets, Utica.

F. MIDLAM & CO.

Successors to Stephen Thorn & Co.

MANUFACTURERS OF

Beer, Porter, Ale & Malt.

Half & Quarter Bbls. of Ale & Beer expressly for Family Use.

ORDERS THROUGH THE POST OFFICE PROMPTLY ATTENDED TO.

Ad from 1861–62 *Utica City Directory*.

in Amsterdam, F. Midlam & Co. in Utica, G. Ralph & Son in Utica and M. McQuade in Utica.

George Ralph had been working at the brewery for some time. In 1864, he left to form his own brewery with his son. It was located at 59 Columbia Street in Utica. It was called the Columbia Street Brewery and produced ales exclusively. The following year, Ralph came back to the Oneida Brewery and became partners with Midlam. They formed the Ralph, Midlam, & Co. The partnership operated both breweries until 1867, when the Columbia Street Brewery was closed down.

A fire was discovered on the morning of April 7, 1868, at the Sash and Blind Manufactory of Walter Embley, which was located in the rear of the brewery. The flames spread quickly, completely destroying the building. By noon, the firemen had left to go to other fires. The Oneida Brewery was on fire in several places early in the morning, caused by

COLUMBIA STREET BREWERY,
G. RALPH & SON, Proprietors,
(For the last 23 years connected with Oneida Brewery,)
MANUFACTURERS OF
PALE, CREAM & STOCK ALES,
Are prepared to fill orders from any part of the Country on short notice,
AT THE LOWEST CASH PRICES,
Office and Brewery, Nos. 57, 59 & 61 Columbia St.
UTICA, N. Y.
CASH PAID FOR BARLEY & HOPS.

Ad from 1863–64 *Utica City Directory*.

ONEIDA AND COLUMBIA ST. BREWERIES,
RALPH, MIDLAM & CO., Proprietors,
Cor. of Court and State Streets,
AND NOS. 57, 59, & 61 COLUMBIA STREET.
MANUFACTURERS OF
Beer, Porter, Ale & Malt,
THEIR STOCK OF
PALE, CREAM & STOCK ALES,
Wnich for FLAVOR AND PURITY are UNSURPASSED, they are prepared to deliver either in town or country at the shortest posible notice.
Half & Quarter Bbls of Ale & Beer Expressly for Family Use.
ORDERS THROUGH THE POST OFFICE PROMPTLY ATTENDED TO.
USE THE GOLDEN BITTERS

Ad from 1864–65 *Utica City Directory*.

sparks coming from the other fire. These additional fires were quickly found and put out.

At 3:00 p.m., smoke was seen issuing from the icehouse of the brewery. It was found that sparks from the burned building had lodged in the sawdust that covered the ice, and this material had started to burn. The flames were quickly put out.

In 1872, both Midlam and Ralph Sr. retired, leaving the operation of the brewery in the hands of George Ralph Jr. The company was known after this as the George Ralph Jr. & Co.

The brewery produced 5,758 barrels in 1874 and 4,722 barrels in 1875. Francis Midlam died in 1875. Joining George Ralph Jr. at the brewery were his younger brother Thomas P., who was listed as brewmaster starting in 1876, and his sons George F. and William L. In 1879, William L. Ralph graduated from medical school and became a physician.

On Wednesday, April 6, 1881, George Ralph Sr. started bleeding from the nose and became dangerously ill. He died on April 8 at 1:00 a.m. at the age of seventy-nine. George Ralph Sr. was born in Kent County, England, in 1802. He came to America in 1826 and resided in Schenectady before moving to Utica. He was one of the founders of the St. George Society and was an active member of the Utica Cricket Club. He was an earnest and enthusiastic believer in the doctrine of spiritualism and took great comfort from the frequent seances he attended around the country with other believers.

The Oneida Brewery produced 9,030 barrels of ale in 1881, making it the second-largest brewery in Utica. The brewery occupied most of the block bordered by Court, State and Broadhead Streets and Chenango Avenue by 1884 and was only a stone's throw away from the Chenango Canal.

The brewery consisted of a two-story L-shaped malt house with a sprouting room on the first floor and storage on the second floor. The office was located in a two-story building facing Court Street that contained coolers on the second floor. Also on the premises were two wood kilns, several icehouses, a cooper shop, a wagon shop and several miscellaneous buildings. Light was provided by kerosene lamps. Heat and power was provided by coal and wood. In 1884, George Ralph Jr. had a two-story frame dwelling, eighteen by twenty-six feet in dimension, with a one-story addition of ten by twenty-two feet, built to house his family for $1,500.

During the summer of 1885, a decision was made to incorporate the company. Articles of incorporation were filed in the county clerk's office on September 7, 1885. The company changed its name to the Oneida Brewing Company and issued $40,000 of capital stock, divided into four hundred shares of $100 each. In a meeting held that same day, George Ralph Jr., William L. Ralph, George F. Ralph, Alexander T. Goodwin and Henry J. Ralph were elected trustees to serve the first year. The incorporation papers stated that the business of the concern was the manufacture of beer, ale and all kinds of malt liquors.

A fire badly damaged the barn and stables of the brewery on April 12, 1886. The building was in the rear of the brewery and fronted Chenango Avenue. The fire was discovered about 2:20 p.m. by William Near, one of the brewery employees, who was at work in the yard. The fire department responded quickly to the alarm and by hard work succeeded in confining the fire to only the barn and stable building. The interior of this structure was completely gutted, leaving just the shell.

The edifice was a two-story frame building, twenty by sixty feet. The stables were located on the first floor, where Ralph kept his private carriage horses and the brewery teams. At the time of the fire, five horses, one colt, one cow and one calf were in the building. Several of the brewery wagons and related equipment were also in the building. The second floor contained about two tons of hay at the time of the fire. All the animals and wagons were saved, but everything else was lost.

The origin of the fire was unknown, but the owners thought it was deliberately set, as there had been no light taken into the building and smoking was not allowed on the premises. The loss was estimated at $1,800, which was covered by various insurance policies. A new barn was built shortly afterward.

The brewery was located on land that was owned solely by George Ralph Jr. On May 1, 1886, he sold the property to the Oneida Brewing Company for $10,000.

George Ralph Jr. died on February 4, 1889, after a prolonged illness. He was born in Schenectady in November 11, 1836, coming to Utica shortly after. Once he grew up, he lived in Binghamton and Elmira for a time before returning to Utica in 1869, at the solicitation of his father, and erecting the Columbia Street brewery. He was a prompt and energetic man. He was a prominent Freemason and did much charitable work.

In 1889, Dr. William L. Ralph became president of the brewery after the death of his father, but he was never active in the business. William Ralph died in 1907. He was a distinguished ornithologist who was for many years a curator at the Smithsonian Institute in Washington, D.C. His brother G. Fred Ralph became secretary and treasurer of the brewery, and Henry J. became manager.

Henry J. Ralph sold his interest in the brewery in 1889 and moved to New York City. His brother George Fred Ralph became president and sole manager. George used his middle name, Fred, for most of his life, not liking the name George. He was born in Holland Patent on May 29, 1833. His parents moved to Binghamton, where he was raised. In 1874, he joined his father at the brewery.

In early 1897, extensive improvements were being made to meet increasing demand for its products. A new sixty-horsepower boiler, made by the Utica Steam Engine and Boiler Works, was installed. The cellars were extended and numerous minor improvements made. A new brew house was also erected at a cost of $4,000.

Sayer Spedding, who ran the Ilion Brewing Co. in the 1880s, was brewmaster in 1898. He may have been brewmaster as early as 1887. The brewery produced between fourteen thousand and sixteen thousand barrels in 1898. The Oneida Brewing Company was the only brewery in Utica to make its own malt in 1898.

In 1899, G. Fred Ralph's son George A. joined the brewery as master brewer, replacing Spedding. He had been sent by his father to New York City to learn the brewer's art. He remained brewmaster through 1902, when he became superintendent.

In the July 1899 issue of the *American Journal of Health*, the brewery received high praise for the quality of its products. In an article titled "Malt Liquors from a Hygienic Viewpoint," written by Robert R. Hamilton, MD, it was stated "that the ale made by the Oneida Brewing Company of Utica demonstrated such qualities of purity and wholesomeness as to deserve specific notice in the editorial columns of the *American Journal of Health.* If all malt liquors were as pure as this brand the most critical hygienist would never object to their use. A purer or more wholesome article never entered our laboratory. In fact it has so thoroughly demonstrated its worth that we do not hesitate to bestow upon it the unreserved editorial endorsements of the *American Journal of Health.*"

In December, responding to an article in the local papers about a price war between Utica brewers, G. Fred Ralph said, "There is no war among the Utica brewers and no movement from any quarter for a reduction in prices. The publication of such a story is ridiculous. A little investigation would have discovered that it had no foundation. It simply makes annoyance for the brewers and their customers. That is all there is in it."

Lewis Metz became brewmaster in 1902, remaining in that position until June 1904, when he left the company and moved to New York City. The

Oneida Brewing Company letterhead from 1898. *Author's collection.*

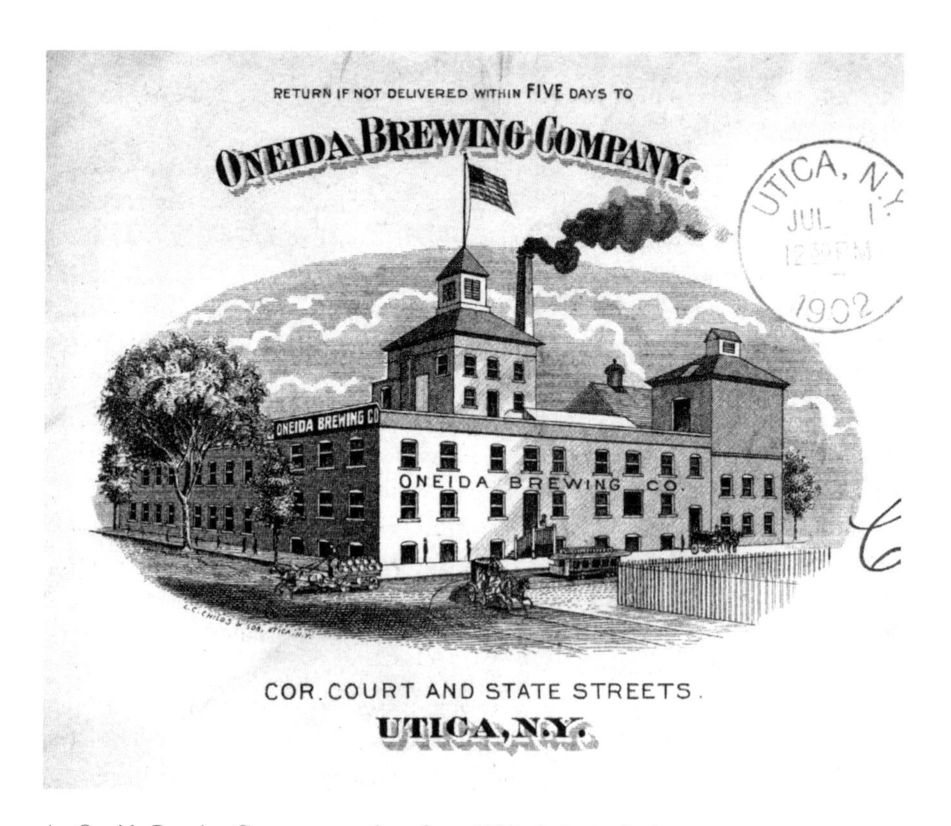


An Oneida Brewing Company envelope from 1902. *Author's collection.*

brewery had undergone few changes since 1884. Power and heat were now provided by coal-fired steam, and lights were gas and oil lamps.

A fire was discovered at the brewery on March 1, 1902, around 9:00 a.m. Upon arriving at the brewery, firemen saw volumes of smoke issuing from the windows and along the cornices of the building. No blaze was seen on the exterior. The firemen forced an entrance from the rear and side while the doors leading from the office proper were opened, thus causing a draft to be created. This sent flames out in all directions. The main blaze was found to be in the kiln on the second floor, beneath which were the pipes used for drying the malt. One of these pipes became overheated and ignited the malt nearby. The tiny blaze spread rapidly and, creeping along under the perforated iron, soon ignited other beds of malt.

Before the arrival of the firemen, employees were using fire extinguishers on the fire. They kept the blaze under control. The size of the kiln greatly handicapped the firemen, but they managed to keep the blaze confined to that section of the building. The loss did not exceed $1,000 and was covered by insurance.

The fire temporarily crippled the working of the plant, but the storage cellars were filled, and no delay in filling orders was anticipated.

Extensive additions were started in March 1902 that included a new fermenting house and storage cellar. The capacity of the brewery was approximately seventy-five thousand barrels. A small fire broke out at the brewery, causing $1,000 worth of damage on April 1, 1902. The brewery experienced some union trouble in 1902. Three coopers stopped working when the supervisor told them to report in writing each evening how many barrels they had fixed during the day. They told him that they performed day work, not piecework, and that the foreman could keep track if he wanted, but they weren't going to. A special meeting of the brewery workers' union was held later that night to consider the matter. It was decided that no strike was necessary. The matter was resolved amicably on May 10 in favor of the coopers, who did not have to report how many barrels they did.

Mathias Isele, an assistant brewer at the brewery, died on October 11, 1902, after a seven-month illness. He was born in Baden, Germany, in 1839 and came to this country in 1866. He found a job in Utica at the brewery and had worked there for thirty years.

The brewery purchased a new delivery wagon and team of three Canadian grey horses in November 1902. Business at the brewery was increasing to a point that it was necessary to increase the capacity of the plant. By December 1902, a 240-square-foot addition had been made to the wash house, making it the largest and most complete in Utica. The brewery also built a 60-square-foot new cooper shop. A new storage cellar, holding twelve casks, each cask having a capacity of 125 barrels, was constructed. A big addition to the stables was also made.

In early 1903, a new seventy-five-ton ice making machine and a one-hundred-horsepower boiler were added.

In May, the brewery accepted plans for finishing the remodeling. It planned to add a new brew house, storage house and office building. Costs were expected to be $75,000. The changes increased the capacity of the brewery to two hundred barrels per day. On August 4, 1904, the brewery held a banquet to mark the completion of the alterations. About 350 guests were invited and enjoyed the company's hospitality.

George A. Ralph became superintendent of the brewery in 1903. During the early 1900s, India Pale Ale, porter, brown stout, stock ale, sparkling ale and cream ale were being produced by the brewery. An ad run in April 1904 stated that the formula used in 1832 was the same formula used in 1904 in the brewing of Oneida Ale. This was probably stretching the truth, as brewing methods had greatly improved over the years, affecting how the ale was made.

The brewing process in 1904 began with the malt being delivered to the brewery and stored in large bins. The first operation at the brewery began with the crushing of the malt as it passed between iron rollers of a malt mill. It was then stored in a malt hopper. From the hopper, the malt was added to the mash tub, where it was mixed thoroughly with water at high temperature by means of revolving rakes.

After this process was completed, the resulting liquid (wort) was strained through the perforated false bottom of the mash tub and conveyed by gravity to the brew kettle. In 1904, Oneida had the largest brew kettle in the city, with a capacity of two hundred barrels. The brew kettle was a large copper vessel in which the wort and hops were boiled for a time. Once this was completed, the resulting liquid was pumped into the surface cooler. This receptacle was a long, shallow iron tank in which the wort was allowed to aerate and cool to the proper temperature. It was then conveyed by gravity to large Baudelot coolers. In these coolers, the wort was reduced to very low temperatures, after which it was pumped to the fermenting vessels. Yeast was then added, and fermentation was begun. This lasted for about six to eight days. The yeast was then separated from the beer, and the beer was placed in storage vessels to age.

After it had aged for the correct amount of time, it was passed through a filter to remove all suspended yeast cells that were left. It then passed through a meter, which was used to measure the amount of ale put into trade casks

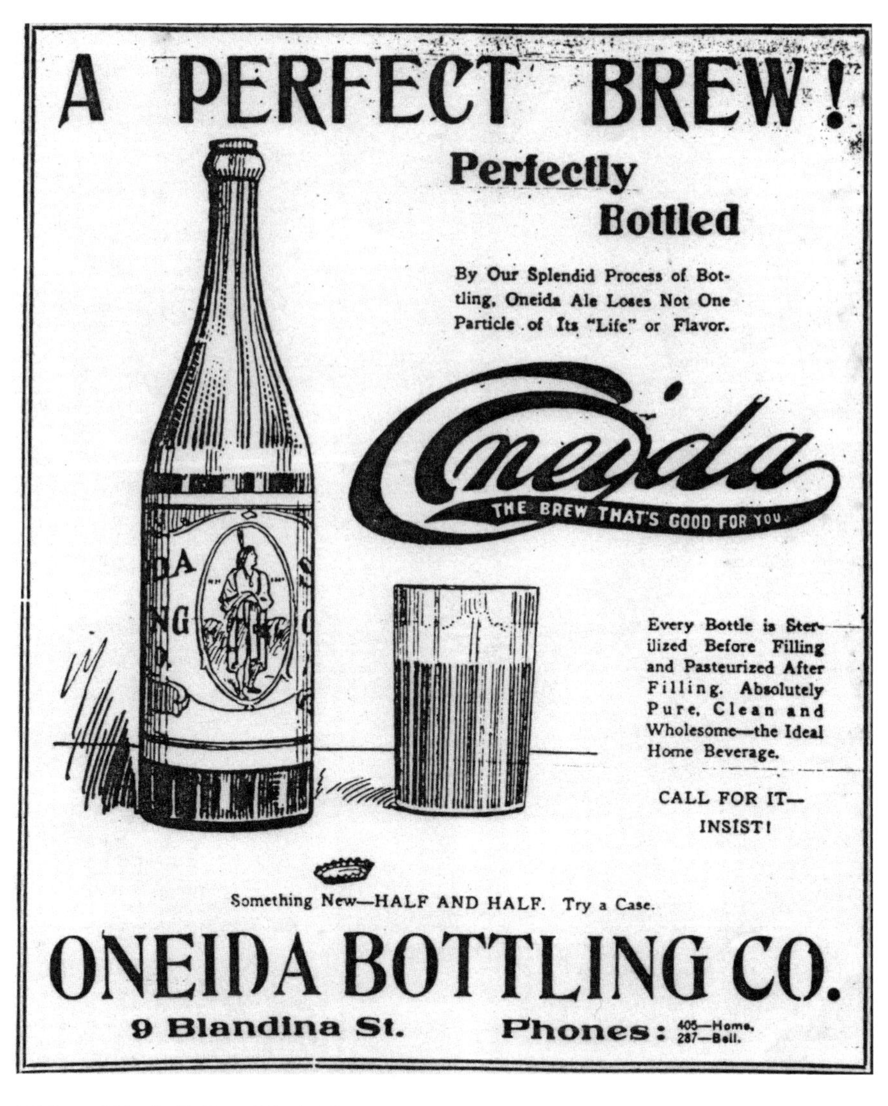


Ad from *Utica Daily Press*, July 1908.

of stock ale. These casks were then rolled through an underground tunnel to an elevator where the casks were hoisted to the shipping floor. From there, they were shipped out by rail cars or trucks to the customer.

E.A. Edwards became brewmaster in 1904 and remained in that position until April 1915, when he resigned. The last couple years he was with the brewery, he also carried the title of superintendent.

Oneida Brewing Company tray from 1915. *Author's collection.*

Ad from *Utica Daily Press*, June 1906.

In 1906, Oneida started advertising heavily in local newspapers. Through 1910, it produced some of the most entertaining ads of any of the local breweries, including many series ads featuring sports or political themes and many in the form of poems.

The year 1907 saw the first use of Oneida's trademark, the standing Indian chief. The Indian chief pictured in the trademark represented Skenandoah, a chief of the Oneidas. Chief Skenandoah died in March 1816 at the age of 110. This was also when the brewery started using the slogan "Call for it—insist."

The brewery ran a series of thirty ads during 1907 in local newspapers over a thirty-week period, explaining the various steps that were followed in the making of its ales. It had done a similar thing in 1904 using illustrations to show the brewing process. This time, photos were used. The quality of the photos was not great, but they were some of the earliest actual photos of the brewery equipment in use in 1907.

The brewery was capable of mashing and brewing two hundred barrels of ale in seven hours and at that time had the largest brewing vessels in central New York. In 1908, Oneida products were being bottled by the Oneida Bottling Company, located at 9 Blandina Street. Up until this time, Oneida ales were only available in kegs. It bottled Oneida's cream ale, stock ale, India pale ale, porter and half and half, which was just introduced.

George A. Ralph, son of G. Fred Ralph, was found dead in his home on May 12, 1908, at the age of thirty. He had been ill for a long time and had undergone an operation for gallstones and also suffered from depression. George was born in Utica in 1878, and when he was old enough worked at the brewery as a brewer. He took courses at the National Brewers' Academy in New York City and became proficient in the art of brewing.

By 1909, the brewery had erected its own bottling works. The brewery also became a distributor of Pabst Milwaukee Lagers during the summer of that year. The following year saw most of the advertising generated by the brewery touting Pabst lager. Few ads even mentioned Oneida Ales. The brewery came under attack from the Eagle Brewing Company for selling out-of-town brews. Eagle campaigned very successfully over the next few years to buy locally, which hurt sales of Oneida products.

In 1912, G. Fred Ralph was still president of the company, with C.M. Ralph serving as vice-president and Wilbur B. Ralph serving as secretary. Around 1915, the brewery moved its offices from Court Street to the corner of Lincoln Avenue (formerly Chenango Avenue) and Roberts Street (formerly Broadhead Street).

Ad from *Utica Daily Press*, March 1908.

The brewery erected a new office building in 1914 at a cost of $3,000. The officers for the brewery in 1914 were G. Fred Ralph, president and treasurer; C.M. Ralph, vice-president; and W. Booth Ralph, secretary. Ernest Edwards, who had been brewmaster at the brewery for the last twelve years, left at the end of 1914 to go into business with his father. A banquet was held in his honor at the Maennerchor, where he was given a beautiful silver loving cup.

In 1915, the brewery hired John F. Ryan as secretary. W. Booth Ralph became treasurer. Gustav Detlefsen joined the brewery as brewmaster/superintendent when E.A. Edwards resigned in April of that year. He remained in that position up until Prohibition.

On November 29, 1915, an accident occurred between an Oneida Brewing Company delivery wagon and an automobile. The accident occurred at the corner of South and Leeds Streets. The automobile was completely wrecked and one of the horses was so badly injured that it had to be killed. Automobiles were becoming more common, and these kinds of accidents increased.

During World War I, there was a lot of anti-German sentiment. The government passed the Espionage Act, which outlawed, among other things, abusive and seditious language. In August 1918, Benjamin Smith, a driver for the Oneida Brewery, was charged with violating the new law. Smith entered a restaurant on June 24 and asked for beef steak and potatoes. He was told by the owner that it could not be served to him that day, as it was a beefless day.

Smith swore and said, "The s— of b— that make the law eat what they want, and I will eat what I want. They can't tell me what to eat, but they think they can tell me what to eat. The soldiers are no better than I am. They have what they want."

He was then asked if he was pro-German and replied, "I am a German. You can call me what you like." Smith was sent to jail, as he was unable to post the $1,000 bail.

Smith had his day in court and was eventually released. This incident shows how high the anti-German sentiment was at the time. Many of the local brewers were of German origin, and they had to walk a fine line during both World War I and II.

The years prior to Prohibition saw many improvements to the brewery with additional buildings being added, along with electricity. The brewery was assessed at $56,000 in 1918 and paid $2,026 in city and county taxes. It was the third-largest brewery in Utica at this time.

A small fire started in the pitch room at the brewery on January 28, 1919. The fire department was called and quickly put out the blaze.

The Oneida Brewing Company became the first Utica-area brewery to apply for a real beer permit to manufacture medicinal beer on November 9, 1921. The company's application was before the federal Prohibition director in New York and the federal prohibition commissioner in Washington, D.C. The brewery bond received the formal approval of collector Jesse W. Clarke of the Syracuse Internal Revenue office and, with the application for the permit, was forwarded to Acting Prohibition Director E.C. Yellowly in New York City. A week later, still no word had been received on approval of the permit. The West End Brewing Company and Eagle Brewing Company had in the meantime applied for their permits. All three breweries were denied permits to produce medicinal beer.

G. Fred Ralph died at his home, 4 Avery Place, on January 28, 1923, after a long illness. He had been confined to his home for the past two months. He was sixty-nine years old. The Oneida Brewery was idle for the rest of Prohibition. On April 1928, all property and buildings belonging to the Oneida Brewing Company were transferred to the Lincoln Realty Corporation.

In December 1932, the local newspaper reported that the brewery owned by Wilbur Ralph and the Ralph estate might be sold. By early 1933, the brewery had been on the market for some time. The realtor, Harry Duffy, had received many inquiries and thought a deal would be reached shortly. The plant had been operating until a short time earlier as the Oneida Liquid Malt Company, manufacturing wort, a legalized ingredient of near beer.

Frank B. Steele, who was a consulting engineer at the time, was picked to become president of the brewery. He was formerly vice-president of the Utica Gas & Electric Company and was vice-president of the Utica Rotary Club.

Vice-president Henry Hoffman was engaged in the wholesale and retail meat business, as well as president of the Utica Maennerchor Society. The treasurer was Seward B. Eric, who was president and director of several corporations. The secretary and assistant treasurer was Harry McDuffy.

The management obtained the services of Otto Selg as brewmaster. Selg had been a master brewer since 1893. He had been brewmaster and superintendent of the Crown Brewery Company of Cincinnati, Ohio; Adolf G. Hupfel's Sons Brewery in New York City; and the Obermeyer & Liebman Brewery in Havana, Cuba.

Selg pointed out that this brewery, erected nearly one hundred years ago, was designed to brew ales and was ideally equipped for the purpose. The brew house, of modern steel, brick and concrete construction, as well as the cooling room, fermenting room, storage cellars and their equipment, were intact. With minor overhauling, they would be ready for operation in a short time.

"With this equipment," he said, "together with installation of modern electric-driven refrigerating apparatus, the plant will again be in a position to produce the well-known 'Oneida Sparkling Cream Ale.' The old established methods used in the art of brewing this ale will be combined with the latest processes, thus insuring [*sic*] an ale even better than that so favorably received by the people of this community in years gone by." The brewery would concentrate on brewing only cream ales to start.

The brewery began undergoing renovations to bring it up to modern standards. Besides general repair and painting, new electric refrigeration machinery was installed. The roofing was repaired by Stanley Weiss, and the painting was being done by the E.P. Walter Company. To raise money for these renovations, the new owners offered stock (58,000 shares at $2.50 each) to the general public in the new company. The company had an authorized capital of 150,000 shares. The directors of the company had been given options good for six months after the payment of an initial dividend on the stock to purchase 8,250 shares of stock at $2.00 per share. The total authorized capital stock in the brewery was 150,000 shares. While waiting for its permits, a number of experimental brews were tried. The new owners wanted to come up with a brew that would be an immediate hit.

The first board of directors included Richard Metzler, publisher of the Utica Deutsche Zeitund; Frederic A. Willis, director of public affairs and foreign relations of the Columbia Broadcasting System; T. Edward McDermott, president and treasurer of the Mohawk Valley Brick and Supply Co.; T. Harvey Ferris, general counsel of the company; and Drs. James G. Douglas and F. John Rossi.

On May 25, Earl Bowman, a workman at the brewery, was injured when a wall of dirt from a ditch was being filled in the yard caved in on him. Other workmen at the plant rescued him. He suffered shock and injuries about the head and shoulders.

The brewery obtained its federal permit (U-254) on June 10, 1933, but did not get its state license until August 14. This made it one of the last breweries in Utica to be able to sell its products to the public. On August 15th, the first shipments of Oneida Sparkling Cream Ale were made. Oneida made its first shipment of ale in big red trucks, which replaced the horse-drawn wagons of old.

The company did not bottle its products immediately after Prohibition, preferring to distribute the ale it produced in half and quarter kegs to begin with. Bottling would start up later when the supply of ale allowed.

In mid-June, Henry Wanger and Ira Guilden of New York City and Leonard W. Ferris of Utica were added to the board of directors, increasing the directorate to eleven. The capacity of the brewery at this time was nearly fifty thousand barrels a year.

On September 29, the brewery had to run an ad saying that it had run out of Oneida Sparkling Cream Ale due to public demand for the product and that the next batch would not be available until October 3. On October 24, at a meeting of the board of directors, Frank J. Winslow was elected chairman of the board. Wilbur B. Ralph, formerly connected with the brewery, assumed the duties of production manager, and James H. Penrose became brewmaster, replacing Otto Selg.

James H. Penrose graduated from the National Brewers' Academy in 1909 and was the brewmaster with Penrose & McEniry in Cohoes until accepting the job with Oneida. Frank J. Winslow had long been identified with the

WE ARE GRATEFUL

•

In expressing our sincere appreciation to the people, for their ready acceptance and approval of ONEIDA SPARKLNG CREAM ALE

We Regret to Announce

Owing to the steadily growing demand of the public for ONEIDA SPARKLING CREAM ALE we are unable to fill any more orders

Until Next Tuesday

•

SINCE 1832
a well deserved reputation for Quality and Flavor

ONEIDA BREWING COMPANY
INCORPORATED
915 LINCOLN AVE., UTICA, N. Y. Phone 4-5131

Ad from *Utica Daily Press*, Sept. 1933.

brewing industry in Utica as the owner and operator of the Fort Schuyler Brewery that in 1933 was leased to the Utica Brewing Company.

By 1935, Wilbur B. Ralph had become president and treasurer of the company again, with Henry B. Hoffman serving as vice-president, and Harry B. Duffy serving as secretary and assistant treasurer.

On May 11, 1939, the brewery announced plans to build a new bottling plant at a cost of $40,000. The authorized capital stock for the brewery was increased from 72,000 to 150,000 shares in $1 common shares to cover the expansion.

In 1941, the brewery closed temporarily due to a labor dispute. Officials said that negotiations were underway for the resumption of operations in the near future. The brewery employed forty people at the time.

The Ralph family sold the brewery to New York City interests in 1942. They ran it only briefly before it closed its doors in August 1942, succumbing to the shortages of raw materials caused by the war and other factors. The brewery was put up for public auction on August 26, 1942. Offered for sale was all of the brewery equipment, machine tools, supplies, steel and wood tanks, pipe, barrels and office furniture.

A small fire was caused by a blowtorch on September 3, 1942. Firemen were called to the scene and put out the blaze. Little damage was done.

On November 25, 1944, the Utica Oldsmobile Corporation bought the brewery buildings from the City of Utica. It received permission to demolish the brewery buildings on December 28, 1944. By 2013, the only building to remain standing was the one-story office building.

On November 20, 1950, Henry J. Ralph died at the age of ninety. He had been ill for several weeks before. Since 1939, he had been living in New York City at the Hotel Latham. He was born on May 29, 1860, in Holland Patent, a son of George and Mary Wells Ralph. Henry had served as secretary of the brewery for many years. He never married.

# CHAPTER 22
# EAGLE BREWING COMPANY

## 1888–1943

In July 1888, a group of men associated with the local brewing industry met to form a lager beer brewery in East Utica. They included John Quinn, Moses Barney, James O'Toole, William F. Welch, Francis Moore, Martin McGarvey, Edward Callahan and John Myres.

From this meeting, the Eagle Brewing Company was formed. A site was found for the new brewery at the corner of Jay and Third Streets. Well-known Philadelphia architect A.C. Wagner was chosen to design the new facility. This brewery was to be the largest, most modern brewery in the city of Utica.

On September 14, 1888, ground was broken for the immense brick brewery. Contractor John Redmond was awarded the contract for the stone and mason work. P. Thomas' Sons were awarded the carpentry work. The overall construction of the brewery was supervised by Frederick Brunet of Philadelphia. The old Gulf brewery was located across the street from the new brewery.

The foundations of the building were made from Canajoharie stone, laid in Portland cement. They were three feet thick and were built on solid rock. The first of the 1.5 million bricks that were used in the construction was laid in place on October 30. The bricks were made by Callahan & Doyle of Utica. The pillars and girders used in the buildings were made of riveted wrought iron made in Pottsville, Pennsylvania, at a cost of $11,000.

The main building rose to a height of 60 feet and consisted of four stories with a cupola on top. Atop the cupola rose a flagpole, on top of which sat a large gilded eagle. This eagle was 120 feet from the ground and could be seen over a large distance. Contained in this building were four distinct departments: a mill room, a malt storage room, a brew house and a beer storage room. The building measured 70 by 132 feet, not including a detached two-story powerhouse. The floors of the building were covered with asphalt. The walls and ceilings were plastered, kalsomined or painted, depending on the location.

At the time the Eagle Brewing Company buildings were erected, great strides had been made in the scientific field of brewing technology. The new brewery was the first one in Utica designed and completely equipped for year-round production of ale and lager in accordance with the latest nineteenth-century developments in brewery technique and practice.

Eagle was the first brewery in the area to be equipped with a mechanical refrigeration system, which allowed it to manufacture all year long. This system consisted of a thirty-five-ton consolidated ice machine, which was built in Chicago by the Consolidated Ice Machine Company. The machine was sixteen feet high and had two ten-foot-diameter fly wheels. The machine was similar to one installed in the Crystal Spring Brewery in Syracuse but more modern. The machine was installed in the brewery under the supervision of R.M. McDonough and Andrew Richardson.

A roadway entered the building from the Third Street side of the brewery, where wagons, loaded with bag of malt, were unloaded and emptied. The malt was emptied into a tightly covered hopper, which contained a conveyor belt of buckets that conveyed the malt to the top floor of the building.

On the top floor, the malt was weighed and then dropped into huge holding bins on the floor below. Each bin could hold twelve thousand bushels. When the malt was needed, it went through a revolving screen located at the bottom of the bins that sifted out all foreign substances and then was conveyed to another weighing hopper.

After being weighed again, it was conveyed to the cupola of the building by another conveyor belt of buckets. From here, the grain was gravity fed down into a grinder and then into the mash tank, where it was mixed with water.

The resulting mash was drawn out of the tank when ready into a huge copper boiling kettle with a capacity of 175 barrels. This kettle cost $3,300. Hops were added to the kettle at this point, and after a vigorous boiling of three to four hours, the resulting brew was drawn off through a strainer called a hop jack.

The strained brew was then pumped to the top of the building into a large, shallow steel tank called the cool ship to be cooled. This tank was twenty-five by fifty feet in size. After being partially cooled, the brew was let down into large copper pans near the ceiling of the room below. Through a series of small holes in these pans, the brew flowed over what was known as the Baudelot cooler.

This machine was made by the grouping of thirty-two two-and-a-half-inch copper pipes, sixteen feet long, in a horizontal position. A stream of cold brine from the ice machine was forced through the pipes, and the brew, flowing down and around these tubes from the pans above, became very cold by the time it reached the copper receptacle below.

The mash tub, hop jacks and coolers were made of steel and cost $6,000. The bottoms of the tanks were moveable and cost $300 each.

The fermenting room was located on the floor below. The cooled brew was pumped to one of twenty-nine huge cedar vats occupying this room. Each vat had a capacity of seventy-five barrels. The walls of this room were twenty inches thick, and the windows were made with three separate panes of glass to keep out heat. Ice coated all the pipes and coils in the room, helping to maintain a low temperature.

After the beer had fermented for the required length of time, the beer was pumped to the storage or lagering room on the floor below. Here the beer was stored in one of twenty-nine cedar casks that had a capacity of 150 barrels each. Each of the casks was tightly covered, and this was the first time in the process that the beer was not exposed to the atmosphere. Coils of pipes containing brine from the ice machine surrounded the beer, keeping the room just above freezing.

The beer remained in these casks for at least three months to properly age. Once the beer was ready for the market, it was pumped to the cellar below into oak casks, and from these casks, the beer was racked into kegs. At this point in time, the brewery did not have its own bottling works. Bottling for the brewery was handled by Patrick McGuiness at 179 Bleecker Street in Utica.

The mill machinery was furnished by Haas, Parsons & Co. of Philadelphia, the copper and tank work by the Cast Copper and Sheet Iron Company of Buffalo and the cedar vats by George J. Buskhardt's Sons of Philadelphia. The plumbing and steam fitting was done by Edward Martin and Nugent & Mooney of Utica.

The two-level detached power house contained two eighty-horsepower steel boilers, built by the Phoenix Foundry Company of Syracuse, and a fifty-horsepower engine. This equipment supplied all the power needed by the brewery. The smoke stack attached to this building rose to a height of one hundred feet. Construction of the brewery was scheduled to be completed by February 1889. When complete, the brewery could do two to three brewings per day and had a capacity of between forty-five thousand and fifty thousand barrels per year.

Articles of incorporation were drawn up and filed in the county clerk's office on September 24. The existence of the corporation was fixed at fifty years with capital stock of $100,000. This was divided into one thousand shares at $100 a share. Named as trustees of the new firm were John Quinn, James O'Toole, Martin McGarvey, Edward Callahan and William F. Welch.

For the first year of operation, John Quinn was chosen to serve as president. Other officers for the first year were Edward Callahan, vice-president; William J. Barney, treasurer; Martin McGavey, secretary; and Thomas S. Geary, bookkeeper.

The brewery was expected to employ fifty people when fully operational. Joseph Lauer of Rochester was hired as master brewer for the firm. He had previously worked as a master brewer for the Bartholomew Brewery (six years) and the Genesee Brewery (ten years) in Rochester.

In the spring of 1889, P. Hammes, a West Utica wagon maker, was contracted to build two large wagons for the brewery after the pattern in vogue among the New York City breweries at the time. They were the largest in Utica.

Accidents seemed to plague the brewery as it was being built. On February 27, 1889, William T. Hickey and William Collins, both fifteen years of age, fell from the cupola of the brewery. After dinner of that day, both boys decided to explore the new brewery being built across the street from where they lived. They entered the building unnoticed and climbed up into the cupola, which represented the highest point accessible in the brewery. Hickey lost his balance and fell through an opening sixty feet to the ground floor. Collins attempted to save his friend but, in doing so, lost his balance and also fell through the opening. Collins landed on top of Hickey, completely crushing Hickey's chest. Workmen in the brewery heard the noise and rushed to find out what had happened. Hickey died from a badly crushed chest shortly after medical helped arrived at the brewery. Collins, whose injuries did not seem severe at the time, developed complications. He died from lockjaw on March 6.

The brewery was scheduled to start its first brewing on Wednesday, April 17, but tragedy struck again. There was a fire in which three men, James Quinn, Martin Knorr and Fred Knorr, were severely burned. They were coating the interior of one of the huge cedar vats with shellac. Someone knocked over the kerosene lamp that was being used for light, turning the interior of the vat into an inferno. The men somehow managed to get out of the vat alive. Quinn was taken home and treated by a doctor who came to the house. Fred and Martin Knorr were taken to the city hospital and treated. Martin Knorr was the most severely burned, with all of his hair burned off and first degree burns over most of his body. Damage to the brewery was confined to the cedar vat.

Martin Knorr died from his burns on May 2. This was the third death at the brewery in less than three months. Both James Quinn and Fred Knorr recovered completely from their injuries.

The brewery managed to start its first brewing the next day. The total process from beginning to end took three months, with the brewery's first brew reaching the consumer June 22, almost one year after the brewery was first formed.

John Quinn was scheduled to tap the first barrel of brew at the Genesee Cafe in Bagg's Square at 10:00 a.m. However, an ad ran in the June 22 *Morning Herald* by Charles & Fenner of 14 Genesee Street in Bagg's Square that claimed that they had tapped the first keg of Eagle beer. On June 27, the Eagle brewery held an open house where people were invited to inspect the brewery and sample its products. A very large crowd came to visit the brewery. On July 1, the first official ads for the Eagle Brewing Company appeared in newspapers.

The brewery introduced Eagle Extra Pale Liebotschaner Lager to the public on August 8. At the beginning, the Eagle Brewing Company produced mainly lagers. Liebotschaner, export, bohemian, bavarian and stock lagers were among the first products produced at the brewery.

In August, the brewery began drilling an additional well to supply the water necessary to keep up with demand. The well was 23 feet in diameter. In a similar well sunk by the Utica Star Ale Brewing Company, drilling 400 feet had failed to secure water. By September 7, the well was 117 feet deep but had not hit water in sufficient quantity to stop.

The Eagle Brewing Company participated in the local Labor Day parade on September 3 by entering one wagon. The Utica, Star, Gulf, Hutten, People's and Fort Schuyler breweries also entered one wagon each in the parade. The Oneida Brewery entered two wagons, and the West End brewery did not enter any.

A warehouse was built for the brewery in 1889 by Phillip Thomas' Sons for $3,000. On November 22, John Bredt, a cooper at the brewery, was severely injured by the fall of a pile of barrels. His ankle was dislocated and his leg broken.

In June 1891, Joseph Lauer, the master brewer, tendered his resignation to take effect on August 1. He had been offered a position at the Stoppel Co-operative Compression Brewing Company of Cleveland, Ohio, which he decided to accept. There had been rumors that he and others were considering buying the Hutten Brewery, but he denied any involvement. He was replaced by Henry J. Luebbert, who remained in that position until after Prohibition. Luebbert had worked as a plumber before joining the brewery. On August 12, a major thunderstorm passed though Utica, causing damage to the northeast corner of the brew house roof. A large number of trees were blown down around the brewery.

Ad from *Utica Daily Press*, August 1890.

Fire struck the brewery on November 28, 1892. Shortly before 3:00 p.m., the brewmaster, Henry J. Luebbert, noticed fire in the cupola of the building and summoned help. The fire was thought to have started in the malt mill located on the third floor.

Before the malt was ready for brewing, it was ground up thoroughly in this mill. A magnet device was located in the machine to remove any metal items that were mixed in with the malt. It was thought that a nail got by this magnet and the friction caused by the rollers and the nail set fire to the very flammable malt dust. The flames shot up the machine into the cupola of the building, which was made of wood. Extinguishers and hoses were brought into service by the brewery help, and before the fire department responded to the alarm, the ground malt in the mill had been saturated with water. The firemen succeeded in speedily extinguishing the blaze in the cupola, although a large portion was burned. The flagpole with the huge brass eagle tumbled one hundred feet to the ground shortly after. Fortunately, no one was hurt by the falling object.

A 1890s Eagle Brewing Company trade card. *Author's collection.*

Because the brewery was constructed with very little wood, the fire did little damage. The insurance adjusters paid the company $1,400 for the building damage and $400 for the lost malt. The malt grinder where the fire started was not damaged badly in the fire. Brewing was expected to resume in a few days.

A two-story wash house and pitching house was added to the brewery in 1894. A special brew of lager beer, called "Salvator," was made for the July 4 holiday. McGuinness' Eagle Bottling Works, located on Bleeker Street, was bottling all the brews from Eagle.

A small fire broke out at the brewery on October 20 in a shed used to store empty beer kegs. The shed was partially destroyed.

In late 1894, a new three-story wash house was built. It was twenty by forty feet and was located in the rear of the main building. A one-story pitch house, thirty feet square, was constructed to replace the one destroyed by fire. The improvements cost $3,000.

The brewery workers' union held a lively meeting on April 5, 1895, in which it discussed the Utica brewers' refusal to accept the new schedule of payment for brewery workers. As a result, it was voted to withdraw the union label from the Eagle and Oneida breweries and to declare their products unfair. The reason these breweries were singled out was because Quinn and Ralph were believed to be the leaders of the opposition to the new schedule.

Several weeks later, both sides made some concessions, and the boycott was removed. The newly signed agreement contained the following pay grades: coopers, $12.00; practical engineers, $15.00; firemen in lager breweries, $12.00 for seven days work per week of twelve hours per day; firemen in ale breweries, $11 per week per week for sixty hours work with pro rata increase for extra days; foremen of wash house in lager brewery, $11.00; helpers, $10.00; men in fermenting room, $11.00; kettle men, $11.00; first cellar men, $11.00; first teamster in ale breweries, $10.50; assistant teamster, $9.50; lager peddlers, $12.00; helpers, $10.00; barn men, $10.00; men in bottling works, $10.00; and indoor men for labor over sixty hours per week would receive twenty-five cents per hour. Coopers were required to take care of leakages on Sundays, and teamsters would take care of their horses on Sunday without charging overtime.

By 1896, Martin McGarvey was no longer secretary for the brewery. William F. Welch assumed the secretary position, in addition to his treasurer's job. Capacity at the brewery was between sixteen thousand and eighteen thousand barrels annually in 1897. The brewery added the manufacture of stilled and lively pale ale in early 1898. It was also producing bock beer at this time. The new ales were a big hit, and their popularity grew rapidly. Capacity at the brewery had increased to between twenty thousand and twenty-five thousand barrels annually. P. McGuinness on Bleeker Street was still the bottler for Eagle products at this time. Products produced by the brewery in 1899 included bohemian, extra pale liebotschaner, export, bock, stock lagers and stilled and lively pale amber ales.

By 1899, business at the brewery was growing nicely, enabling it to add a new cold storage building, a barrel shed, a wagon shed and an icehouse, all of which were one-story buildings. Power and heat were generated by coal-fired steam, and the lights were gas powered.

A small fire took place in the brewery on Friday, June 8, 1900, when a stopcock on a gas pipe in the cellar blew off as an employee was passing with a lighted candle. The fire department was called, but employees put the fire out before they got there.

The fire department was called back to the brewery on August 20, 1900, at 1:52 p.m. when a kettle of pitch caught fire. The fire was extinguished before any damage was done.

A horse attached to one of the delivery wagons belonging to the brewery became spooked in front of the Utica jail. It ripped up the iron fence to which it was attached and dragged the fence and the wagon until it finally broke away from the wagon. It then took to the road and ran a short distance over Bleecker Street until captured.

The post to which the horse had been attached was knocked over, and many portions of the iron fence were broken. The animal also succeeded in badly damaging the wagon. The driver, who was about to jump into the wagon when the horse started, quickly stepped away and avoided being injured.

In February 1902, a rumor was circulating in Utica that the local breweries were merging in the near future. For the past five years, the brewery business in Utica had not been paying as well as it had in former years. The output had been increasing, but the profit had not increased proportionately. Within seven years, competition and expense had closed the National brewery, the People's brewery and the Utica Star Ale brewery. The Consumers' brewery met with setbacks from various causes, and New York maltsters, who were the heaviest creditors, sent Theodore Rhinebeck to revive it. A poor product defeated Rhinebeck's efforts and those of his partners, and the brewery failed. He spent the next six months in Utica to work on the consolidation.

The Eagle, Oneida, Fort Schuyler and West End breweries had agreed to the terms proposed. The Gulf Brewery held out for $150,000, but the merger's offer was $110,000, take it or leave it. The combined company would be formed with a capital of $1 million. Of this amount, the Eagle and West End breweries would receive each one-fourth, the Oneida one-fifth and the other two breweries one-eighth or more. All payments were to be in stock, and each brewery would be represented on the board of directors according to its stock interests.

The object of the merger was not to close down any of the breweries but to increase the profit of each by a loose combination that would decrease expenses, work in a larger market and buy materials in greater bulk. In the end, the plan fell through, and each brewery proceeded along on its own.

A new stock house, racking room and cooper shop (thirty-nine by fifty-two and a half feet) was added in 1905. In April, the brewery installed a device for consuming smoke. Manufactured by the American Economy Engineering Company of Houston, it was known as the Brasle Steam Generator and Smoke Consumer. It was installed under the personal direction of Jacob Brasle, the inventor. The device was said to consume about 80 percent of the smoke coming from the brewery chimney and had previously been installed in Buffalo, Fort Plain, Gloversville and Amsterdam.

February 1906 saw a large force of workmen engaged in enlarging the brewery. They were preparing the plant to receive and install two of the largest filters used for filtering beer. The filters were purchased from the Loed Manufacturing Company of Cleveland, Ohio. They were installed in

June. Each filter could fill thirty barrels an hour. The brewery also purchased and installed a new mash washer.

By 1907, the brewery decided its brew house was inadequate to cope with its increased business. As a result, it built a new wash house adjoining the racking room with dimensions of sixty-two and a half feet by fifty-one and a half feet. There was twenty feet clear beneath the steel trusses, which was covered with corrugated galvanized iron. The dome was sixteen feet in diameter and had a skylight to provide ample light for working. In the cellar was a temporary place for storage. The building was fireproof, the only wood being in the doors and windows.

The floor consisted of steel beams, hollow tile with two layers of waterproofing and four-inch vitrified brick, and the points were filled with asphalt and tar. New machinery was installed throughout the building.

In late 1907, the brewery's products were bottled by R.W. Cahill at 56 South Street and John B. Kenney at 589 Bleecker Street. The brewery's association with Mr. Kenney only lasted for one year and with Mr. Cahill for only two years until the brewery built its own bottling works.

John Quinn, the president of the brewery, died suddenly when he suffered a stroke of apoplexy at his home on April 14, 1909. He was sixty-nine years old. His brother Daniel had died a couple days before. John Quinn was born on January 6, 1840, in Boonville, where he lived until 1855. From there, he moved to Arizona Territory, where he stayed until 1861, when he came to Utica and got a job at the Gulf Brewery. In 1874, with John Myers, James O'Toole and Thomas Quinn, he formed a partnership under the firm name of J. Myers & Co. The firm built the Utica Star brewery. In 1888, he and others formed the Eagle brewery, of which he became president.

A kettle of pitch in the rear of the brewery caught fire on the afternoon of August 20, 1909. It was quickly put out by the fire department. Another small fire occurred on August 30. A fireman walking by the brewery was told there was a fire on the roof of the pitch shed. He investigated and saw a small blaze, which he quickly extinguished with some water.

In June 1909, the brewery began its "Boost for Utica" campaign. This campaign came about as a response to the growing influence of the national brewers in the area. The Fort Schuyler Brewing Company (Budweiser distributor) and the Oneida Brewing Company (Pabst distributor) were the main targets of the campaign, along with the national breweries. The Eagle Brewing Company really stressed the fact that it produced and sold only local products, as did the West End Brewing Company, to a lesser extent. The campaign proved to be very

Ad from *Utica Daily Press*, July 1909.

successful, with Eagle sales growing tremendously—to the detriment of the breweries selling national brands.

As a result of this increased business, the brewery decided to build a modern bottling plant of its own in December 1909. The new bottling works was completed on April 18, 1910. The bottling plant adjoined the brewery on the east side of Third Street near Jay. The building was constructed of brick and stone and had forty and a half feet of frontage with sixty and a half feet of depth. It was two stories high with a basement. The floors were of steel and concrete construction, making them fireproof. The bottling shop had an asphalt floor.

The basement was used for storage of empties. The first floor proper contained the bottling shop, and the second floor was used to store new bottles, barrels and cases. The bottling shop had the latest equipment and design. The shop had a twelve-spout Bishop & Babcock bottle filler, a Crown Cork & Seal capper, a New Era pasteurizer and an Ermold labeler. For the preparatory work, there was a twentieth-century soaker with a capacity of fifteen thousand bottles, an Eycke thirty-thousand-bottle washer and a Voltz thirty-thousand-bottle rinser. The capacities stated above were the amount of product the equipment could process in a ten-hour workday.

On January 22, 1910, the brewery announced a contest to name the brewery's new bottled lager and ale. The brewery offered two prizes of ten dollars in gold to the person who entered the name used by the brewery for the products. Each winner would also receive a double case of lager or ale when the bottling works began operations.

The winners were announced on Thursday, February 3. Mr. A.J. Dutcher, of Court House, Utica, was the first to send in the name "Peerless" and won the ten dollars in gold and a double case of Peerless Eagle Lager. Mr. Morris Splain of 205½ Morris Street, Utica, was the first to send in the name "Monarch" and won the ten dollars in gold and a double case of Monarch Ale. The response to the contest was great, as more than one thousand replies were received by the brewery. Brewery officials stated that much deliberation on the part of the judges was required to make a fair selection of the names and winners.

The first shipments of Peerless Lager and Monarch Ale from the new bottling works began on April 18. An ad run by the brewery stated that the enormous output of the opening days had surprised even the most optimistic of the owners. The brewery was operating the bottling works at full capacity right from the start.

Around 9:15 a.m. on July 20, 1910, the fire department was called to the brewery to put out a blaze in the shed used as a storage house for barrels. The fire was caused by the ignition of some pitch by the heat of a smoke stack in the shed. Little damage was done.

Three large casks were delivered to the brewery on April 18, 1911. They were shipped from Buffalo on the New York Central Railroad. The casks were made of oak and measured ten feet, six inches high when lying on their sides. End to end, they were twelve feet, two inches long. It was said that the contents of 200 ordinary beer barrels would fit in one of these casks. To get these casks

Ad from *Utica Daily Press*, April 1910.

into the brewery, it was necessary to remove a large section of brickwork in the wall. The three new casks replaced seven smaller ones that had from 120- to 140-barrel capacity. The casks were made by Peter Pfeil of Buffalo.

In November 1911, the brewery was granted a building permit to construct a new boiler house. The new building was twenty-five by forty-five feet and adjoined the old boiler house. The new building was needed to house pumps, which were located in another building, and a new 175-horsepower boiler. Total cost for the project was $3,500.

## Home Pleasures

The man of the house should not be selfish. If he enjoys a glass of cool, refreshing Lager or Ale---and what real manly man does not?---he should remember that his wife, his daughters and in fact all at home would find pleasure in a glass if he would but send a case there. Now it's only a matter of very little trouble to telephone us and we will see that the home is provided with just what it wants.

GIVE US A CHANCE TO CHECK THE THIRST, DRIVE DULL CARE AWAY AND MAKE LIFE WORTH LIVING...WE WILL DO IT WITH OUR CELEBRATED

**PEERLESS LAGER and MONARCH ALE**

**IN WOOD AND BOTTLES...MADE IN UTICA BY THE ORIGINAL UTICA BOOSTERS**

*Order a case for the folks at home. Do it today. Put in a supply for*

**"The Glorious Fourth"**

*and the National Holiday will be celebrated in proper shape.*

Ad from *Utica Daily Press*, July 1910.

By 1912, William F. Welch was president of the company, as well as serving as the president and treasurer of the Gulf Brewery. John T. Quinn was now secretary and treasurer of the Eagle Brewing Company.

Even though the brewery had erected a bottling plant several years before, by mid-1914, it felt that it was necessary to erect a new one with greatly increased capacity. The new building was constructed of brick and concrete and faced Jay Street. The building was 44 feet 2 inches wide, 102 feet 8 inches in length and 37 feet high. Puckert & Wunder of New York were the designers, and R. Richards & Son Co. was the builder. The cost of the project was $30,000. The new bottling works was equipped with Barry-Wehmiller soakers and pasteurizers with the capacity of 150 barrels. The new building was completed in early 1915.

During the years before Prohibition, the brewery constructed a large two-story office building on Third Street, added a building to house ice-making machines, expanded the power house and converted the old icehouse to an auto repair shop to service its growing fleet of delivery trucks. Electricity was added to many of the buildings during these expansions.

John T. Quinn, secretary and treasurer of the brewery, died on April 9, 1916, at the age of forty-six. He had been in failing health for more than a year. He was the son of Thomas Quinn, one of the founders of the brewery.

On June 11, 1917, a major storm came through the area. Both the Gulf and Eagle breweries were surrounded by water, which rapidly filled the cellars. While the breweries kept working, the horses used to pull the delivery wagons had to swim at times to reach the buildings. The Eagle brewery had last suffered flood damage in 1915 when the bottling department was filled with water. Around $700 damage was done.

The brewery prospered up until Prohibition. The brewery was assessed at $111,650 in 1918 and paid taxes totaling $4,104. It was the second-largest brewery in the city at that time. Like most of the other breweries in the area (except West End), the brewery closed its doors and remained idle throughout Prohibition.

Just before Prohibition became the law of the land, the Eagle Brewing Company offered Extra Pale Liebotschaner, Bohemian Lager, Ruby Ale, Old Stock, Porter, India Pale Ale, Peerless Lager, Amber Monarch Ale and XXX Pale Monarch Ale in kegs. Peerless Lager, Monarch Ale, Old Stock and Porter were offered in bottles.

The brewery filed an application with the Internal Revenue Bureau for permission to manufacture real beer for medicinal purposes. Locally, both the Oneida and West End breweries had also filed an application. All three breweries were refused their permits, and the law for making real beer for medicinal purposes was changed.

In early 1921, the brewery was selling pure apple cider for thirty cents per gallon in barrels and half barrels. Prohibition was tough on the firm. In 1922, it sold two of its delivery trucks (a White and a Republic truck). In 1924, it sold its single and double sleighs.

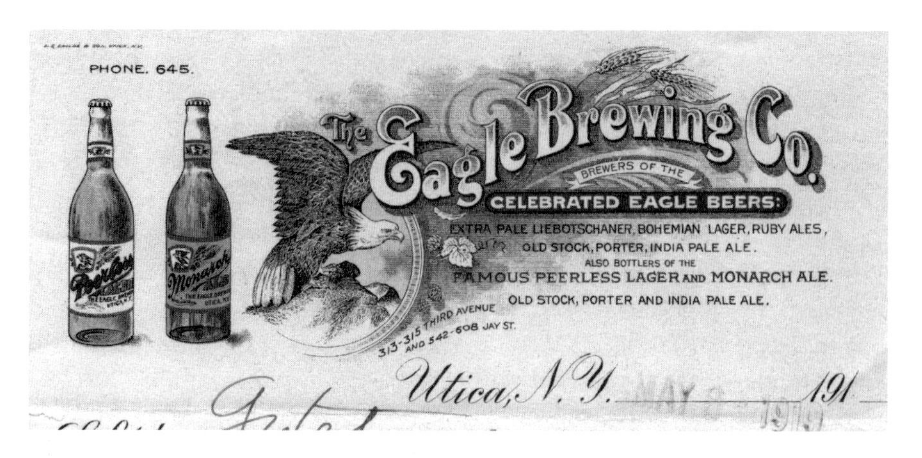


Eagle Brewing Company letterhead from 1919. *Author's collection.*

In September 1925, the brewery ran into trouble with the Prohibition agents. R.Q. Merrick, acting prohibition administrator for this district, said, "We have concentrated our brewery squads on the Utica breweries for the past several months and were successful a few weeks ago in making a very splendid case against the Eagle Brewing Company and they will be prosecuted criminally as well as cited for revocation of their permit."

The action marked the first of its kind against a Utica brewery since Prohibition had become law. It was believed to be based on the seizure of a truckload of beer near the brewery a few weeks before. At the time, the agents seizing the truck were attacked by a gang of young men.

In September 1931, the business was terminated, and the company was in the process of liquidation. Thomas Quinn objected to the tax assessment against the brewery. The assessment was for $77,000. He said the company would be glad to get $40,000 to $50,000 for the plant and that insurance on the plant was $32,000. There were no buyers, so when Prohibition ended, the Quinn family still had the brewery.

With the end of Prohibition, the brewery made ready to resume brewing. John M. Quinn, son of one of the original founders, John Quinn, was now president of the brewery.

Henry J. Luebbert, who had been master brewer and superintendent for over forty years, left the company to work at the Utica Brewing Company. To replace him, the brewery hired William Lafferty, who had been the brewmaster at the Gulf Brewery for the past thirty-five years. By 1940, William J. Brill had become brewmaster.

Matthew C. Quinn served as vice-president. His father, William, was a brother of John and one of the original stockholders. John M. Slaven, grandson of John Myers, another original stockholder, served as secretary and treasurer. Arthur O. Gray was office manager at the brewery.

After receiving its federal (U-244) and state permits (D-42), the brewery resumed brewing on July 1, 1933, exactly forty-five years from the day (July 1, 1888) when the plant first began making beverages. Previous months had been spent bringing the brewery up to operating condition. Distribution of Monarch Ale and Peerless Lager to the general public began on Saturday, July 22. The brewery changed the names of the offerings shortly after. They became Eagle Lager, Amber Ale and Pale Ale. The reason for the change is unknown. The brewery was issued license BR-81, which allowed it to sell beer at retail.

When the Eagle Brewing Company first opened in 1888, the Erie Canal was still a bustling nearby waterway, and Utica's famous "gulf" was a popular sylvan retreat, crossed by a wooden footbridge just beyond the brewery. The ravine was filled in during the 1930s, and part of it, facing on Rutger Street, was made into a playground named after Harry V. Quinn, the youngest son of John Quinn and a brother of John M. Quinn and a hero of World War I who was killed on the Hindenburg Line on September 29, 1918.

On January 16, 1934, George H. Finn, who was assistant brewer, died suddenly while engaged at work. He was sixty-eight years old. Finn had arrived at the brewery around 7:00 a.m. About two hours later, employees were trying to locate him. They called his house but were told he had gone to work. After much searching of the brewery, they located his body in a cupola. The coroner was called, and it was believed he died of natural causes. Finn was born in Utica in 1865. He worked at a brewery in Rome before coming back to Utica to work at the Eagle brewery when it started.

Arthur Gray, office manager for the brewery, reported to the police that burglars had broken into the brewery offices on February 10, 1934, but that nothing of value was taken.

Things went well for the brewery for the first few years after Prohibition, but then production steadily declined. William J. Brill was brewmaster in 1940. The Food Distribution Administration ordered brewers in 1943 to hand over 15 percemt of their production to the troops. This edict, along with the rationing of brewing materials, finally proved to be too much for the brewery, which closed its doors for good in early 1943. The last brewmaster employed at the brewery was John Defren, who had been hired in February 1943. Defren had previously been brewmaster at the Adam C. Jaeger Brewing Company plants in Philadelphia and Reading, Pennsylvania.

By 1947, the Utica Brewing Company had purchased some of the brewery buildings, using them primarily for storage and office space. The old bottling works became home to a wholesale grocery business.

In 1948, John Lalor, former president of the Utica Brewing Company who now owned the Eagle Brewing Company, reported to the police that boys were breaking windows at the brewery while playing after school.

A high wind and heavy rainstorm came through Utica on April 15, 1951. A brick ornament atop the brewery fell to the street. No one was injured.

The 1960s brought an end to the buildings that made up the Eagle Brewing Company. As a result of urban renewal, all the buildings were torn down. The eagle that sat on top of the brew house was taken by John Lalor's daughter, Anne Millard, who placed the eagle in her garden in Barneveld, New York.

# CHAPTER 23
# WEST END BREWING COMPANY (F.X. MATT BREWING COMPANY)

## 1888–PRESENT

### THE PRE-PROHIBITION YEARS

The history of the West End Brewing Company begins with the demise of the Columbia Brewing Company. On February 14, 1888, the Columbia Brewing Company was offered for sale at public auction at the sheriff's office in Utica. The business and property were bought by a group of men who would transform it into the West End Brewing Company. Included in the sale of the premises were all the fixtures, machinery, vats, pipes, hogsheads, barrels and all other personal property used in and connected with the business of the manufacture and sale of ale and lager, including all the horses, wagons, sleighs, harnesses and other equipment used around the premises.

On March 28, when the new owners formed the West End Brewing Company, they continued operating the brewery on Edward Street. The six trustees elected to manage the brewery for the first year were Henry Roemer, Robert Cromie, Sylvester D. Powers, Frank X. Matt, John J. Fuess and George H. Bierbauer.

A deed was filed at the county clerk's office on May 18, by which Barbara Bierbauer transferred to Sylvester D. Powers six lots on Edward Street, known as the Bierbauer brewery property, for $13,930.96. A mortgage on the property for $10,000 was given by Bierbauer to secure a portion of the purchase price. The next day, Powers filed a deed that transferred the property to the West End Brewing Company.

The purchase price of the brewery was $20,000. The new owners could only raise $17,000 cash when they bought the business and agreed to issue $3,000 capital stock to Barbara Bierbauer as the balance of the purchase price.

Henry Roemer served as the first president and Sylvester D. Powers, who owned the Senate Saloon at 116 Court Street, was the first vice-president. F.X. Matt was chosen as superintendent and brewmaster, with J.J. Fuess serving as secretary and treasurer.

The brewery was one of the smallest in the Utica area, employing twelve people and producing only four thousand barrels of beer annually, which it distributed over a six-block area. The new company commenced operations on April 2, 1888.

F.X. Matt, who was born in Igelschlatt Im Schichthal, Baden, in the Black Forest region of Germany in 1859, began his brewing education as a boy working for his father, Theodore Matt, and continued as a teenager at the famed Duke of Baden Brewery. The Matt family moved to the United States in 1878 when F.X. was nineteen. His father opened a meat market in Utica, but F.X. got a job at Charles Bierbauer's West Side Brewery. He then went to Canajoharie briefly to work at a brewery run by Louis Bierbauer before returning to Utica to help form the West End Brewery. Matt said of his desire to come to America, "I was in love with America and the American way, I believe, from the time I first began to read. Though, in those days in Germany, life was not too hard for a boy."

To make the brewery a success in 1888 required an aggressive manager not only to produce a quality beer but also to market it. F.X. Matt proved to be this energetic and forceful leader. Matt kept a close eye on sales figures and came to the conclusion that sales were not increasing satisfactorily since he was convinced that his beer was the finest in the city. He decided to take over the route of one of his salesmen for one day. By the end of the first day, he had more than doubled beer sales. From that day on, he combined the duties of a brewmaster with those of a salesman. As F.X. told the story years later, "I would come in very early to start the mash in the brew house and to see that the brew was well started. Then I would go out and sell the beer, stopping only because the horses got tired at the end of the day."

F.X. had reddish hair and a stocky build. His method of selling was to go around from tavern to tavern and make a speech to the people in the tavern. He would tell them about how he made his beer using only the finest ingredients. He said it was much better than competitive products. One

F.X. Matt. *Author's collection.*

time, a couple hecklers made some disparaging remarks while he was trying to speak. Supposedly, F.X. picked up the two offenders by their shirt collars and threw them out of the tavern and went back to his speech. This selling approach worked, and business grew.

Over the next three years, sales quadrupled. During this time, other Utica breweries cut their price to only one dollar per barrel. F.X. decided not to follow suit, as he believed that he was brewing the finest beer in the city. The other brewers kept the new price for three years, during which four of the breweries went out of business. Sales at West End during this time jumped from eighteen thousand barrels to sixty-five thousand barrels.

In May 1889, the 11 Edward Street property, which was known as the old Bierbauer brewery, became a music hall. The grand opening took place on May 27. The Koehl & Perkins orchestra provided the entertainment. The place also had a summer garden attached. All were invited to attend free of charge, and a fine zither concert was one of the features of the evening. Matt Harrer was manager of this new enterprise occupying the saloon that Bierbauer ran.

Around 10:00 p.m. on September 2, Manager Harrer of the West End Music Hall was sitting in his restaurant when the bookkeeper of the brewery rushed in and told him that the brewery to the rear of the hall was on fire. Harrer and several other men formed a fire brigade and by the use of ladders and buckets succeeded in putting out the blaze. The fire had started on the roof near one of the chimneys and was thought to have come from a flying spark. Damage to the brewery was minimal. During the 1890 stockholders meeting, the following officers were elected: Henry Roemer retained his job as president; Michael McCormick was chosen as vice-president, replacing S.D. Powers, who remained as a trustee; and F.X. Matt was elected to be secretary and treasurer, in addition to his duties as superintendent. S.D. Powers and George Bierbauer were chosen as inspectors of elections. Michael McCormick also owned the Eureka Coal Yard in addition to his duties at the brewery.

In 1890, city residents were complaining that the local breweries were dumping waste into local streams. The drainage consisted mainly of water with which the beer barrels had been rinsed. The streams were not swift enough to carry this water away and allowed some of it to stand in pools, which fermented and gave off a sour and disagreeable odor. The health officer notified the breweries that they would have to connect to the sewer lines or face fines. West End had little trouble complying, as sewer lines were near the brewery. The other breweries had more trouble, as the sewer lines weren't near the breweries.

A 1910s West End Brewing Company postcard. *John Jones private collection.*

On Friday, July 25, 1890, at around 5:00 a.m., a fire broke out in the roof of the brewery. The fire department quickly extinguished the blaze. Considerable damage was done by water, and the loss was estimated at $350, which was covered by insurance. A small fire also occurred in the same place on July 22. It was thought that the flames in each instance originated from sparks from the brewery's smoke stack.

Later that year, the brewery ordered a new ice-making machine so it could brew all year. The brewery also became unionized for the first time and has never had a strike right up to present time.

When the West End Brewing Company purchased what was known as the Columbia Brewing Company, the capacity of the brewery was 5,000 barrels a year, which was ample to meet demand. During the first four years of operation, the demand for its product increased so steadily that the brewery had to increase the capacity to 12,000 barrels a year. The brewery used all of the original buildings constructed by Charles Bierbauer until November 1891, when demand finally exceeded what could be produced in the old buildings. Plans were made to increase the output of the brewery to 20,000 barrels a year. A new fermenting cellar, forty feet by sixty feet, was constructed adjoining the old cellar. Twenty new fermenting tubs of

100-barrel capacity and a new boiling kettle of 150-barrel capacity were purchased. A new twenty- by forty-foot racking cellar was also added so that the brewery would have a storage capacity of 5,000 barrels. The new improvements were expected to be completed by January 1, 1892. The last remaining structure built by Bierbauer, a small wooden shed, remained in use until the early 1940s, when it was finally torn down.

Frank Schmelzle, owner of the West End Bottling Works, bottled the brewery's products in 1892–93. The building was located at 11 Edward Street, next to the brewery. By 1897, the brewery had built its own bottling works.

By 1895, demand was exceeding the brewery's capacity, and more improvements to the plant were necessary. A new thirty- by seventy-foot wash house was added. The ice machine's capacity was increased from ten to thirty tons. Several other improvements were also made.

On February 9, 1897, a large wooden tank burst, and several workmen narrowly escaped injury. The tanks were supposed to withstand a pressure of forty pounds per square inch. As beer was forced through a filter into the tank, it was only under a pressure of ten pounds per square inch. The tank burst and spilled about one hundred barrels of beer in every direction. A flaw in the riveted iron making up the tank was found to be defective. The brewery produced between twenty-five thousand and thirty thousand barrels that year. This increased to between thirty thousand and thirty-five thousand barrels in 1898.

The brewery introduced two new beers in early 1897. They were called Lorelei and Walhalla beers. They were made from pure imported Canada malt and Bohemian hops.

The brewery purchased a forty-ton ice machine in early 1898. Up until this time, it had been using a seven-ton machine. A bigger machine was needed to keep up with increasing demand. The new machine could make ice blocks weighing two hundred pounds each. A new eighty-horsepower boiler was installed at the brewery in early 1899.

In June 1899, an Eastern syndicate was attempting to purchase some of the breweries in Utica. The West End Brewing Company was offered $260,000 for its property. The company considered the proposal but finally decided to reject it. The brewery leadership felt that the company was worth at least $300,000 under terms such as those set forth by the syndicate. In the end, the syndicate was not successful in acquiring any brewery in Utica.

Joseph Schmitt, a foreman at the brewery, was badly burned about the face and hands by escaping steam on July 21, 1899. The large steam pump

An 1898 West End Brewing Company letterhead. *Author's collection.*

stopped, and the engineer opened the valve in front of the boiler and went to the rear to ascertain the cause of the stoppage. Schmidt stood in front of the open valve, and when the machinery started, he was badly burned. He was treated by a doctor in his home and later recovered.

On March 1, 1901, two boys stole a copper machine for mashing grain from the brewery. They carted it on a sled, late at night, to Joseph Perroula's place and sold it to him for a couple dollars. The machine was brand new and valued at $350. Perroula was tried a year later and was found guilty of knowingly receiving stolen goods.

About 6:00 p.m. on August 12, 1901, a westbound Bleecker Street car ran into a West End delivery wagon at the corner of Kossuth Avenue. A more serious accident was averted by the alert actions of the motorman. Both the wagon driver and his assistant were thrown forcibly to the payment. The horses were knocked down, and the harnesses were badly damaged.

Louis Lauer was brewmaster in 1902 through at least 1906. He was replaced in 1909 by W. Daubenspeck, a large man, six foot four inches tall, and reputed to be a count from Germany. After he left the brewery, he worked at the Lone Star Brewery in Texas. He was replaced by Robert L. Neidhardt in 1910.

There was almost a strike at the brewery on March 15, 1902, because of the absence of the union label on a carload of malt. The brewery bought its malt in carload lots in Buffalo. The malt had been shipped by the Charles G. Curtis Company of Buffalo, which was a union concern, as were all other malt houses in Buffalo. The brewery workmen who started to unload the car could not find any union label, and they refused to work and left the brewery. There was a meeting of the Brewery Workmen's Union that night, and the president said there would be a strike.

F.X. Matt said the shippers had neglected to place the label on the car. When the brewery ascertained the source of the trouble, it contacted the malt company in Buffalo. The malt company took the blame and sent the missing union label by express. It reached Utica on Saturday night. Assured that the malt was union malt, the workmen called off the strike. Matt said the company had not received fair treatment from the men. He said no fault could be attached to the brewery. Every malt house in Buffalo was a union concern, and the employees of the brewery knew it. He said the representatives of the union ought to have conferred with him before taking steps toward ordering a strike.

In late 1902, the brewery decided that it would erect a new four-story stone bottling house and storage building that would be equipped with all the latest technology. The Fuller's Electric Stone Works was awarded the contract for the stone to be used. The new building was complete by May 1903. The new building was forty by sixty feet with a brick exterior. This building is still standing at this writing in 2013 and has been renovated into part of the Tour Center. The brewery then purchased property next to the brewery on which to build a new wash house and shipping department. This building was completed by August 1903.

In April 1903, the brewery installed two brass filtering machines with a capacity of 1,800 barrels. The machines were made by the Lowe Filter Company of Cleveland. Three new pumps of six horsepower each were also installed. These were run by electricity and were part of the refrigerator plant. A new hot-water tank costing $1,000 and having a capacity of 320 barrels was being completed. The tank was made by the Cast Copper & Sheet Iron Company of Buffalo.

Henry Roemer, the brewery president, died on February 6, 1904, at the age of sixty-six. He had been ill for four months with a compilation of diseases. He was confined to his house. Roemer was born in Hamburg, Germany, on January 1, 1838, and, in 1852, came to America, where he worked as a farm hand in Deerfield. He bought his own farm in 1866 and helped form the West End brewery in 1888.

F.X. Matt replaced Henry Roemer as president of the company in 1905. Matt still retained his positions of treasurer and superintendent but gave up the secretary position.

As head of the company, F.X. Matt never allowed German to be spoken in the brewery. He believed that if you came to America to live, then you should speak English. West End was one of the few breweries in this country where German was never spoken, in an industry that was predominantly of German origin. The brewery had been unionized since the 1890s, but F.X. was a man of strong character and strong beliefs. When F.X. caught a worker not working, he would come up to him, put the worker's hand in his pocket and say, "If you want to rob me, take my money—not my time."

F.X. Matt left Utica on September 12, 1905, to visit several large brewing plants in New York City and Philadelphia. He wanted to study the construction of these large plants as he was planning on expanding his brewery to meet demand.

Work on a new building was started in October 1905 and was completed in May 1906. The new building was situated just northwest of the buildings on Edward Street. It was 93 feet wide by 115 feet long and was two stories high. The building was of brick with a concrete foundation, all cement floors and was fireproof. The building was used for storing beer and as a wash house, barrel storage and cooper shop.

A song extolling the virtues of West End products was written by Fred J. Hamill in 1907. It was called "Hurrah! For the West End Brewery." Published by the brewery, it cost fifty cents a copy.

Louis Lauer, a brewer at West End, resigned on September 5, 1907, after he accepted a position as head brewer with the Bartel Brewing Company of Syracuse.

The brewery registered its Miss Columbia trademark on June 13, 1908. It claimed that it has been in use by the brewery since about May 1, 1890.

George Swanenburg, a worker at the brewery, was severely injured on March 23, 1909, when his clothes got caught on a shaft in the washroom, and he was whirled around the shaft. He was rushed to the hospital, where his leg was amputated. He died shortly afterward.

A similar accident occurred on January 6, 1910, to Anthony Springer. Springer was at work plating the ceiling just above some heavy shafting. His clothes were caught in the shafting as it revolved, and he was thrown heavily against the ceiling. Unlike Swanenburg, his clothing gave way, and thus he received only bruises and lacerations with no broken bones.

Walter Daubenspeck, who had been the brewer at West End for the previous three years, resigned on March 10, 1910, to take a position with a large brewing concern in Sacramento, California.

In early 1910, the West End Brewing Company purchased several Reliance trucks to deliver its products in the Utica area. The trucks were capable of carrying a load of three and a half tons. This meant the end of the horse and wagons that were used by the brewery up until this point. The brewery began constructing a large storehouse and office building in late 1910. It was of brick construction, two stories high, and it cost $20,000. The first floor was used as a storehouse and office. The second floor had apartments.

At 2:10 a.m. on June 20, 1910, a fire was discovered in the cooper shop of the brewery. The blaze was extinguished with slight damage. The origin was not known.

A building permit was granted to the brewery in September 1911 to erect a smoke stack and chimney at a cost of $4,700. The N.W. Kellogg Company of New York City was the contractor.

In 1911, the brewery erected a storage depot in Rome, New York. A small fire broke out at the storage depot in Amsterdam, New York, during the summer. Little damage was done. The brewery also planned to build a $20,000 storehouse in Schenectady. The two-story building was constructed of brick and contained the offices of the local branch, a barn and a harness room. R. Neidhardt left the company and was replaced by R.L. Middlehart as brewmaster. Middlehart did not last long; he was replaced as brewmaster in 1912 by Charles H. Hummerl. Hummerl, in turn, was replaced by Robert L. Neidhart, who returned as brewmaster in 1913.

During the period between 1910 and 1912, the brewery produced a temperance beverage known as malt mead. It was a non-intoxicating, fermented malt liquor, containing a little over 1.5 percent alcohol.

Several lawsuits resulted when people claimed they could not tell this product apart from real beer. One occurred in St. Lawrence County in northern New York. In 1910, there were several no-license towns where alcohol could not be sold. The brewery had sent its new brew to these towns and was doing a good business. Because of the very low alcohol content, the brewery believed the beverage could be legally sold in these towns. It did admit that the only way the new brew could be distinguished from real beer was by a cross mark made on the barrels with chalk. The jury came back with a guilty verdict. The brewery promised that no more temperance drinks would be shipped to no-license towns in St. Lawrence County and admitted that the company had been operating under a misapprehension of the statute.

The other case happened in 1912. A man was charged with violating the liquor tax law. The man was a drunk and had deserted from the army and navy. He said he was drinking malt mead and wasn't drunk. The climax of the trial came when two men were asked to take a blind taste test to see whether they could tell the difference between real beer and the malt mead produced by the brewery. Three bottles were used, two with real beer and one with malt mead. They said they could not tell the difference. In the end, the barrel of malt mead was found to be a mismarked barrel of real beer. The man was found guilty of drunkenness and was sentenced to jail time.

In December 1975, a brewery employee conducted an interview with Tony Springer, who worked as a bottler at the brewery in the early 1900s. Springer was born on January 16, 1891. He started working for the brewery in 1902 in the bottling department, which, at the time, was in the rear of the office. He stayed at the brewery until 1912, when he took a two-year tour of the country. He first went to Detroit and worked at Goebbel's and Stroh as an apprentice. Then he worked at Schoenhoefer's in Chicago. From there, he went to the San Francisco area, where he worked at the Mondale Bottling Works. After that, he worked at the Golden West Brewery in Oakland. Next, he worked at the East Side Brewery in Los Angeles, where his wage was $22.50 per week in gold. While at the East Side Brewery, he apparently had an adventure that took him to Mexico. There was a Mexican brewery that was offering premium wages of $25.00 per week in gold to experienced bottlers. Apparently with the East Side Brewery's blessing, Tony and a number of others went down there, only to be stopped at the border by bandits and sent back to Los Angeles. He resumed his employment at the East Side Brewery. He left Los Angeles and went to New Orleans to visit, after which he returned to Utica to work at West End again. It was a fairly common practice for breweries to send apprentices back and forth between them as a means of gaining experience. It was believed that he went where he went with a letter of introduction from F.X. Matt and that the intention had always been to return to Utica and work at West End.

A fight broke out in the brewery washroom on July 13, 1912, between John Evans and his brother-in-law, John Holland. As the argument progressed, Holland hit Evans in the head with his fist, dropping him to the floor. Evans struck his head against a hard object, which resulted in his death. The coroner ruled that the death was accidental and that Holland had not purposely tried to kill Evans.

In 1913, the brewery erected a three-story addition of 130 feet by 90 feet. Work was started on erecting a four-story addition that was used for clarifying and storage purposes in February. The building was 92 feet by 54 feet and constructed of brick and reinforced concrete. The building was

A West End Brewing Company delivery truck is pictured in this 1910 photograph. *Author's collection.*

A West End Brewing Company delivery truck is pictured in 1916. *Author's collection.*

insulated and cost $45,000. J.C. Schultz of Buffalo was the architect, and Pius Kerner & Son was the general contractor. The building was ready for use in August.

Later that year, the brewery obtained a building permit to erect an additional story on its recently built storage building. The additional cost was $25,000 and gave the building four stories. The piers and columns in the building were of brick construction and needed to be reinforced by steel box posts from the basement up. The additional story was 92 feet long and 75 feet wide and was used for storage. Agne, Rushmer & Jennison were the architects, and Pius Kerner & Son was again the general contractor.

In 1914, the brewery had plans prepared for the construction of a garage, barn and ice storage buildings to be built the following year.

During the summer of 1914, the brewery placed a large electric sign on the highest point of its buildings, showing the company's name in gigantic letters. In late 1915, the brewery erected a three-story storage and stable building. The dimensions of the building were 75 feet by 175 feet. They also installed a horizontal rice cooler and a Baudelot cooler with a copper pan, which was made by Emil Schaefer of Philadelphia. The cost of construction was about $75,000.

At the turn of the century in Utica and on through the peaceful years of 1900 to 1914, the big summer event in town was the German Day parade held on August 7 of each year. Everyone anticipated these occasions, which were marked by the music of top bands and marching organizations that included the Maennerchor and the Turn Verein. But outstanding in the processions were the floats, dozens of them, contributed by local businesses. Elaborately decorated, they competed for prizes. Each year, prominent Uticans acted as jury members and selected the winners. The floats of Fritz Heim & Son, proprietors of a wholesale and retail delicatessen, were particularly ornate. The company won three times. West End had great displays and usually finished in the top three. Oneida and Eagle also won prizes.

The vice-president of the West End Brewery, Sylvester D. Powers, died at his home on May 13, 1916. He had a protracted illness from pneumonia and resulting complications. Powers was born in Ireland in 1845 and was brought to America as an infant by his parents, who settled in Massachusetts. His mother died shortly after they arrived, and the family moved to Utica. He fought in the Civil War and was a prisoner at the notorious Andersonville Prison. Powers was a natural organizer and was one of the original founders of the Columbia Brewing Company and the West End Brewing Company.

The inside of West End Brewing Company's bottling works is pictured in this 1930s photograph. *Author's collection.*

A powerful storm came through Utica on July 11, 1917, causing Nail Creek to overflow its banks and flood the brewery yard and stables. The floodwaters reached eleven feet at the peak of the storm and remained at a high level for several hours. The stables were located on ground that was lower than most of the surrounding area. Of the twenty-two horses the brewery had in the stables, three of them drowned. A rowboat was used to get around the stables. Barn boss Joseph Meyers and drivers Joe Leuthauser, Henry Lockwood, James Bean and William Colwell worked hard at rescuing as many horses as they could. The dead horses were named Tom, Margery and Baby. Tom was one of the best team horses, and Baby was a carriage horse. Margery was floating around the yard for several hours.

The brewery sued the City of Utica, saying it had been negligent in providing culverts of sufficient size to eliminate flooding that occurred during heavy rains or heavy spring thaws. Sometime between 1905 and 1917, a new culvert was put in, but the contractor made it shaped like a funnel. The wide part of the funnel was on the upstream side, with the narrow end downstream. This constricted the water flow and caused the water to overflow the culvert banks. The brewery wanted $4,821.77 to cover the losses caused by the latest flooding. The case was finally decided on April 13, 1921, in favor of the brewery. The courts awarded the brewery

$6,047.20. The City made improvements to the culverts, lessening the chance of flooding.

On November 21, 1917, the West End Brewing Company announced the construction of a new bottling plant. The building was located facing Schuyler Street, Farrell Street and Nelbach Avenue. Dimensions of the building were 150 feet by 72 feet, and it was 48 feet high. The building consisted of two stories and a basement. The main floor contained an office and the machinery used in bottling. The second floor was used for storage of kegs and other packaging materials, while the basement provided storage for empty bottles. The exterior of the building was red brick, with the interior finished in white buff brick. The entire building cost over $47,000 to construct. Some of the equipment ordered in this expansion consisted of two Ermold Automatic fillers, made by the Edward Ermold Co., of New York; four O.&J. Automobile labeling machines; and two Barry-Wehmiller soakers. Construction of the new bottling house was completed in 1918.

The brewery erected a new concrete icehouse in late 1917. The building was thirty-two feet wide, forty-nine feet long and thirty-six feet high. It cost $2,000 to erect.

Peter Stamberger became brewmaster in 1917. Stammberger came from working at the Standard Brewing Company in Rochester, New York, where he was an assistant brewer.

The name "Utica Club" was first introduced in 1918. The company wanted a name that represented the city where the brewery was located. Up until this time, the brewery's products all had the West End name on them. When Prohibition started, the company was going to make soda and near beer, so it did not want to use the West End name on these products in case they were not well received. The brewery was assessed at $196,500 in 1918 and paid $6,178 in city and county taxes. The brewery was shipping seven to ten railway carloads of beer a day, making it the largest brewery in the Twenty-first Internal Revenue District.

## The Prohibition Years

On September 7, 1918, the government said that it would order the closing of all breweries on December 1. Local brewers were taken by surprise, as they had lots of material on hand that had to be used up. If the order was delayed until May or June, they felt that they could use up the material. The West End Brewing Company had on hand sixty thousand bushels of malt and twelve thousand pounds of hops. It had a contract for delivery that fall of fifty thousand additional pounds of hops. Earlier in the year, the government had ordered that no malt could be made from July through September. To meet this requirement, the brewers had ordered a six-month supply.

Another federal order required brewers to cut down their manufacture to 70 percent of normal levels. The brewers said they could convert their plants to manufacture near beer but were not certain the government would allow it.

In 1918, the West End Brewing Company employed 151 men; the Oneida Brewery, 35; the Fort Schuyler Brewery, 16; and the Eagle and Gulf breweries, 84. The closing of the breweries would put 284 men out of work.

The brewery erected a framed storage shed on Edward Street near Schuyler in April 1919 at a cost of $1,000.

West End was the first of the local brewing concerns prepared for a dry wave in the state and country. Starting in early June 1919, the brewery started manufacturing root beer and ginger ale, in addition to near beer and 2.75 percent beer. These products were on sale at leading hotels and cafes.

F.X. Matt stated that he intended to operate his plant even if the country went dry. By this, he meant that he was prepared for dry times as well as wet, and he had prepared for the inevitable by starting the manufacture of light beers and soft drinks.

The brewery hired Dr. Frederick Hallock, a chemist from New York City, to look after the soft drink end of the business.

In June 1919, the brewery's output of soft drinks was 2,300 dozen bottles a day. Output could be increased to 5,000 dozen bottles per day. The company was manufacturing a high-grade ginger ale, called the Utica Club brand, as well as Dr. Sweet's root beer. It had the distributorship for Dr. Sweet's in New York and Pennsylvania, and it also expected to manufacture loganberry juice, grape juice, birch beer and a cocoa drink.

Joseph Lenhardt, manager of the brewery, stated that while the West End Brewing Company was manufacturing the so-called 2.75 percent beer, not much of it was sold in Utica as yet. The brewery also had been manufacturing WEBCO near beer, which was sold in no-license towns, for some time past.

An ad from 1919, describes Utica Club Ginger Ale as follows:

> *It's 100 percent pure. Hold a bottle to the light, note the crystal clearness. Such faultless purity can come only from the most perfect and painstaking processes.*

AGENTS NOT ALLOWED TO PURCHASE OR INCUR ANY LIABILITIES FOR THIS COMPANY

THE WEST END BREWING CO.

"WEBCO" CEREAL BEVERAGE "PEVA"

Less than half per cent alcohol by volume

UTICA CLUB BEVERAGES

F. X. MATT, Prest. and Treas.

GINGER ALE, ROOT BEER, LOGANBERRY,
CAFFEE COLA, GRAPE JUICE,
ORANGE KISS, ETC.

COR. VARICK AND COURT STS.
COR. SCHUYLER AND FARRELL STS.
COR. NELBACH AVE. AND FARRELL STS.

OFFICE, NO. 11 EDWARD STREET
LONG DISTANCE TELEPHONE NO. 608

Sold to C Denslow

Dec 20. 1919

Utica, N.Y.

West End Brewing Company letterhead from 1919. *Author's collection.*

*Every drop of water used in its make-up is purified and rendered bacteria proof by the most modern processes. It is scientifically carbonated in the most modernly equipped and immaculately kept bottling plant in the East.*

*As a result of this extreme care in the manufacture and blending of Utica Club Ginger Ale a product that is different and of distinct individuality is the result, with it's pure genuine ginger flavor, it's beautiful sparkle, delightful effervescence, it's gentle and moderate warmth, without the pungent, peppery heat, it's mildly stimulating and exhilarating effect, makes it easily the preference of discriminating folk, once the luscious, smooth, mellow and refreshing bouquet is known.*

A soft drink called Utica Club Caffee Cola became available in October 1919. It was described as a drink that has a kick in it.

Two workers at the brewery, Fred Schnetka and Joseph Rothdiener, died on September 25, 1919, when the vat they were working in caught fire. They were burned and suffocated. The men were applying pitch to the inside of a big tank at the brewery. They had to enter the tank through a small opening sixteen by thirteen inches near the floor. There was another opening of eight by twelve inches on top of the tank, but it was closed.

Once inside the tank, the pitch was heated to 250 to 320 degrees on a gasoline stove placed on the floor of the tank. Meanwhile, the tank itself was heated with a gasoline torch before the pitch was applied with a brush. Then the gasoline torch was used again to heat the pitch to even it out on the surface.

All of the employees at the brewery agreed that the pitch was not flammable or explosive. They all agreed that it was the gasoline that had leaked from the torch that caused the fire and explosion. Peter Stammberger, the brewmaster, said that the men had completed the sides of the tank and some of the floor when the accident occurred.

Henry Bick, the chief engineer, was working in the machine shop 250 feet away from the tank. He said that fire appeared to occur near the lower opening. He thought that the torch might have gone out and the men, in relighting it, spilled some gasoline, or one of the torches might have leaked. The accident was caused by a gasoline explosion.

Albert Bassett, a utility man, was painting in the basement about fifty feet away when the accident happened. He heard a muffled sound and then one cry. Bassett put a hose in the top of the tank, but the flames and smoke drove him off the tank. He said he had talked with Rothdiener outside the tank three minutes before the accident.

The coroner asked all the witnesses if it was not dangerous to work in a tank with no more ventilation than this one had. They agreed that the pitch was not explosive or inflammable unless it became so from being over heated. The coroner ruled the deaths accidental.

The Volstead Act (National Prohibition Act) became the law of the land on January 17, 1920. The manufacture, sale, transportation and/or consumption of any beverage exceeding one-half of 1 percent alcohol was illegal.

At a special meeting of the stockholders held at the brewery on January 22, the certificate of incorporation was changed to include other purposes, powers or provisions, "to wit, the manufacture, production, and sale of non-alcoholic cereal beverages of every description ginger ale and other soft drinks of every name and nature, ice, cold storage, packing preserves, ice cream, confections, dairy products, food products, syrups, vinegar and industrial alcohol, in addition to those now set forth in the certificate of incorporation." West End was preparing to be in a position to produce anything the law allowed.

The brewery introduced Hydro Crystal Distilled Water in July 1920. The water was available in one-gallon bottles and five-gallon carboys. In 1920, the brewery offered the following beverages; Champanetto-Mum, Ginger Ale, Root Beer, Loganbero, Uta-Cola, Orange-Jo, Cherro-Fruta, Blackbero-Punch, Lem-JU, Quaker Birch Bru, Apa La Champagne, Cremo-Choclat, Cuban Hot, Conco-Grapette, Burgundie-Mum, Lime-Jo and Sassa-Bru. All these products were made with distilled water.

The brewery also manufactured pilsener and wuerzburger lager that was made with the famous Heuser System. They claimed it had the original taste and flavor of old-style lager.

The commissioner of Internal Revenue made several rulings on July 22. In the first ruling, he said that corporations already using the words "alcohol," "distilling" and "brewing" in their names may continue to do so. Price lists, solicitation of orders—even where the person held a booze permit—and distribution of business cards or stationery mentioning booze were all banned, which particularly affected Utica druggists.

The second ruling took specific steps to forestall a recurrence of the Utica booze case that had landed three men before a federal court, accused of breaking the Volstead Act in transporting liquor. It said that those transporting booze must have a valid permit, which stated that the product could only be delivered to the name on the permit and that this person must be known to the driver of the truck.

Dr. Hallock left the brewery shortly after he was hired in 1919. He was replaced with J. William Wells, who came to Utica from the South. Wells created the line of Utica Club Fruit beverages and ginger ale and the Seneca Club line of fountain syrups and concentrates. Like his predecessor, Wells resigned after less than one year on the job. In December 1920, he left to take a job in Kansas City, Missouri. He was replaced by his son, James R. Wells. His son would continue to use the same methods, processes and formulas as his father.

Products manufactured in 1921 included wurzburger, bock and pilsener at $2.00 per case, plus $1.00 extra deposit refunded on the return of the bottles. These contained one-half of 1 percent alcohol by volume, which was the legal limit during Prohibition. Soft drinks included ginger ale, champanetto-mum with white grapes, champanetto-mum with champagne grapes, burgundy (red grapes), loganbero, birch beer, orange kiss, lemon sour and root beer. These sold for $3 per case, except for the burgundy and champagne-style champanetto-mum, which sold for $4.50 per case.

The brewery filed an application to make medicinal beer in November 1921. The Eagle and Oneida breweries had also filed applications.

In June 1922, a glassful of Utica Club Ginger Ale contained seventy-six calories. It was made from pure cane sugar, Jamaican ginger, distilled water and the fragrant essences of lemons, oranges and limes.

In December 1923, a case of bottles cost $1.75 for the standard size and $2.25 for the 15.5-ounce bottles.

Soft drinks were offered in sixteen-ounce, ten-ounce and six-and-a-half-ounce bottles in 1924. The brewery produced Gold Top Pale and Extra Dry Ginger Ale, Champanetto-Mum, Champagne Cider, Birch, Cherry, Chocolate, Cream Soda, Lemon, Lime, Grape, Orange, Root

Beer, Strawberry, Sasa' and Uta-Cola. You could also buy distilled water, carbonated water, Gold Seal Table Syrup, soda fountain syrups, concentrates, extracts, emulsions and liquid colors. Utica Club Pilsener was still available.

Officers of the company for 1925 were F.X. Matt, president and treasurer; F.J. Roemer, vice-president; Henry Elting, secretary; F. Milton Matt, assistant secretary and treasurer; Frank Dugan, controller; and Peter Stammberger, superintendent. Directors were F.X. Matt, F.J. Roemer, Charles Roemer, Henry Elting and and F.M. Matt.

During the Prohibition period, production ranged between 23,000 barrels and 170,000 barrels per year. During one year, the bottling department had done more than 500,000 cases. A sales record was broken in June 1926 in the sales of Utica Club beverages. Utica Club Pilsener, Wuerzburger and Brown Stout were very popular.

A building permit was issued to the brewery on November 1926 to erect a brick boiler house for $30,000. The new boiler house was 185 feet long, 135 feet wide and two stories high.

Matt refused to cooperate with criminal elements in their attempts to sell bootleg beer. As a result, he and his family lived under constant kidnap threats. His home and his children's homes were guarded by elaborate burglar alarms as a precaution against these threats. Matt refused to break the laws of the country that had been so good to him.

F.X. relied on the ingenuity of his employees and his own keen knowledge of the beverage business he had been a part of most of his life to survive. One of the items that became popular during the dry years was West End's near beer or malt tonic. The malt tonic was so good that many people claimed it was regular beer. Malt tonic was touted as a boon to nursing mothers and was good for coughs, colds, pulmonary conditions, loss of appetite and loss of weight. Malt tonics could only be sold in drugstores. Other near beers included Brown Stout, Webco (an acronym for West End Brewing Company) and Utica Club Pilsner, which contained less than one-half of 1 percent alcohol. The brewery used a process known as the Heuser process, which used vacuum equipment, allowing the alcohol to be boiled out of the beer at lower temperatures and making for a better-tasting near beer. This product sold fairly well—until the bootleggers came to town with their illegal brews.

Another successful product was malt syrup, which was made from concentrating the contents of the brew kettle into a thick heavy syrup that was then canned. The malt syrup cans were rather amusing as they gave instructions to add water and yeast, which was really an instruction on how to make home brewed beer. But not all products were as well received.

Several products that didn't do well were chocolate milk and barreled cider. The brewery had a homogenizer for the chocolate milk that apparently didn't work, because after two weeks, all the chocolate settled to the bottom of the bottles.

But inventing new products was not the only problem faced by the brewery. By 1929, people were spending what little money they had on bread and clothing. Soda did not rate very high on the list of essentials.

In January 1928, a notice of change of corporate name from the Seneca Products Corporation to the Seneca Food Products Corporation was filed with the state department.

The brewery was offering the following products in 1928: champagne cider, pale dry ginger ale and champanneto-mum in twelve-and-a-half-ounce bottles at $3.60 per case; golden ginger ale, root beer and lime and lithia in sixteen-ounce bottles at $3.25 per case; Adirondack water in twelve-and-a-half-ounce bottles at $2.25 per case; birch, cherry, chocolate, creme, grape, ginger ale, lemon, lime, loganbero, orange, root beer, sasa-brue and strawberry sodas in six-and-a-half-ounce bottles at $1.50 per case; pilsner, wuerzburger and bock in twelve-ounce bottles at $2.80 per case; brown stout and India pale ale in twelve-ounce bottles at $2.90 per case; and Utica Club bohemian style hop-flavored and plain pure barley malt syrup at $0.60 per can.

A fleet of seven Brockway trucks were used by the brewery in 1928 to deliver its products. Six of the trucks were one-and-a-half-ton versions, and one was a five-ton version.

The brewery received an order to discontinue at once the manufacture of 12 percent malt tonics on July 13, 1929, as did all other brewers in the country making malt tonics. No other Utica brewery had been engaged in making such a product, which was originally limited to drugstore sales. Disappointment over the ruling was expressed by an official at the brewery, who commented on the order, "This means quite a loss as the brewery had special equipment to turn out the product."

Officials said, "Hereafter malt tonics must contain a minimum of 18 percent solids derived from malt and not more than 2 percent alcohol by volume." The previous December, the Prohibition department authorized the manufacture of malt tonic containing 12 percent solids obtained from malt and not over 2 percent alcohol content by volume. It was supposed to be manufactured entirely from malt.

Retail drugstores were limited to twenty-five cases each week. All advertising of the malt tonic had to be medicinal in nature, and the labels had to be approved by the Prohibition Department.

Some of the companies receiving permits were negligent in carrying out the provisions of the rulings, and the malt tonic found its way to roadside stands, grocery stores and menus of soda fountains. Instead of revoking the permits of the violators, the Prohibition Department made a general ruling by which the innocent would suffer.

Then, in 1930, F.X. was diagnosed as having a severe heart and kidney illness. A noted heart surgeon from New York City told his family that it was only a matter of time. However, shortly after this diagnosis, he miraculously recovered.

The brewery was in federal court on June 9, 1931, to defend its permit for beverage making against the federal government. Testimony on June 9 and 10 revealed that the federal government was moving to revoke the company's permit to sell hop-flavored malt syrup on the grounds that the product was being used for illegal purposes by the purchasers.

An inspection was made by Federal agents of stores in Syracuse and Rochester where malt syrup made by the brewery was sold. The agent asserted that one proprietor told him that he was a former brewmaster and that the malt syrup was not used for baking purposes but only in making beer and that was the purpose for which his customers used it.

No records of customers were kept in most of the stores where the syrup was sold. The agent described the contents of the stores as being mostly barrels, filter paper, hops, malt syrup and, at one store, brewer's yeast.

In federal court on June 10, F.X. Matt testified that the brewery took extreme caution to sell malt syrup only to legitimate customers. Matt said he instructed his salesmen to investigate all customers thoroughly to see that they were not selling to any persons who might be considered bootleggers.

Matt asserted he did not require any written report from his salesmen on investigations but stated that a salesman could generally tell whether the product was being used for illegal purposes. Asked if he ever refused to sell malt syrup to anyone, Matt asserted that he had refused hundreds of persons. He was asked if he could name one of them and replied that he could not. He was then asked if he ever had any suspicion as to what the malt syrup was used for. He said that he had not.

Frank Dugan, company controller, testified that the smear marks on the company's records were made by the government inspector. He then demonstrated how it had happened. Dugan was then questioned concerning the abbreviations on the ledgers that had been changed to read "merchandise." He testified that these items had originally been compressed yeast, but because the yeast was not made in the plant, the records for the purpose of better bookkeeping had been changed to the word merchandise. Dugan said that no yeast had been sold by the plant in 1931. Dugan further denied that he had ever told the inspectors that 80 to 90 percent of the West End product was hop flavored.

The mayor of Utica took the stand to testify to the character of Matt and the reputation of the company. He said he had known Matt most of his life and knew him to be a man of the highest caliber. Speaking of the brewery, the mayor asserted that, to his knowledge, it had always had a satisfactory reputation.

The brewery lawyers made a motion to dismiss the charges. They claimed that the alleged violations of permit provisions in 1930 could not be considered as evidence in a move to revoke a 1931 permit.

An extension was granted to the brewery lawyers until July 18. The judge stated that after receiving all the papers, his decision would come sometime in August, but it wasn't until December 24 that the case against the brewery was dismissed by the Treasury Department.

When informed of the dismissal, F.X. Matt expressed his delight and remarked on the timeliness of the action as a bit of Christmas cheer. He stated that he was confident from the very beginning that the proceedings ultimately would be dismissed for the reason that he would never tolerate a company that he was in charge of violating any law.

Despite this favorable outcome, the financial position of the company was grim by the last half of 1932. The business was getting so bad that Matt got the employees together and asked them to take a 10 percent cut in pay. He said that it would keep the company going. Matt was running out of ideas to keep his company solvent, so he began frequent trips to the nation's capital, clinging to the hope that the Eighteenth Amendment would eventually be repealed.

## The Post-Prohibition Years

On March 13, 1933, in what was then called the briefest presidential message in history, Roosevelt asked Congress to legalize the manufacture and sale of beer, ending over thirteen years of Prohibition. His seventy-two-word request caught most Americans and even many in the idled brewing industry off guard. The president was only asking for the passage of a beer bill at the federal level.

Each state had to pass its own beer control plan in order for the taps to flow when the federal bill became effective at 12:01 a.m. on April 7, 1933. Only nineteen states passed the necessary laws to lift the ban by then. In New York, the state legislature dumped the muddled situation into the lap of Governor Herbert Lehman. "We haven't had any beer or liquor control machinery operating for the last fifteen years," one of the governor's advisors said, after it became known that the state had no hope of licensing drinking places by April 7. Governor Lehman declared that the state would get its plan into operation just as quick as humanly possible.

The next day, the New York State Brewer's Association met in New York City to draft a message to the state legislature urging a quick adoption of a fair control plan. Named to serve on the committee to outline the brewer's position was F.X. Matt.

Matt remained in Utica, however, to prepare his brewery for the days ahead and sent his son to represent him on the committee. After the meeting, Frank Matt, then secretary of the company, remained in New York overnight.

President Roosevelt signed the new beer bill, which had easily passed in both the House and Senate, at 2:02 p.m. on March 22. By 3:28 p.m. that same day, Frank M. Matt and company attorney Murray L. Curtin obtained a permit (U-218) from the Industrial Alcohol Bureau in New York, making the West End brewery the first in the country to secure a license to manufacture and sell beer.

Under the new permit, storage limitations were removed and the brewery could store beer to its capacity of fifty thousand barrels. Under the dry law permit it had previously held, it could store much less and had to dealcoholize the beer, but this still put West End Brewing Company ahead of other formerly operating breweries. West End was the only brewery in the area that had a cereal beverage permit by which beer could be kept on hand, thus ensuring the release of aged beer as soon as it became legal.

Matt went to the Internal Revenue office in Syracuse with $15,695. Of this, $4,000 in cash was paid for beer already in bottles. A certified check for $10,625 was paid for barreled beer, $1,000 for the first brewer's license, $50 for the yearly wholesaler's license and $20 for a yearly retailer's license permitting the brewery to sell directly to the public.

The West End Brewing Company was the most successful local brewery to keep up operations through Prohibition. By maintaining the proper permits that allowed it to have 3.05 percent beer in storage, the brewery was ready to issue properly aged beer when it became legal.

A storage capacity of 50,000 barrels gave the company confidence that they could keep up with demand. The bottling works was automated and capable of filling 50 million bottles a year. The brewery could fill 1,400 barrels of draft beer a day. To prepare for the big day, the company purchased thousands of new kegs, cases and bottles.

On March 31, the brewery placed an order for beer revenue stamps worth $497,500 with the Internal Revenue Service in Syracuse. This was to cover the estimated federal tax of $5 per barrel generated by the brewery's expected summer output.

As the brewery continued to gear up for April 7, problems still existed. In Albany, after legislative leaders failed to reach an agreement on a state control plan, Governor Lehman attempted to break the deadlock by submitting a bill setting up a five-member Beer Regulatory Board.

By the last day of March, his plan was killed by opposition from Republican leaders in the assembly. They opposed the granting of complete control to a central board. On that same day in Utica, F.X. Matt and his brewmaster, Peter Stammberger, were ready to fill the barrels to be sold to thirsty people from all over the state on April 7. But federal inspectors from the Industrial Alcohol Bureau appeared and demanded to see proof that the firm had complied with all laws. Matt showed them his receipt signed by Jesse W. Clark, collector of Internal Revenue at Syracuse, but the inspectors demanded further proof before they would allow the beer to pour.

The next day, Saturday, April 4, Clark drafted a statement showing that the brewery had complied with all laws, signed it before a notary and made a special trip from Syracuse to allay the fears of the inspectors that the beer production was illegal. Convinced, the inspectors unlocked the tanks from which the beer flowed into the first of several thousand barrels. On April 5, the state legislature was still unable to decide on a suitable control plan after Governor Lehman's measure failed.

With legal beer sales less than two days away, many cities throughout the state were preparing to deal with beer under the local soft drink or special refreshment ordinances. Mayor John P. O'Brien of New York City called a special meeting of the board of aldermen asking them to be ready to enact an ordinance in the event that the state legislature failed to adopt a beer control measure before Friday.

Utica's mayor Donnelly was deciding whether or not to introduce a soft drink ordinance at the Common Council meeting that night. The morning of April 6 began with great news from Albany. Although the deadlock on an overall control plan still existed, the Senate and the Assembly had passed a bill imposing a one-dollar-per-barrel tax on 3.2 percent beer. Governor Lehman signed the bill that afternoon. This enabled the state to collect revenue from beer when the federal bill became effective at midnight, whether a control measure was put into effect or not. More importantly, it allowed New York State to join eighteen other states and the District of Columbia to go off the near beer standard at 12:01 a.m. the next day.

In New York City, the mayor decided that his city would see few, if any, public celebrations at the end of the thirteen-year drought. Brewers in the city had agreed that no beer would be shipped until 6:00 a.m. to avoid a "wet carnival." In upstate New York, however, there would be no such limitations. Of the region's several dozen breweries, only three were licensed and prepared to sell beer. One was in Albany, one was in Rochester and the third was in Utica.

The West End brewery was filled with anticipation and excitement. Trucks began to line up in the afternoon from all over New York State, Pennsylvania and even New England. By 5:00 p.m., trucks were lined up and down Varick Street and across Columbia Street, several blocks away.

Because of all the traveling back and forth to Washington, F.X. Matt was ill. He was under a lot of stress and had a bad cold. His wife begged him to stay home, but he insisted on being at the brewery because of stories that there might be a hijacking and trouble with bootleggers.

Brewery cashier Ida Graf and billing clerk Julia Mullin spent the time between 8:00 p.m. and midnight preparing the books and sales slips. They were set up in the shipping office, where Ida Graf would handle the money and Julia Mullin would take care of the sales slips. She was not allowed to make out any sales slips until after midnight. Just before midnight, a crowd of about one thousand had gathered along the iron fence by the shipping office on Edwards Street. They were ready to celebrate. Court and Varick Streets were jammed, and twenty-five police officers were there to direct traffic.

Directing operations in the brewery's yard was Frank Dugan, the company's controller. A few minutes before midnight, Dugan gave the order to warm up the delivery trucks, told Henry Bick to stand by the gate and then climbed on the hood of a truck to address the crowd. Dugan thanked them for being orderly and said that 800,000 glasses of Utica Club Beer were about to come through the gates. He said that most breweries had not acted with West End's speed and were not ready for production.

At exactly midnight, the brewery's whistle blew, the crowd cheered, and Dugan yelled, "Fling them wide!" Bick opened the gates and out rolled track

The West End Brewing Company shipping area pictured in 1933. *Author's collection.*

number B-31 with a load of beer. Nine other brewery trucks were right behind, followed by the private trucks.

Suddenly, it was like an open house at the brewery. People were running through the bottling works. It was apparently free beer for all those in the brewery. A lot of beer went over the fence that night. West End stopped loading trucks at 4:00 a.m., its workers totally exhausted. Dugan estimated that ten thousand cases and two thousand half kegs of beer went out of the brewery during those four hours.

F.X. Matt stood on the loading dock. "I am dumbfounded at the whole thing," Matt said. "I had expected we would have a busy time, but the enormous demands went way beyond anything I imagined. I have never seen anything like it."

Matt thanked the city, county and state police for their help. There had been rumors that some of the beer trucks would be hijacked, so the beer trucks were escorted to the city line by Utica police on motorcycles. Deputy sheriff and state police picked up the escort duty from there.

At least one hijacking was reported. Five days after beer was legalized, two drivers operating a truck for a Pennsylvania distributor were held up by three highwaymen on the Paris Hill Road, just outside of Utica.

The two men told police that they had just gone to the West End Brewery and were returning home with 140 cases of beer when they were ordered to stop by three armed men. One of the robbers drove the truck, and the other two bound and gagged the truck men. After taking approximately fifty dollars in cash, they drove the victims to Washington Mills, where they were abandoned.

Police from throughout the state were asked to aid in combing the highways for the truck and its cargo, and the state police initiated an investigation. The results of that investigation are unknown, but police continued to provide protection for the drivers for at least one month after the incident.

As for local delivery, a special truck was sent to the Hotel Utica, and beer went on sale there at 12:30 a.m. The hotel's chef, Barnard del Valle, dressed in a high white hat and white coat, marched into the hotel's main dining room carrying the first bottle of beer on a silver tray. He was followed by an orchestra playing "Happy Days."

Business continued to be brisk. The beer went out so quickly that the brewery was running out of it, as capacity was limited. Rather than sell green beer, F.X. rationed his product. He knew he could have sold three or four times the beer, but he would not risk his reputation. Eventually, a sense of normalcy returned to the brewery. The 10 percent pay cut that was necessary just months before was lifted almost immediately. Having been told by his doctors that it was almost as if he had grown a new heart, F.X. was able to begin plans for a new brew house.

In the first four days that beer was legal, the brewery had distributed eight thousand barrels of beer. F.X. Matt said that while his company had 350 men working three eight-hour shifts, the brewery couldn't possibly take care of demand.

The brewery had paid $40,000 in federal tax on the eight thousand barrels. The output of the brewery was eight hundred barrels a day, and orders were running close to two thousand barrels a day. Since the beginning of the year, the brewery had been broadcasting a radio program from station WGY in Schenectady. The show, *Utica Club*, aired Saturday nights at 8:45 p.m.

Not all breweries in New York State were ready to produce beer on April 7. The Gerhard Lang Brewery in Buffalo was one of those. Since 1931, it had contracted with the West End brewery in Utica to make its near beer. To meet initial demand, West End produced 3.2 beer for the Gerhard Lang Brewery and shipped several hundred cases to Buffalo for it to sell.

By the summer of 1933, the brewery was regularly shipping beer to nine states. It was operating twenty-one hours a day with two shifts in the bottling

The West End Brewing Company back lot as it appeared in the 1930s. *Author's collection.*

department and three shifts in the brew house. Employment had risen to 278 people. Shipments required three to four railroad shifts a day and continuous truck traffic for the twelve-hour business day. Demand for West End beverages had been received from every state, Puerto Rico, Panama and Haiti. The brewery estimated that from April to July, it had sold over 40 million glasses of beer. On June 5, the brewery started selling its second product, Sparkling Ale. Brewing of this product had started on March 27 and only now did Matt deem the product to be properly aged.

Due to the volume of business the brewery was doing, it was decided that several additions to the facilities were needed. The first was an addition of a second story to the bottling plant, which would be of steel construction and would double the capacity of the bottling department.

A new steel and concrete two-story garage that would house 50 trucks was built and provided the addition of more office space.

On July 11, 1933, the brewery filed a patent on its slogan "The Famous Utica Beer," which it said had been in use since 1890.

In July, threats were received by F.X. and his son Walter. These threats were made by bootleggers who had been supplying beer to people during Prohibition and getting rich from this illegal activity. Selling of beer legally would mean the end of the bootleggers' profitable business, and they weren't happy about it. This prompted the police to station guards around the Matt family. Nothing ever came of the threats, however, and police guard was removed after awhile. In June 1935, a police guard was again provided to F.X. Matt based on a warning letter received by him. Nothing came of this letter, however, and after a few months, the police guard was removed.

By the fall of 1933, the brewery's radio program was carried on WGY and WIBX. F.X.'s oldest son, Walter, joined his father at the brewery and was made vice-president. He had previously worked at the Utica Cutlery Company as general manager.

On July 30 of that year, F.X.'s first grandson was born. The child was named after his grandfather and would become the brewery president in 1980. During September, Pierce Jones, a local contractor, was awarded the general contract for building an additional story on the bottling works.

A July 1934 newspaper article about the brewery described the operation, writing:

> *Currently malt was received in bags and the present malt house had a storage capacity of 16,000 bushels. A new and larger malt house was to be built where rail cars of malt would be unload by vacuum and stored in bins.*
>
> *By enlarging the ale fermenting room, the capacity of brewing would be increased about 7,000 barrels a month. There were two brewings a day and there was no interruptions in the process. Malt, hops, and water are the only ingredients.*
>
> *The malt was crushed, not ground, and water is added. This makes a mash which separate the soluble matter from the malt. This liquor is drawn off and pumped up two flights and boiled with hops in two brew kettles. It is then called wort. It is separated from the grain and hops, and yeast is added, starting the fermenting process.*
>
> *When the fermenting process has stopped, the product must be given time to ripen or age. Lager beer is aged three to five months or more, while ale is aged six weeks to two months, and stock ale is aged six to eight months. During all this time the product is in huge steel, glass lined tanks of 300 to 400 barrels each. Some of the tanks used in fermenting ale are of cedar. The total capacity of all the tanks is 50,000 barrels. In aging of lager by storage it creates its own life. There is no artificial carbonation.*

*The hop storage capacity was to be increased from 100,000 to 330,000 pounds. The hops used are domestic and imported. Those raised abroad are used only in the making of pilsener and wurzburger beer. The hops are kept at a low temperature, ranging from 35 to 40 degrees. By this process there is no chance for the oil in the hops to become rancid, and their flavor and aroma can be preserved.*

*After the beer has been sufficiently aged, it is passed through filters, of which there are five in the basement. There it is passed through cotton, linen, and asbestos fiber and clarified, which makes it more brilliant in appearance.*

*The bottling plant in a separate building has several large machines in which the bottles are filled rapidly and effectively. The cap is applied in the same way and a test is made to show that it is airtight. The label is also applied by machinery, six at a time, 200 a minute or 36,000 bottles labeled in eight hours. The cleansing of returned bottles is done thoroughly by using a solution of caustic soda, six times in each bottle at a temperature of 167 degrees. The bottle is then rinsed, and its absolute cleanness assured after the bottle has been filled it is pasteurized by giving it a hot water bath. This assures the preservation of the contents.*

*When beer is shipped in barrels it does not come in contact with the wood, but touches only the pitch made from pure resin, with which each barrel is lined. When an empty barrel is returned from a customer, it is examined by putting a light inside. If found necessary, the old pitch is removed by heating and new pitch, heated to 380 to 400 degrees, takes its place. The new coat is smooth and shines like varnish. After they have cooled, the barrels are filled with water and, after soaking several days are emptied and refilled. Barrels which have received injury in any way are repaired by having new heads or staves put in. Before filling with beer or ale, barrels are tested for leaks with the use of 75 pounds air pressure. All barrels are washed and sprayed inside and out and after being cleaned and sterilized, they are rinsed in fresh water.*

*The boiler plant generates steam not only for brewing, but for power and light. It was equipped with two 1,000 horsepower Union Iron Works horizontal water tube boilers. The fuel which comes in the plant by rail is fed to the boilers from above automatically.*

*In the engine room is a Cross compound engine of 250 horsepower. This is directly connected with three ammonia compressors able to make 250 to 300 tons of ice in 24 hours. Electric light and power used in every building are generated by two 158 horsepower DeLaval steam turbines, directly connected to four generators. There are also tow air compressors, one electric and one steam driven.*

*A new garage was built in 1934 of pressed brick and is two stories high. It is 145 feet x 135 feet. On the first floor there is room for 32 trucks. The second floor which is reached by a ramp can hold as many trucks. It also contains the engineer's office and a machine shop. The old garage is used for the storage of empty barrels and bottles. A carpenter shop and repair shop are close by.*

A small fire broke out in the pitch room of the brewery on June 27, 1935. It was put out quickly once the firemen got there. One brewery worker was treated for minor burns on his hand.

Utica Club Beer was first packaged in cans in 1935. The brewery went with the cone-top cans, which could be run on existing bottling lines with minor adjustments. They were essentially metal bottles. They used both twelve-ounce (1935) and thirty-two-ounce (1937) cans. The Utica Club Beer cans were white, the Pale Ale cans were red and the Sparkling Ale cans were blue, all of which had a German slogan around the top part of the can.

In 1936, the Seneca Food Products Corporation officers were F.X. Matt, president and treasurer, and C.H. Roemer, secretary. The directors were F.X. Matt and C.H. Roemer. The production of various non-beer items that were introduced during Prohibition continued until just before World War II.

The brewery's advertising activities were extended to include the entire New England area in 1938. Newspapers and radio announcements were used through Compton Advertising, Inc. On March 3, 1938, the brewery received a building permit to erect a brick addition for use as an engine room. It was estimated to cost $14,000. The brewery added showers and a locker room to the plant in 1938 at a cost of $3,000.

F.X. Matt was an enthusiastic booster of New York State hops. In 1938, he wrote many letters to prominent brewers in New York City and elsewhere urging them to encourage the local hop-growing industry by purchasing state hops.

He wrote in one letter, "Undoubtedly you will realize that the leading brewers in the state should purchase the hops grown by farmers in the state. Last year this brewery was forced to purchase the major portion of the New York State hops and while we are willing this year to again purchase what we can use, yet it should also be the duty of the big brewers in the state to purchase their share in order to create a friendly feeling among the farmers and legislators."

The West End Brewing Company office, brew house and storage facilities in 1937. *Author's collection.*

In reply to this letter, an unnamed brewer reported that he had purchased thirty-four bales of state hops, and another brewer wrote, "I quite agree with you that the brewers of the state should do all they possibly can to encourage the growing of hops in our state, not alone because of the high quality of New York State hops but also because of the psychological effect it would have on the farmers."

In 1939, the brewery replaced the original large electric sign on top of the brewery with a new one promoting Utica Club Pilsener and Utica Club Ale. F.X. Matt II said, "My grandfather, F.X. Matt I, had the sign built to help promote our new beers. The sign also served as a symbol of quality and was a tremendous morale-booster for employees." The sign took six months to build and used twenty tons of steel. The sign stood seventy-five feet tall, with each letter standing eight feet by four feet. The sign used 1,950 bulbs that were clear or frosted. In 1964, the letters "U" and "C" used red bulbs to emphasize the "U.C." in Utica Club. The total cost of the sign was $25,000, and it was considered a landmark by Utica residents and travelers approaching the area. In 1971, during the country's energy crisis, the sign was shut down to conserve electricity and save money.

The sign was relit briefly in 1989 to signify a new beginning after the Matt family regained control of the company. Upon the death of F.X. Matt, his will stipulated that the brewery ownership would be handled by a trust that contained all branches of the family. In 1989, the main branch of the Matt family bought out the other members of the trust so that it could proceed on the path the family thought was the correct one for the brewery. During the summer of that year, the sign was lit from 9:00 p.m. to 12:00 a.m. During the winter months, it was lit from 6:00 p.m. to 11:00 p.m.

Rupert Berner became master brewer in 1939 upon the retirement of Peter Stammberger. Berner started working at the brewery in 1928 as the supervisor of the malt syrup department. He left in 1935 to join the P. Ballantine & Sons brewery in Newark, New Jersey, but came back to West End in 1936 to become assistant brewmaster to Stammberger. Berner retired in 1975 after thirty-six years as master brewer. He died in December 1990 at the age of eighty-six.

In March 1940, after a lapse of a year, the brewery reappointed the firm of Moser & Cotins, Inc., which had local offices in Utica, as its advertising agents. Plans were made to use newspapers, posters and radio to advertise the brewery's products. In July, Alfred Holz was hired as assistant master brewer. Holz was formerly with the Fergus Breweries, Inc. in Fergus Falls, Minnesota, and was a 1936 graduate of the Siebel Institute of Technology.

In 1941, the brewery gave its workers their annual Christmas gifts in the form of United States defense bonds and stamps. The brewery usually gave money but decided the bonds and stamps were the soundest investment possible to keep the country safe. All brewers associations were united under the United States Brewers Association in 1941.

On June 14, 1941, the State Liquor Authority ordered the brewery's license canceled on the grounds that the licensee made gifts or rendered services, entered into restrictive agreements, sold at wholesale without appropriate license, had interest in retail premises and did not keep adequate books and records. Walter J. Matt said that the cancellation did not mean that the brewery must suspend operations, though it probably would be necessary to secure a renewal of the license.

The annual fee for a brewery license, which expired on June 30, was $2,500. Where the renewal is for a period of less than six months, renewals were sometimes permitted for $1,250. Matt said that pending further inquiry, he could not say if the brewery would be required to pay that sum for a license that would expire in two weeks.

Between 1933 and 1942, the brewery added several new buildings and invested in new equipment, keeping pace with the latest advances in modern technology. The brewery now included an engine room, where two steam-driven electric generators supplied a 150-kilowatt-per-hour direct current; a refrigeration system of three hundred tons daily; a five-story cold storage building; and a bottling works in which 440 bottles could be filled per minute, with an average day's run of 6,240 cases. An automatic pasteurizer and automatic labelers completed the operations of bottling. Modern racking machines filled about 1,400 half-barrel kegs per day. A big garage, built in 1938, housed a fleet of sixty-one motor trucks in 1942. West End was one of the first breweries in the world to use the then new concept of pneumatic unloading of grain. This was a great labor-saving innovation that was eventually adopted by all breweries. In 1942, the West End Brewing Company had branch offices and warehouses in nine cities and over three hundred employees. Utica Club brews were shipped throughout the northeastern states. The brewery even ran a six-line ad on the front page of the *New York Times* in May advertising its Utica Club Pilsner.

World War II caused significant problems for the brewing industry. Brewing was classed as a nonessential industry, thereby making equipment and ingredients hard to obtain. Every Sunday, the Matt family would go for rides in the countryside to try to convince farmers to grow hops, usually without too much success. They usually made a stop to see two mechanics who helped keep the brewery equipment in running order despite the severe lack of parts.

A fire occurred on the roof of the six-story brick storage building at the brewery on April 23, 1942. Huge clouds of black smoke attracted a large crowd of three thousand people. Although the fire was confined to the roof, damages to the large electric sign, cooling system and roof were estimated at $20,000. Walter J. Matt praised the firemen for halting the flames and keeping them entirely outside the building.

A fifteen-inch concrete roof kept the flames from spreading. This was covered by tarpaper. Principal damage caused by the fire was to the spray pond on the roof, used to cool the air for the ice machine and to the roof itself with the sign. The fire was believed to have originated in the pitch room on the second floor, where barrels were given an interior coating. It was thought that a vent became coated with pitch and ignited, carrying the fire to the roof.

Two years later, on May 25, 1944, another fire struck the brewery in the pitch room. The contents of a pitch kettle caught fire, and flames spread through a ventilator. The fire was confined to the pitch department on the second floor of the building in the southwest corner and a ventilator, which extended to the roof.

When flames shot from the room into the ventilator, the one-hundred-foot extension ladder was raised, and firemen carried a line of hose to the roof, where they poured water into the ventilator. The firemen put the fire out quickly, and most of the damage was water related.

The brewery applied for and received forty supplementary gasoline cards in May 1942. Gas was rationed during World War II, and the cards were needed so that the brewery could continue delivering its beer to all its customers. They would be used by salesmen of the company. The shortage of manpower caused by the war meant that the remaining workforce was required to work long hours to maintain production. By mid-1940, anti-German sentiment caused West End and other brewers to change any brands and advertising that looked or sounded German. West End removed its slogan "Hopfen und malz gott erhalts" from its products. Starting on March 1, 1942, the canning of beer was prohibited by the government due to shortages of metal caused by the war. The brewery maintained a workforce of 275 employees in 1943. Starting in this same year, the Food Distribution Administration ordered brewers to allocate 15 percent of their production for military use.

When F.X. Matt was in his eighties, he kept a fairly constant schedule. Just before noon, he would leave for lunch at home. There he would eat, take a quick nap and then return to the brewery around 2:30 p.m. One day, as F.X. Matt was leaving for lunch, a fire was discovered on the roof of the brewery. Walter Matt stopped his father and told him about the fire. F.X. replied that there was nothing he could do and went home for lunch. When he returned, the fire was out with little damage to the building.

F.X. Matt greatly disliked the power company. One time, Walter Matt came to his father with a problem. The power company was going to run a power line across the brewery parking lot, but Walter did not like the idea. His father said that the parking lot was very dirty and that Walter should place an employee there with a fire hose to clean the lot. It should take a long time, as it was very dirty, and nobody should get in the way. The power company finally backed down and rerouted the power line.

On the evening of February 26, 1944, the female employees of the brewery held a sleigh ride. The sleighs started from the brewery and ended at Wally's Restaurant, where refreshments were served and followed by dancing. Due to the war, the brewery was employing a large number of women in its workforce at the time.

In 1944, the government allowed the larger breweries in the country to supply limited amounts of canned beer for use by the military. Utica Club Pilsener was produced in an olive drab cone-top can. Most of these cans were shipped to the Pacific. The brewery has one example of this can brought back by a local soldier who was stationed in the Pacific. In the spring of 1947, canned beer was again made for general consumption. West End started using the slogan "Dry—not sweet, not bitter—Just right" on its cone-top cans. The cans were red (pale ale), white (pilsener) and blue (sparkling ale). The brewery had branch offices in the following locations in 1944: Buffalo, Syracuse, Schenectady, Binghamton, Amsterdam, Newburgh, Rome, Fort Plain, Oneonta and the Bronx in New York City.

In late 1944, F.X. Matt began planning for building a new state-of-the-art brew house. The firm of J.C. Schultz & Son, Architects & Engineers, of Buffalo, New York, was hired to develop the plans. An agreement was signed between the two companies on December 19, 1944. The plans for the new brew house were to be ready by May 1945. Due to shortages of materials caused by the war, the project was put on hold. The agreement entitled the architectural firm to collect a portion of its fees for its work if the project was put on hold and 60 percent of its fees if the project was cancelled. The brewery paid for services rendered up until the project was put on hold.

F.X. Matt announced on December 6, 1945, that preliminary work on improvements and enlargement to the brewery were underway. The brewery had signed contracts with the John W. Cowper Company of Buffalo for construction of a new seven-story brew house and additions to the bottling department, the stock house and the powerhouse. Approximately $300,000 was involved in the program. He said the contract marked the resumption of the company's improvements program, which had been halted by the war. The project finally got underway in 1946.

The brewery slogan for 1947 was "The Tang's All Here." This was followed in 1948 with the slogan "Preferred by Millions." The brewery used the slogan "UC for Me. Flavor at its Finest." from 1949 to 1951. In 1952, it was replaced with "Tastiest Beer in Town."

After World War II, the policy of reinvestment in the business was continued, for this was Matt's way. Though a daring and original thinker, capable of great eloquence, he preferred a simple example to make his point. One of his favorite expressions was, "A business is like a man—you have to feed him to keep him alive." In line with this belief, two new bottling lines were installed in 1947 when the end of World War II made the machinery available again.

In 1946, work was begun on F.X. Matt's lifelong dream, a million-dollar brew house with the most modern equipment and facilities in existence. An article in *Fortune* magazine described it as "the model brew house."

By January 1949, the new eight-story brew house was complete. Walter Matt said, "The new structure was three years in the building. It took that long because of the difficulty in getting material and the time it required for assembly." Because of the size of the equipment, openings had to be left in the side of the building until the apparatus could be installed.

The new brew house had twenty-six thousand square feet of floor space. The equipment included a mash filter believed to be the largest in the world at the time rather than the traditional lauter tank, two huge six-hundred-barrel gleaming copper brew kettles and an automatic control system that takes the malt through the mills, distributes the correct weights and sends the ingredients to the proper containers accurately measured and mixed for the brewing process. Entering the brew house on the second floor and looking up from the section set aside for the giant copper kettles, the balconies with their trim railings of stainless steel give the impression of a giant ocean liner.

When the filter, which was forty-two feet long and had 108 frames, was under construction, visitors from Europe who had inspected breweries around the world pronounced it the largest of its kind in the world. It was made by Shriver Company of Harrison, New Jersey. The copper and stainless-steel equipment was made by the Bufalovak Division of Blaw-Knox and installed under the supervision of Gordon Driver. The construction of the copper kettles, wort tank and hot water tanks was done by the Central Copper Company of Cincinnati, Ohio.

The brewery was the largest user of New York State–grown hops. Although these hops cost about twenty cents a pound more than western hops, the brewery bought them because it believed they came the closest to matching the European hops that are considered ideal for brewing.

Under the supervision of Robert Berner, the brewmaster, the brewery was making lager, ale, stock ale, bock beer, porter and old english premium ale. A new flat-top canning line was added in 1950, replacing the cone-top canning line. A new quart bottling line was added in 1951.

In 1951, ninety-two-year-old F.X. Matt turned over the control of the brewery to the oldest of his two sons, Walter. F. X. became chairman of the board, a position he held until his death in 1958. As a tribute to his father,

Photo of Walter Matt. *Author's collection.*

Walter had the brewery create Matt's Premium Lager, which was first released in 1952.

At F.X. Matt's ninety-third birthday party on March 25, 1952, he was asked to briefly describe the progress of the company that he had ran since the beginning. He recalled, "I became brew master and general superintendent in 1888. With 12 brewery workers and three salesmen we produced and distributed 16,000 barrels of beer each year. Today, with 300 employees and 40 salesmen, we distribute 355,000 barrels in about 10 states." He also recalled starting with three horse-drawn wagons and in 1952 having sixty-five short-haul trucks and sixteen larger over-the-road transports. There were eleven brewery depots around the state in 1952. On Prohibition, Matt said, "It was impractical. But the people made it the law and the law I observed closely. There are men today who refuse to buy our product because they remember that we refused to attempt manufacturing our product on the side. During prohibition, I not only did not make beer, but I stopped drinking it because it was the law."

By 1952, the brewery decided to make use of the new medium of television to advertise its products, and it was one of the first breweries in the country to do so. One of the first programs it advertised on was *Royal Playhouse*, a half-hour dramatic program produced by Bing Crosby Enterprises in Hollywood.

When Francis and Thomas Dufle of Crogan, New York, and a party of eight other men went on a weekend hunting trip in late 1952, they took along forty-five cases of Utica Club beer from William Steiner. They ran out of beer, so one of the men returned to the village of Long Pond and sent an SOS to Mr. Steiner for more Utica Club. Bob Powers, a local pilot,

A West End Brewing Company cardboard sign from the 1950s. *Author's collection.*

immediately took off with a cargo of UC Pilsener and Cream Ale in his Beechcraft Bonanza plane. There was no landing place available, so he dropped the beer at a height of one hundred feet while flying more than ninety miles an hour. Every can dropped on target, with slight damage to only one, and a good time was had by all.

An expansion of the bottling shop was done in 1952 followed by a conversion to palletization in 1953. In 1953, the German city of Birkendorf presented F.X. Matt with a plaque making him an honorary citizen. It was presented to him at an open house held at the brewery. The open house was a two-day affair that was expected to draw five thousand people. This was the first open house program at the brewery since before World War I. The brewery employed around 350 people at the time.

By 1953, the steam whistle at the brewery was one of the few whistles operating in Utica. The brewery's whistle was sixty years old. It got its steam from the brewery boiler when the fireman on duty pulled a rope leading to the roof of the boiler house. The whistle gave off a three-toned signal eight times a day.

Originally, workers lived close to the brewery where they worked, and the whistle started their day by warning them they had five minutes to walk to work. As workers started living farther and farther away, the whistle did not serve the same purpose. No longer did workers arise, start trudging to work, knock off for lunch, return to the job and put away their tools according to its signal. The whistle did have a functional source. The necessity for keeping certain plant areas cool, an odd use for steam, keeps the boilers busy driving two giant wheels. The steam at 175 pounds of pressure that trembles its way to a rooftop toot eight times a day isn't much of a waste. Although it is hand operated, the whistle involves no waste of manpower, either. A fireman on duty in the boiler plant reaches up and pulls a dangling cord beside the boilers, synchronizing his pull with a clock controlled by a master clock.

Richard Evans assumed the duties of general sales manager for the brewery on January 5, 1953. This was a new position, created to consolidate wholesale sales and branch sales. Evans was replaced the following year, 1954, by Robert E. Welch, who had been the wholesale sales manager for some years previous. It is unknown whether Ryan retired, died or was inept.

The new AFL Teamsters gained bargaining rights at the West End Brewing Company and the Utica Brewing Company on March 30, 1954. The consent election for the two breweries showed that of the 253 eligible voters, 202 voted yes and 12 voted no. The workers had formerly all been members of the CIO Brewery Workers Union.

In 1955, the brewery completed the first stage of a new expansion plan. The project involved a three-story addition to the bottling house and a third-floor addition to the garage building. The addition to the bottling house provided a new railroad loading platform on the first floor and over eleven thousand square feet of storage on the top two floors. A new freight elevator and pallet lift was installed between floors to improve handling of the finished product and raw material.

Construction of a new $800,000, two-story brick storage building was announced by chairman of the board F.X. Matt on May 25, 1956. The structure, designed by H.A. Kuljian of Philadelphia, was built to house twenty-two glass-lined steel tanks that were to be used for the aging and storing of beer. This building increased the brewery's storage capacity by 50 percent, which was needed to keep pace with the 50 percent rise in sales experienced by the company during the previous five years. This sales spurt came at a time when the brewing industry in general was having a hard time. West End saw sales increase from 329,000 to 440,000 barrels a year. Each storage tank had a 1,014-barrel capacity, which equated to 31,941 gallons or approximately 500,000 glasses of beer.

The building was constructed between the existing storage facilities and the old bottling works. An additional two stories were planned and built later. This building was part of a $3.5 million expansion that the brewery had been continuing since the end of World War II. A new bottling line was added in 1957 that ran at six hundred bottles per minute. At the time, it was the fastest in the United States.

Other improvements and additions made during this period and through the early 1960s included: practical doubling of the bottling and warehousing space, a new can line, a new thirty-thousand-square-foot garage, a completely new steam boiler plant and further renovation of the brewing department. It was also during this period that the brewery completely converted its case and handling procedures to palletized operation, as well as replaced its fleet of more than one hundred vehicles to fit in with this new and more efficient concept of warehousing. New branch warehouses were built in Schenectady, Binghamton and Glens Falls.

The founder of the brewery, F.X. Matt, died on Friday, June 27, 1958, at the age of ninety-nine. He had been seriously ill for the ten weeks prior. For the previous two years, his health was precarious, but a will to live and determination to stay at the helm of his business kept him active almost to the end. In both world wars, he was an indefatigable worker in bond drives and for the local war chests. He served actively during World War I on the Home Defense Committee. Besides founding the brewery, he helped organize the Utica Cutlery Company and the Utica Hotel Corporation and had been active in banking and textile affairs. His interest in charitable ventures was varied, and his religious devotion was an example for others.

After the death of F.X. Matt, the controlling stock of the brewery was placed in trust under the terms of his will. Income from the trust and eventually the principal and the residuary estate would be divided among Matt's descendants. F.X. Matt directed that the trustees should not consent to any indirect or involuntary disposal of stock through the medium of any liquidation, dissolution, merger or consolidation of the company, nor consent to any change in the financial structure of the company by reclassification of stock or otherwise as would defeat his intentions.

In 1958, the brewery saw that rising costs were demanding that peak production efficiency be reached and maintained. The canned beer business was steadily increasing, so the company decided to put in a new canning line. Walter J. Matt gave the okay to proceed with the new line in September 1958. He appointed F.X. Matt II to coordinate the project. F.X. Matt II had just joined the brewery earlier that year after graduating from Princeton.

The engineers at the American Can Co. designed the line, which had to fit within the existing building and be installed with as little disruption to production as possible.

The final design for the canning line involved eleven major pieces of equipment representing an investment of $500,000. The installation was accomplished in three phases. In the first phase, the new filler and closer were connected to the old equipment. During the second phase, the old filler and closer were removed, and the rest of the new equipment was installed. The third phase removed the remaining old equipment. The old equipment was kept set up until the bugs were worked out of the new installation.

The new canning line was a two-floor operation and could accommodate twelve- or sixteen-ounce cans with an easy changeover. The line started on the second floor, where the cans were dumped into an Atkron Dumore unscrambler. From there, the cans moved along in single file on a 240-foot-long cable line through a Barker accumulator. After a two-minute accumulation of cans in order to maintain an uninterrupted flow of cans to the filler, the cans were carried down to the first floor by gravity. There they passed through a Barker rinser before being fed into a sixty-spout Cemco filler from the Crown Cork and Seal Co., Inc. and the Canco eight-spindle closing machine. From here, the cans were divided into two lines and passed into a double deck pasteurizer. The cans spent forty of the fifty minutes it takes to move through the process in the pasteurizer. After the cans came out of the pasteurizer, they passed through the rotary filers, which arranged them in single file and discharged them through twisters to twin flat-top conveyors. The dual conveyors passed the filled cans through bulged can detectors, ink markers and Hytafills, which were mounted in tandem. The cans were then returned to the second floor, where they went to a R.A. Jones and Co., Inc. six-packer. This machine opened, filled and glued the six-pack carton and discharged it to the Jones case packer. The six-packs were put in case boxes and moved by conveyor to the warehouse.

Walter was a quieter man than his father but was equally effective as a leader. His special skill was to be a motivator and the facilitator who drew the loose weave of a small family business into a tight competitive corporate fabric. He was very community oriented, being part of the group of community leaders who, after World War II, worked to bring new industry in to replace the textile firms that had fled south.

On May 20, 1959, the West End Brewing Company and the Utica Brewing Company announced that they were consolidating their operations. The announcement by John H. Lalor, president of the Utica Brewing Company, and Walter J. Matt, president of the West End Brewing Company, said that production of Fort Schuyler Beer would be continued at the West End plant through a separate division to be known as the "Fort Schuyler Division." The Utica Brewing Company buildings were left vacant with no plans for use. Sales of Fort Schuyler were to be continued with the same sales personnel and as many as possible of the forty Utica Brewery employees were to be absorbed by the consolidated operation.

The two presidents stated, "We are taking great care to keep the individual character of Fort Schuyler Beer. It will continue to be brewed in the same way as it has in the past." Walter Matt said, "We feel we have an excellent product in Utica Club. But we realize that other people have other tastes. Fort Schuyler has its following and we plan to service it and if possible to increase it. With proper promotion we hope to expand the Fort Schuyler Division." On May 25, the Fort Schuyler Division of the West End Brewing Company opened with Charles H. Pugh in charge as sales manager. Mr. Pugh had formerly been employed by the Utica Brewing Company for a few years.

At the time of consolidation, the Utica Brewing Company was producing 50,000 barrels annually, and the West End Brewing Company was producing 450,000 barrels annually. The final truck moved out of the Utica Brewing Company on Friday, May 22, 1959. Its destination was Auburn, New York.

Sales dips were encountered from time to time during these periods of growth and expansion. A sales dip in 1957 and 1958 resulted in the hiring of the Doyle, Dane, Bernbach Advertising Agency in 1959 and the complete revamping of the sales and merchandising divisions of the brewery. The firm previously used was the Cohen & Aleshire Agency.

The new advertising agency came up with the concept of two talking beer mugs, "Schultz and Dooley," for Utica Club ads. This idea was an immediate hit, and sales increased by more than 50 percent. Schultz and Dooley were brought to life on the television screen by Bill Baird, the famous puppeteer who made them move, and by comedian Jonathan Winters, who did all the voices. The Schultz and Dooley used in the commercials were made of wood and the material used to make dentures. In June 1959, West End placed an order with Schmetzer Inc. (an export-import company) of New York City for five thousand sets of Schultz and Dooley stems. These were to be manufactured in Germany and delivered to the brewery for $4.70 per set. Schmetzer was allowed to sell Schultz and Dooley stems to individuals for $9.95 per set and to stores and other wholesalers for $6.00 per set.

As Schultz and Dooley's popularity grew, other characters were added to the television commercials. The following characters starred in at least one commercial: Officer Sudds; The Countess; Farmer Mugee, who represented whole grain; U-Cee, who represented rice; Old Man Stein, who represented natural aging; Bubbles La Brew, who represented natural carbonation; Cousin Irma; and Uncle Rudolph. Altogether, there were ninety-six commercials made. All except two were in black and white, according to F.X. Matt II.

West End discontinued its Old English Ale as a packaged brand in 1960. The brewery sponsored the first Utica Club New York State Bowling Tournament in 1960. It also started sponsorship of the *North Country Sportsman*, a weekly outdoor television program seen on WWNY-TV in Watertown.

In 1960, the brewery decided to spend about $1 million to enlarge its boiler plant and its bottling, warehouse and garage facilities. W.J. Matt reported that 1959 was the biggest year in the history of the brewery. Sales during 1959 were 12 percent higher than 1958. A new sixty-thousand-square-foot warehouse was erected on land purchased from Utica Knitting Company plant on Schuyler Street. Construction began in early summer.

During the fall, a new high-speed bottling unit was installed and the garage was enlarged. The company directors for 1960 were Walter J. Matt, F. Milton Matt, H.R. Ellis, J.S. Elting, R.E. Welch, Henry Witte, Whitney Clark, Mrs. E.B. Welch and F.X. Matt II. Officers for the company were W.J. Matt, president; F. Milton Matt, vice-president, secretary and treasurer; H.R. Ellis, vice-president; R.A. Swartwout, assistant treasurer; A.H. McCaffrey Jr., comptroller; and R.E. Welch, sales manager.

At a January 1962 sales meeting, F.X. Matt II announced that construction was underway in the warehouse for new loading facilities. Later that year, the first of three new gas boilers was installed. These new boilers would replace the old ones and eliminate the job of breaking coal slag.

Gustav Guentert, who had been a brewer at West End for seventy-one years, died on August 16, 1962, at the age of eighty-nine. He had retired in June. Guentert was born in Baden, Germany, in 1873 and came to New York City as a young man. He married in 1891 and moved to Utica, where he started at the brewery.

During 1963, a new storage building was constructed called cellar T. Inside the building were tanks that held a total of 12,000 barrels of beer in storage. The increased storage brought the total brewery capacity to almost 100,000 barrels. This project was completed by July. Also, another fermenting room was constructed that contained open fermenting tanks. During the summer of 1963, brewery tours were given at 10:00 a.m. and 2:00 p.m. during the week.

On Friday evening, December 27, 1963, the brewery was faced with a crisis in the form of a fire that started in the pitch kettle and raced up through the ventilating stack. The fire caused much damage but was quickly brought under control. Men from the fermenting room raced upstairs to ventilate rooms so that there would be no possibility of smoke damage to the beer. The pitch kettle was back in operation after only a couple days.

Construction of a new bottling plant and new non-returnable bottling line was begun in 1964. The City of Utica granted permission to the brewery to erect and maintain natural gas lights in front of the brewery in August 1964. Starting in April 1964, the brewery began the construction work on the Utica Club Brewery Tour Center. Two floors of an empty warehouse (formerly the old bottling works) were re-created by Walter Pfeiffer, a renowned architect, into a reception area and an 1888-era tavern to handle the ever-increasing number of tourists interested in inspecting brewery facilities. Construction was completed in early 1965 at a cost of over $600,000.

In January 1965, the brewery hired Benton and Bowles, Inc., of New York City to handle its advertising. The advertising budget was set at $1,275,000. In May 1965, the ad agency came to the brewery to shoot a tour commercial that was to be aired during the summer months. Over the course of three days, the cameras shot almost twenty-four thousand feet of film. From this amount, only one sixty-second and one thirty-second commercial would be made. If run in its entirety, the total film shot would have run for one and a half hours.

A tour guide traveled to Danforth, Ohio, on June 11 to pick up a second trolley to be used at the tour center. He first delivered the trolley to Madison, New Jersey, for customization. The brewery received the finished trolley on July 26. In July, the brewery contracted with Raymond E. Kelley, Inc., to do a complete facelift on all the old brewery buildings. This was the first time such an endeavor was undertaken. A three-step process was followed. First, the buildings were steamed and chemically cleaned, not sandblasted. Second, all the old bricks were repointed and badly damaged ones replaced. Finally, a silicone finish was applied to the bricks. Receiving this facelift were the malt building, the main office, parts of the new brew house, the old brew house, the boiler and engine rooms and parts of the old bottling building.

The employees' parking lot was paved, which increased the parking spots from 86 cars to 123 cars. Also during this year, the brewery installed a new keg washer, a final filter, an electrical distribution system and the equipment to handle three new packaging operations: eight-pack seven-ounce bottles, eight-pack twelve-ounce non-returnable bottles and twelve-pack twelve-ounce cans.

The 1888 Tavern as it appeared in the 1960s. *Author's collection.*

West End Brewing Company in 1968. *Author's collection.*

A 1960s West End Brewing Company tour group is seen arriving back at the tour center to go up to the 1888 Tavern for a few free beers. *Author's collection.*

In April 1966, ground was broken for three new grain storage silos that were located between the new storage building and the boiler house of the brewery. Construction was complete in August. Each silo (navy blue in color) was sixty feet high with a diameter of seventeen feet. Each silo had a storage capacity of 335,000 pounds. The new silos doubled the storage capacity of the brewery. The four original silos held 250,000 pounds each and were internal to the buildings. June of 1966 saw a 17 percent increase in sales of Utica Club, breaking the record for barrels sold (71,529) in any other month in brewery history.

In mid-August 1966, the brewery changed ad agencies again when Wells, Rich & Greene was named to handle the advertising. One of the first ideas coming from this firm in October was to bring back Schultz and Dooley to television in the first "Schultz and Dooley Festival." The festival consisted of seventeen of the greatest and funniest commercials. The festival was run for a limited time only and was very well received by the public.

On June 15, 1966, the tour center finally received guests from Nevada, which was the only state from which someone had not yet visited the brewery. During the week of July 18 through July 22, 10,716 people went on the tour, which equated to an average of 1,786 people per day. This set a new record. On July 26, 2,114 people went on the tour in one day, which was another record. Around 4,228 glasses of beer or root beer were served that day. The trolleys would have made approximately one hundred trips around the brewery.

In October, a new Jak-Et-Pak machine was installed at a cost of $13,000. The new equipment was used to package seven-ounce eight-packs. It ran at a speed of 270 bottles per minute and could pack up to fifty cases per minute. Starting in October, the brewery began a general beautification program. New sidewalks were added on Varick Street and down Edward Street to the shipping office. Sixteen trees were added along the new sidewalks. The brewery paid for these improvements, with the City of Utica providing the curbing.

F.X. Matt II was elected vice-president of operations. Richard A. Swartwout was named secretary, Frank S. Owens was named vice-president of advertising, Robert E. Welch was named vice-president of marketing and J. Kemper Matt was named vice-president of sales.

In 1967, the brewery built a new warehouse addition and completely renovated an old storage cellar to increase capacity by seven thousand barrels. The new warehouse added seven thousand square feet. The project was awarded to S. and D. Construction Company for $200,000. The contract for the new storage tanks was given to the Bishopric Products Co., of Cincinnati, Ohio, for $150,000.

To get the tour center ready for the summer rush in 1967, three major revisions in the tour route were made. A forty- by fifty-foot red-and-white-striped tent was erected in the tour center's parking lot. The tent became the starting point for tours during the summer. A white picket fence, red carpet and blossoming flowerpots adorned the tent area. Inside the center, another bar was added in the downstairs reception room, which had been converted into the 1888 Clubroom. The Clubroom only operated during peak rush hours of the day. Finally, in the Prohibition area, an exact re-creation of a speakeasy front was constructed, complete with a peephole door and shingles. White marble–topped tables and metal chairs from 1915 though 1925 were added.

By November 1967, the brewery tour center had seen 362,828 people visit since it opened in February 1965. Utica Club's advertising and point-of-sale captured nine awards out of twenty-two events at the Twenty-sixth Annual Convention of the Brewers Association of America in Chicago.

A 1968 photo of the Utica Club disco ad campaign. *Author's collection.*

Point-of-sale items include any items made for the brewery advertising its products that are placed in retail stores and taverns. Items include wall signs, glassware, trays, menu covers and the like. The brewery took first place for Best Television Advertising, Best Mass Floor Displays, Best Wall Point-of-Sale, Best Glassware, Best Menu Cover and Best Outdoor Poster. It took second place for it Schultz and Dooley "Natural Beer on the Way" tray. Third place awards in the six-pack carton and coordinated advertising categories were received.

A completely new set of visual aids to help explain the brewing, fermenting, aging and packaging processes was installed on the brewery tour route in August 1967. The Anderson, Hutchins & Seeds advertising agency of Utica designed the new aids, which were produced and installed by Color-Ad Signs of Utica.

The world's largest Christmas wreath was hung at the Utica Club tour center for the first time in December 1967. The wreath, which measured thirty-six feet in diameter and weighed more than five tons, was attached to the side of the engine room at the back of the tour center parking lot. The metal frame weighed 1,600 pounds, and 8,900 pounds of boughs were used in construction. The wreath contained 5,250 miniature GE Christmas bulbs, and it was constructed by Cirascolo Brothers Landscaping of Yorkville. In December 1968, a bright red bow was added to the wreath, along with the words "Seasons Greeting" lit in the center of the wreath.

In 1968, a major renovation to the refrigeration system was done at a cost of $250,000. Four additional beer storage areas were also renovated. The brewery introduced a completely new package (the twelve-ounce NR Club bottle) and label for its products, created by San Francisco designer Walter Landor in 1968. Beer cans also were packaged differently. For the first time, the cans were held together by plastic rings rather than the conventional cardboard wrapper. A continuous spool of plastic rings is stretched over the tops of a line of cans and then separated into six packs and cased.

On March 2, 1968, members of the Utica Club sales force previewed the new ad campaign entitled "Swings" during the annual sales meeting at the Hotel Utica. The campaign was produced by Wells, Rich, Greene, Inc., and began on March 4. The campaign started with introductory television spots featuring a mythical nightclub, the "Utica Club," which embodied the most desirable features of the best nightclubs in the world. The campaign introduced the Utica Club Natural Carbonation Band.

For the production of the commercials, a complete discotheque was created by Libra Productions on the first and third floor of the old Walt Whitman School on the east side of Manhattan. Included in the production built at a cost of $100,000 were six sets: an entrance to the club, an old-fashioned bar, a color wall that flashed lights in a sequential design, a boutique, a woodland scene and the discotheque proper with a mushroom-shaped bandstand springing up from the dance floor to the bar level. The cast numbered over seventy people, including Rocky Graziano (pro boxer), Judd Hirsch (actor), and "Killer" Joe Piro (dancer). A week of filming produced twenty-five thousand feet of color film and resulted in eleven commercials. The length of the commercials varied from ten seconds up to two minutes. Sasha Burland wrote "The Utica Club Natural Carbonization Beer Drinking Song," which was very popular and was even sold on forty-five-rpm records.

An eight-week introductory period to establish the Utica Club concept was utilized in all markets using all types of media. Longer commercials were used at the beginning, with shorter ones following at a greater frequency. Radio advertising was greatly increased during the summer. West End puts 50 percent of its advertising budget in television, 25 percent in radio and 5 percent in newspapers. The remaining 20 percent was used in outdoor advertising.

Coinciding with the new ad campaign, the brewery changed the design of its packaging. The design studios of Walter Landor and Associates of San Francisco created the "Miss Columbia" labels. In the end, the campaign was very successful, with the brewery seeing an increase in market-share. People were even calling the brewery trying to see if they could acquire a Utica Club discotheque franchise.

By late 1968, the brewery decided to terminate its two-year relationship with Wells, Rich, Greene, Inc. The main reason given was the brewery's increasing need for an extensive variety of merchandising programs to assist a strong sales effort. In 1968, Mohawk Airlines, which flew out of Utica, started offering U.C. flights one which travelers could get a cold Utica Club during the trip. Utica Club products were prominently featured in the 1969 Paramount film  starring Liza Minnelli. A large portion of the movie was filmed at the Hamilton College campus and the surrounding area.

In April 1969, the brewery introduced a new advertising campaign with the slogan, "It's tough to argue over a Utica Club. We put too much love in it." The campaign idea was simple. Take two natural antagonists who were really fighting it out, bring them together and make them friends over a Utica Club. Nine different television commercials were made. The commercials featured cartoon characters who became friendly over a Utica Club beer. The cat and dog were the first characters. Later they added commercials titled "McSwipe" (featuring a Mountie and a bad guy), "Landlord" (a landlord and a tenant), "Cowboy and Indian," "Bull and Matador" and "Omnibus" (which featured all the characters). The music was again arranged by Sasha Burland. Three of the commercials that came out in December featured a Christmas theme. The ad agency responsible for this campaign was Delekanty, Kurnit & Geller, Inc. The television campaign won first place in a contest for beer advertising sponsored by the Brewers Association of America in 1969, beating out the Erie Brewing Co. of Erie, Pennsylvania, (second place) and the Burger Brewing Co. of Cincinnati, Ohio (third place).

In the fall of 1969, the brewery replaced nine World Tandem labelers on its non-returnable bottle line with two new Weiss rotary units. Some of the old World Tandem units were then used to replace older units on the seven-ounce and quart bottling lines. The new Weiss labelers could process 400 bottles per minutes. The two units had a capacity of 800 bottles per minute, compared to the 720 bottles per minute of the World Tandem units.

Henry Eichenhofer retired in 1969. He was assistant brewmaster from 1946 to 1969. He began working at the brewery in 1926.

In 1971, the brewery continued making improvements, including huge domed covers for the tanks in Cellar T to permit automatic cleaning, automatic temperature controls for the fermenters (at a cost of $150,000), an automatic control panel for the brew house to control almost all brew house functions ($50,000), a new bottom support plate and interior seam re-welding on one of the brew kettles ($15,000), a new electronic bottle inspector, major changes to the refrigeration system to increase efficiency and many minor equipment upgrades.

Schultz and Dooley steins, which had been made in Germany since 1959, were being manufactured by Ceramate in Brazil starting in 1971. An Officer Sudds stein was added to the lineup in 1973, and the Countess was added in 1978.

Maximus Super beer was introduced in 1971. When Maximus was first introduced, it caught many people by surprise with its alcohol content of 7.5 percent by volume. Many a story circulated that area bars serving this product would find some of their patrons asleep in their cars the next morning after drinking Maximus. Maximus developed a reputation as being far superior to any mainstream, national brand malt liquors and built up quite a following.

The brewery added four new stainless steel storage tanks in 1972. Each tank had a twelve-and-a-half-foot diameter and was seventy feet long and was the largest available to the brewing industry. Each tank holds the equivalent of 27,000 cases of beer and weighs 250 tons when filled. The tanks were lifted by crane to the top of the brewery's storage building and then slid into position in a new cellar on the seventh floor. The addition of the tanks was necessitated by the steadily increasing demand for Maximus Super and other products. In addition to the four stainless steel tanks, the brewery was also adding seven new fermenting tanks to replace smaller units. The new fermenters each held 1,000 barrels of beer. They were each twelve and a half feet feet high, twelve feet wide and thirty-five feet long and contain more than 13,500 cases of beer each. The fermenters were put in place through an opening in the wall. The total cost for both projects was nearly $500,000. F.X. Matt II said, "The new tanks will add to our beer-making capacity and are part of a continuing program of modernization and improvement, which never ceases here."

The great success of the tour center prompted the brewery to add a gift shop in 1972 called the 1888 Village Gift Shop. The brewery placed the gift shop in a trailer parked at the back of the tour center parking lot. The gift shop remained in this location until 1981, when the brewery completed renovations to a building next to the tour center. The renovation matched the decor of the tour center. The old trailer that had previously housed the gift shop was donated to the Utica Zoo, which would use the building for its gift shop. Over fifty-five brewery employees donated the money to cover the expense of transferring the trailer from the brewery parking lot to the zoo. Also that year, the brewery started to filter the water used in making its beer to get rid of possible phenol contamination.

A 1973 brewing industry survey showed a steady drop in West End sales from 1968, with a 1972 sales figure of 550,000 barrels. The brewery changed advertising agencies in mid-1973. The firm DellaFemina, Travisano & Partners Inc. of New York City was chosen.

An aluminum recycling center was opened in the West End brewery garage on June 27, 1974. The center was sponsored by the Reynolds Metal Co. and assisted by the brewery. The brewery had completed the conversion of its canning facility to aluminum cans in March.

On July 2, 1974, the brewery experienced a major flood. Three brewing department buildings were flooded to the first-floor level, the boiler room flooded to eight feet and the basement of the garage to about five feet. The boilers had to be dried out and rewired, and production was suspended for three days. Fortunately, there was enough inventory to supply the July 4 holiday. The damage done by the flood exceeded $45,000. Another smaller flood occurred on August 27, 1974, flooding the boiler room with two inches of water. Nail Creek has been a problem for the brewery for a long time, with floods periodically occurring. Over the years, changes in roads and buildings aggravated the problem. In the late 1970s, the City of Utica completed the Nail Creek sewer project, which helped correct the problem.

In 1975, West End sold 483,385 barrels, which was a 6.50 percent increase over the previous year. The industry as a whole only saw a 1.85 percent increase for the year. The brewery's ad agency, DellaFemia, Travisano & Partners of New York, created a new campaign in 1976 called the "Utica Club Bar Exam." The main premise of the ads was to blindfold a person and have him or her pick out the Utica Club beer from the three choices. If he picked out the Utica Club beer, he passed the exam. The campaign started out in print advertising and was followed with radio and television ads. Schultz and Dooley were brought back to help in the selling and appeared in one spot in which Dooley attempts to blindfold Schultz and give him the bar exam.

For Utica Club Cream Ale, three new funny radio commercials were created. The first ad was called "Hy Diver." One of the characters, Hy Diver, regularly jumps 1,200 feet into a 6-foot pool of Utica Club Cream Ale. He indicates the Utica Club Cream Ale is soft and gentle, and it cushions the blow. The second ad was called "Irish Mike Rosenberg," the name of a fighter who is also a pacifist. He'd rather go a few round with Utica Club Cream Ale than with a sparring partner because Utica Club Cream Ale doesn't hit as hard as a sparring partner. The third ad was called "Yogi Beer." Yogi Beer was deeply into transcendental meditation. He meditated on Utica Club Cream Ale all the time because it is nice, mellow and soft.

In August 1976, extremely heavy rains and an inadequate Nail Creek drain system caused flooding at the brewery and other areas of West Utica. It was the second time since 1974 that the brewery was flooded. In both cases, the Nail Creek subterranean drain system was the cause. Damage to the brewery was not as severe as in 1974, when damage totaled over $50,000. This flood, however, damaged a set of antique drugstore wall cabinets stored in the truck garage. They were to be used in a planned expansion of the tour center and were estimated to be worth $10,000. Also damaged was a tourist's car. Water also entered the boiler room, a dry storage area and the basement of the bottling area.

The brewery made the decision in mid-1976 to install a new laboratory building and make modifications to Cellars D, E and F, where four used beer tanks would be installed. The architectural company of Wm. F. Koelle Sons, a division of Day & Zimmerman, Inc., of Philadelphia, drew up the plans. The new laboratory was built on two levels, comprising more than 2,000 square feet. Plans called for a chemistry section that alone would triple the size of the old lab. A separate room for bacteriological studies, a refrigerated room for beer samples, a taste-testing room and utility and storage rooms were created. The new lab was built to blend in with existing architecture and had decorative brick arches above the windows.

The brewery produced Billy Beer for four months in 1977 before giving the idea up. In 1977, W. Peter Swanson was named treasurer of the company, replacing Richard Swartwout, who retired after working for thirty-eight years at the brewery. Also, Bud McCaffrey was named secretary. A new Krones Starmatic labeler was installed in the bottling department, which gave the brewery the capability of producing unique super premium–type packaging that was usually associated with imported brands.

Starting in early 1977, the brewery ran a contest to rename the 1888 Village Gift Shop. The winning entry would receive a $50 gift certificate. The winning entry was the Brewery Gift Shop, submitted by an anonymous person. The prize was awarded to the second-place entry for the name 1888

Tavern Gift Shop. The winning name would be used when the new gift shop was constructed. This would not take place until 1981.

A major innovation was introduced by the brewery in 1977: the beer ball. It was the first in the nation to use the new container, which held 5.17 gallons of fresh draft beer. The first beer balls were made of amber plastic, though this was later changed to clear. They arrived at the brewery in a test tube shape before they are blown and molded into a beer ball. The beer balls were non-polluting when burned, but they had a variety of other uses such as buoys and lampshades. The state college in Binghamton collected enough of the beer balls to replace all the outdoor glass globes around the campus. West End was also the only brewery at the time to offer its products in short, conveniently sized money-back bottles. This was long before the advent of the deposit law that made all beer containers returnable. Utica Club Light, the brewery's first lower-calorie beer (ninety-six calories) was added to the product line in 1978.

The brewery produced malta, a non-alcoholic malt-based drink, for the Schaefer brewery from 1978 through 1980. It got the business when Schaefer consolidated its Baltimore, Maryland, and Allentown, Pennsylvania plants. The brewery installed a new bottling line in September 1978. Schaefer did not have the capability to produce malta after the consolidation and sought bids from regional breweries. West End got an exclusive contract from Schaefer—even though it was not the lowest bidder—primarily due to its good reputation. Stroh's takeover of Schaefer ended the malta production contract.

In 1979, the advertising firm if Dellfenina & Associates of New York City developed four possible themes for West End's commercials. The first proposed using F.X. Matt II in various situations. The second touted Matt's popularity among visiting foreigners at the 1980 Lake Placid Olympics. The third dealt with people missing Matt's brews after having moved to regions where the beer isn't sold. The final one showed a couple celebrating an important anniversary with a bottle of Matt's Premium.

The first idea was ultimately chosen, with the first commercial featuring F.X. appearing in 1981. The idea of the F.X. commercials was to create a substantial point of difference between Matt's Premium and its competitors, using a limited advertising budget. This series of commercials was very successful as F.X. Matt II came across as being very sincere about his product. Quickly, Matt discovered that his self-effacing charm would catapult him into the world of media folk heroes, where people know you, but you don't know them. The theme for these commercials was "When your name's on the outside."

F.X. Matt II. *Author's collection.*

The management of the brewery has always been concerned about the quality of its products, and any complaints were investigated and handled promptly. Once the brewery received a complaint from a lady saying that a beer can had leaked all over her groceries. She sent the complaint to the brewery in verse. The brewery replied in verse and gave her a purchase order for a free case of beer. Another complaint came from a student in Binghamton, who complained of cloudy beer. The problem was tracked down to a retailer that had accidentally frozen some cases of Matt's Premium. This problem was quickly rectified.

In 1980, Matt's Premium outsold the brewery's regular beer, Utica Club, for the first time. F.X. Matt II was named president of the brewery, replacing his father, Walter. Under his guidance, the brewery's sales and family philosophies continued. In an age where many small breweries were failing, West End survived by reinvesting in the plant, using prudent management and clever advertising and maintaining good labor relations and quality products.

## The F.X. Matt Brewing Company Years

The West End Brewery changed its name to the F.X. Matt Brewing Company in 1980 to honor the brewery's founder, F. X. Matt. F.X. Matt II indicated that "West End" sounded too parochial and it was time for a change. The brewery sold more than 400,000 barrels that year. A major contribution to the brewery's survival has been control of labor costs. The brewery has kept its basic wage in 1981 at $7.50/hr. compared to $10/hr. for the national companies with the help of the employees. Through continually automating as much of the brewing process as possible, the number of brewery employees needed has been consistently low. For example, the brew house once required twenty workers. Now it can be run with one full time worker and one part time worker on a shift, thanks to modern central control equipment.

The Brewery Shop opened on June 15, 1981, adjacent to the tour center, with a ribbon-cutting ceremony. The building was formerly the Rainbow Restaurant. Walter C. Pfeiffer, who designed the tour center, was brought in to design the new gift shop. Pfeiffer's design called for a continuation of the elaborate Victorian theme found in the tour center. The interior of the new shop included a large brass chandelier, stained-glass windows and numerous antiques. In addition to selling many brewery collectibles, the new shop was expanded to include a line of Victorian-period gift items, such as toys and Christmas ornaments. The new location replaced the tiny trailer located in the tour center parking lot, which had been used as the gift shop for seven years.

More improvements were made in the bottling plant in July 1981. They included the purchase and installation of a Meyer four-thousand-case packer, additional bottle and case conveyors and two Jagenberg Solar 50 labelers, which cost $100,000 each. Each labeler could label 500 bottles per minute. The equipment they replaced was capable of labeling only 245 bottles per minute. The new labelers were needed due to the overall increase in demand for Matt's Premium. In total, the brewery spent $300,000 on the improvements. The smoke stack at the brewery was lowered in 1981. When it was originally erected, it had to be very tall to create a draft. The boilers used in 1981 had forced draft fans, which allowed the smoke stack to be reduced in height—important since the smoke stack was beginning to lean toward the brew house.

In September 1981, beer ball sales reached the half million mark. At the time, Matt's Premium was the only beer sold in the unique package in the northeast. The brewery also developed a lightweight refillable deposit bottle with a screw-off top that Matt believes is more convenient than the traditional "export" deposit bottle.

From January 5 through 8, 1982, a crew of twenty people from Paisley and Friends Productions were at the brewery filming a new set of commercials. Most of the location shooting occurred in the brew house and the tavern. The commercial ideas came from the brewery's advertising agency, Drossman Yustein Clowes, Inc. The new commercials debuted on February 22. Twelve different brewery employees were used in the commercials. F.X Matt II, the brewery president, appeared in each commercial as a spokesman. In the commercials, F.X. Matt II discussed some of the history behind the company and talked about using the finest ingredients and natural aging. The new campaign was named "Blood, Sweat and Beers."

In March 1982, the brewery introduced Matt's Premium Light Beer. This was the first line extension of the Matt's Premium brand. At the introduction of the new beer, F.X. Matt II read a short poem to the crowd:

*Look out Bud! Look out Miller!*
*New Matt's Light is a giant killer*
*With taste that's great and body surprising.*
*Look out you guys—a new sun is rising.*
*We're not very big compared to you,*
*But we love our beer and know how to brew*
*A great light beer with malt and hops,*
*Shove over you guys—your monopoly stops.*

Starting in May 1982, the brewery was again leading the industry in being the first brewery to have the in-plant capability to manufacture beer balls. The first beer ball blow-molding machine in the country was installed in the brewery's racking room. The balls had previously been made of high-density polyethylene by Johnson Enterprises in Illinois. The ball produced by the brewery was made of polyethyleneterathalate (PET). The system was designed and built by Cincinnati Milacron and included a large blow-molding machine and three auxiliary units: an air compressor, an air dryer and a water cooling system. The twenty-two-thousand-pound system was installed by Central Steel of Utica under the supervision of Gabe Creo, the brewery's electrical supervisor.

The new system first heated a pre-form (a tube about twelve inches long purchased from Johnson Enterprises) in a radio frequency oven. The hot form was then expanded with a burst of air pressure in a beer ball–shaped mold. The cold walls of the mold, which were chilled to forty degrees by the water circulation system, caused the form to solidify immediately. The mold then opened to release a clear, smooth beer ball, which dropped to a conveyor below. The new system was capable of producing a beer ball every fifteen seconds.

Producing the beer balls in-house provided the brewery with many benefits. Shipping costs were greatly reduced for the empty beer balls, and the new process didn't warp or egg-shape the mouth opening, so a better seal was created when capping the beer ball. Another advantage of the new beer ball was that it could be easily disposed of. Like the original beer ball, it could be crushed, and if incinerated, it would not release toxic fumes. The disadvantages of the new in-house-made beer ball included the fact that it could be punctured by sharp objects and that when empty, they were not as rigid as the old ball, which eliminated some of the uses people made of the emptied balls.

In 1982, the brewery embarked on its first brewing venture with a microbrewer during this year. The brewer was Matthew Reich, who was seeking a producer for New Amsterdam Beer, which would be sold in New York City. Reich, with the help of Dr. Joseph L. Owades, was introduced to F.X. Matt II in Utica. Owades, a brewery consultant, had been a consultant for the Matt brewery on a regular basis for many years. Matt stated that the request from Reich came at a good time. The brewery was working on developing a European-style beer to compete with the imports, and this project offered the brewery an opportunity to get brewing experience with a more full-flavored beer.

In late 1982, the brewery announced that Schultz and Dooley steins, along with the other stems, would now be produced in Germany instead of Brazil. The brewery stated that the change was made because shipping time between the United States and Germany was faster than with Brazil and because the German manufacturer was able to fill large orders on short notice.

The brewery and area was saddened by the death of Walter J. Matt on November 14, 1982, at the age of eighty-one. Walter Matt had succeeded in guiding the brewery to the production of more than 500,000 barrels a year. He was president of the company for thirty very difficult years, as smaller breweries fell victim to the industry giants. Walter Matt was born April 18, 1901, in Utica. He was educated in Utica schools and Cornell University. He married Kathryn Kemper on November 7, 1928. Mr. Matt was production manager at the Utica Cutlery from 1923 to 1927, when he became general manager, a position he held until 1933. He was made vice-president of the brewery in 1933 and became the president in 1950. He retired from active management in 1978, and at the time of his death, he was chairman of the F.X. Matt Brewing Company board.

On September 12, 1983, a new law took effect that required all malt beverages and soft drinks in the state to be sold in deposit containers. After this date, a $500 fine per occurrence would be levied by the government against those still in violation. Inspections by the government would be conducted on a random basis. Working closely with its distributors, the brewery made sure that all the bottles and cans had the deposit information on them when the law took effect.

Season's Best Holiday Amber was introduced for distribution during the Thanksgiving and Christmas seasons in 1983. Season's Best was brewed with 100 percent barley malt and lagered for a longer time than most American beers. Brewing a holiday beer is a deep-rooted tradition that began in Europe many centuries ago when Christmas beers were designed to go with hearty holiday meals and colder weather.

In August 1984, Matt's unveiled a new import style lager called Freeport USA, which was available on tap at the 1888 Tavern at the brewery. This beer was to hit the market over the next three months. However, the ad agency that came up with the original name had second thoughts and changed the name to Saranac 1888. The brewery liked the change, and the beer was introduced the following year. During the summer, the brewery won the award for the "Best American Pilsener Lager" at the Great American Beer Festival held in Denver, Colorado, for its Matt's Premium. Not everything was going the brewery's way, however. The company had an operating loss of $1.1 million on revenues of $17.4 million, mostly as a result of a relatively flat beer market and pricing wars brought on by the big national brewers.

Not being in a position to apply massive amounts of money to its problems and opportunities is a situation that the F.X. Matt brewery has met head on with a potent weapon: the ingenuity of its people. One example is the brew house control panel, which the plant engineer and a local controls specialist devised for a fraction of what it would have cost to buy comparable equipment from an equipment supplier.

Another was a problem with a conveyor system that required an eight-foot turning area in a portion of the brewery where that much space was not available. A bottling mechanic made a rotary turntable that would turn cases 180 degrees in a space only five feet wide—which was precisely the amount of space available.

Beginning in January 1985, the Eric Mower and Associates advertising agency was chosen as the brewery's new ad agency. On May 29, 1985, the brewery introduced Saranac 1888 All Malt Lager, an ultra-premium beer. This was marketed in Colorado; Maryland; Virginia; Washington, D.C.; and New England, in addition to the brewery's normal distribution network of central New York. At the time, industry analysts said that Matt's was taking a chance on its new product because the market for an import-priced ($4.25 a six-pack) domestic beer remained unproven. The risk paid off, as the Saranac line has developed into the brewery's main line over the years.

The year showed a great improvement for the brewery from the previous year, but it still lost money. The brewery had an operating loss of $308,000 on revenues of $15.4 million. F.X. Matt II said the brewery was hurt by cheap mass-produced beers flooding the area and a lack of support. Matt said that too often the community takes its assets for granted.

As a case in point, the local Republican Party served Miller beer during a fundraiser for the mayor of Utica. Matt purchased ads in the Utica newspapers criticizing the mayor for the choice of beer. Another example involved the Utica Blue Sox baseball team. They needed a new scoreboard for their home field, Murnane Field. They asked Matt's if it would contribute to the new scoreboard because Matt's had contributed funds in the past and its beer was sold at the games. Matt's was unable to contribute because of poor earnings over the previous several years. The Blue Sox then approached Miller Brewing Company, which said it would buy the new scoreboard for them if they sold only Miller products at the ball games. The team accepted the Miller Brewing Company's offer, even though the hometown brewery lost out.

In October 1985, the company began brewing Brenner's Amber Light for the Monarch Wine Company. The formula and overall direction for this brew came from Mort Brenner, an internationally known scientist and brewmaster. On September 12, Saranac 1888 was named the official beer of the New York State Forestry Centennial. Season's Best got a new facelift. The label change was made to indicate that the beer was enjoyable throughout the entire season rather than just at Christmas. The new black, gold and white label featuring Miss Columbia was thought to have a much more wintery appeal, signifying a beer hearty enough to drink all season long.

December 14 saw the unveiling of Brewhouse Square, a four-building retail complex owned by the brewery on Varick Street. The shops included the Brewery Shop, the Brewery Tour Center, Tom's Barbershop and the Duxbak Factory Store. An article in the January 20, 1986 issue of magazine praised the brewery for its innovative ideas, citing the development of the beer ball and the fact that it was one of the first breweries to begin contract brewing.

The year 1986 saw many good things happen for the brewery. Saranac 1888 All Malt Lager won a Cleo Award on June 13 for the top packaging in the beer industry. The Saranac 1888 package design was the creation of Eric Mower and Associates advertising agency in Syracuse. Distribution of Saranac 1888 and Matt's Premium was expanded to Maine, while distribution of Saranac 1888 and Matt's Light were introduced to Alaska. Saranac 1888 draft beer was introduced to taverns in central New York and the Saranac Lake–Lake Placid region.

The brewery reopened the tour center during the offseason (September through May) for groups that made reservations in advance. The workforce for the brewery was approximately two hundred people.

Matt's Premium and Matt's Light both received new packaging during the year. Six-packs of both beers show a picture of an 1888 West End brewery clambake. The brewery stated that the change was made to make the beers more visible. Season's Best, Matt's Christmas offering, also received more colorful packaging that stood out to the eye when on the store shelves. The brewery expanded its contract brewing by adding Dock Street Amber to its list of contract brews. Dock Street Amber is brewed for a microbrewery in Philadelphia. Matt's became one of two breweries in the state to gain approval to bottle malt coolers (similar to wine coolers).

F.X. Matt II, president of the brewery, was also named president of the Brewers Association of America, an organization that represents the views and concerns of the small brewers in the country.

The brewery developed Maximus Malt Liquor toward the end of the year to sell in the New York City market. At the time, New York City was known as the malt liquor capital of the world. Maximus Malt Liquor was sold in forty-ounce bottles and contained 6.5 percent alcohol by volume, which was somewhat higher than most other malt liquors. While the brewery introduced some new beers and developed new packaging during the year, 1986 was not a good year financially. The brewery again experienced an operating loss. It lost $551,000 on revenues of $12.4 million, which was almost double the loss in 1985.

The following year (1987), the brewery expanded its contract brews to five. It was producing New Amsterdam Beer, Portland Lager, Dock Street Beer, Sun Country Malt Cooler and Birell Non-Alcoholic Beer. As of 2013, 35 percent of the brewery's production is for contract brews. The brewery will not disclose any of its clients or how much beer it brews for them. If the manifest on a bottle or can indicates Utica, New York, as the place where it was packaged, then the F.X. Matt Brewery bottled, canned and/or brewed the product. An example of this is the recent canning of Harpoon brews, which were brewed at Harpoon in Windsor, Vermont, and shipped to Utica for canning. The Harpoon brewery did not have a canning line at the time. Since then, it has installed one at its Boston brewery and now do not use the Matt brewery for canning. Many small craft brewers make use of the Matt brewery canning line when they want to sell their beer in cans but do not want to make the investment in a new canning line.

In the spring of 1987, the brewery kicked off a new ad campaign to promote its Matt Beer Ball. The campaign included radio and special interest newspaper advertisements, outdoor billboards and a variety of sales promotion programs. The radio ads featured a talking beer ball in three different supermarket situations. The beer ball talks to a store manager, Matt's bottles and cans and kegs of beer. In each ad, the beer ball explains its main selling points, including its no-deposit, no-return, easy-to-carry and easy-to-tap features. The beer ball also explained that bottles, cans and kegs don't like its convenient features and asked consumers to come in and buy it before the other packages take some form of retribution.

The character in the spots had been given life through a newly developed beer ball costume. The costume was shaped like a beer ball box, with oversized hands and a yellow Matt's hat. The beer ball character made appearances at brewery-sponsored events. The company also made use of outdoor billboards that had a theme of "Play Ball" (using the word "play" followed by a photograph of an actual beer ball container). Sales stayed approximately the same from the previous year at $12.4 million but an operating loss of $840,000 was experienced (a 52 percent increase). Matt's Season's Best Amber Beer went on sale on November 29 in the Utica area.

The year 1988 marked the 100th anniversary for the F.X. Matt Brewing Company. To celebrate this feat, the brewery's theme for 1988 was "Cheers to 100 Years!" Many special events were planned for the year. One contest the brewery came up with was the "Matt's Centennial Sweepstakes," in which the brewery gave away one hundred pairs of season tickets for the 1988 Syracuse University football season. Many new events were sponsored during the year celebrating the 100th year. The first-ever Matt's Winter Classic Arm Wrestling Tournament was held at Lily Langtry's in Utica benefitting the American Heart Association. The first-ever Matt's Northeast Chowder Cook-off was held at Hanover Square in Syracuse. The first-annual Matt's Media Challenge Cup ski race was held at Val Bialas Ski Center in Utica in mid-February. The first-annual Fireworks Over Utica event was held on August 27, with the brewery as one of the sponsors.

In mid-March, the New York State Senate and Assembly honored the brewery with a joint resolution to commemorate the brewery's 100th anniversary. During the year, many groups held birthday parties for the brewery. The West Side Merchants of Utica threw a party on July 9 and 10. On July 13, a party was held in downtown Utica, complete with the Schultz and Dooley Band and a twenty-four-foot cake courtesy of Hemstrought's Bakery.

In early 1988, the brewery added Brooklyn Brand Lager, Boston Amber Export and Prior Double Dark to its contract brewing operations. Contract brews accounted for 5 to 10 percent of the brewery's business. It was still brewing New Amsterdam beer, Dock Street beer and Sun Country malt coolers. In August 1988, Walter C. Pfeiffer, who designed the tour center, visited the brewery along with other people connected with the tour center creation. Since its doors opened, the tour center had hosted millions of guests from across the United States and more than one hundred foreign countries.

Even though the Saranac line was launched in 1985 and contract brewing began to fill excess capacity, the brewery was still struggling. In 1989, five direct descendants of F.X. Matt bought the assets from the family trust and reorganized the company. Matt's Special Dry was unveiled.

Per the agreement, two more family members were added to the executive staff. Nicholas O. Matt left his position as president and general manager of Vick's Health Care, a division of Proctor & Gamble, to become president of the brewery. Fred Matt, F.X. Matt II's son, left his post as account supervisor at Grey Advertising to become director of marketing and sales.

## The Saranac Years

In 1990, the Matt family decided to refocus the business to produce specialty beers instead of more mainstream products. They placed their emphasis on the Saranac line of products. So far, the brewery has produced over thirty different types of Saranac. This produced good results. At the Great American Beer Festival in 1991, Saranac won first place in the premium lager category. Saranac Lager received such a positive response during the next couple of years that management decided to increase the Saranac portfolio.

In the summer of 1993, the brewery developed Saranac Black & Tan in answer to a Saranac distributor that wanted a heartier product. The brewery employed 135 people in 1994 and made Saranac Adirondack Amber, Saranac Golden Pilsener, Saranac Black & Tan, Saranac Pale Ale, Saranac Black Forest, Matt's Premium and Utica Club. These Saranac products won two more awards at the 1995 Great American Beer Festival. Saranac 1888 Tavern Root Beer was also introduced in 1995.

In 1994, the brewery occupied 360,000 square feet in floor space, which included the warehouse, offices, production and packaging areas. It had two 600-barrel brew kettles, twenty-five fermenting tanks, sixty lagering tanks, sixty aging tanks, three bottling lines and one canning line. It had a production capacity of 550,000 barrels per year. The brewery added Saranac Chocolate Amber and Mountain Berry Ale in 1995. Another innovation occurred in 1996 when the brewery introduced Saranac Trail Mix, which offered several different Saranac beers in a six-pack or twelve-pack. During the next several years, the brewery continued adding new Saranac products.

Beginning in 1999, the brewery initiated Saranac Thursdays, a weekly summer concert series in which area bands played in the brewery parking lot while the brewery served its products. Of the proceeds taken in, 50 percent are donated to the United Way. The event runs for approximately fifteen weeks during the summer and is in its fifteenth year in 2013.

The year 2001 started out on a sad note for the brewery. F.X. Matt II died on January 15 at the age of sixty-seven. He had been fighting cancer but died of complications from pneumonia. He was a highly visible figure in the American brewing industry, leading the brewery through hard times. News of his death saddened many in the industry, as he had built a reputation for integrity and technical accomplishment. Nick Matt was named chairman and CEO of the brewery in 2008. Fred Matt was named president and COO.

In April 2007, the Lake Placid Craft Brewing Company entered into a supply and distribution agreement with the F.X. Matt Brewing Company. The partnership allowed the Lake Placid brewery to continue to grow and expand distribution into regional areas and extend its availability in new states. Lake Placid closed its brewery in Plattsburgh, moving its production to the F.X. Matt Brewing Company in Utica. The brewery in Lake Placid continues to brew beer at full capacity.

On May 29, 2008, a fire broke out in the second floor of the bottling facility. Welding was being done on some equipment created so much heat that it melted a nearby conveyor belt. This was not noticed right away, and it started to spread to the cardboard and plastic six-pack bindings. The first Saranac Thursday of the year was just getting underway when people started to notice smoke coming out of the building. The fire spread quickly but was confined to that building. The firefighters fought the fire for over fifteen hours before it was declared under control. The roof of the building collapsed onto the third floor, and firefighters spent the next day drowning stubborn hot spots. The fire destroyed the brewery's bottling and packaging operations and storage area. Damages were estimated at $10 million. The company was well insured and planned to invest back into the brewery to make it better. Bottling was resumed on June 30 on the first floor of the burnt building. The High Falls Brewing Company in Rochester was chosen to can for the F.X. Matt Brewing Company beginning on June 23. The brewery received several tax breaks to help it in the recovery process.

Saranac Pale Ale won an international award in 2008 at the World Beer Cup. The brewery purchased the Flying Bison Brewing Company in Buffalo, New York, in 2010. The Flying Bison Brewing was incorporated in 1995 and opened in 2000. The brewery ran into financial troubles in 2009 due to the rising cost of ingredients. The F.X. Matt Brewing Company stepped in and offered to buy the Flying Bison. The agreement allowed the Flying Bison to continue operating as usual while producing small batches of beer for Matt's. The F.X. Matt Brewing Company is looking at relocating the Flying Bison brewery somewhere else in Buffalo to allow for a doubling of its output.

By 2011, the success of Matt products made the brewery the sixth-largest craft brewer in the United States based on beer sales volume. In 2012, the brewery launched one of the first white IPAs on the market.

A two-barrel pilot brewing facility was installed at the brewery in February 2013. It will be used for innovation and testing of new and unique flavors. In June 2013, the brewery used its pilot brewery to create a classic-style Saison with a twist for the NYC Savor event. Joining in the creation of the brew were brewers from the Brooklyn Brewery and the Brewery Ommegang. The brewers used North American two-row barley and a touch of wheat malt. The beer was hopped with German Hallertau Blanc, Mandarina Bavaria and Huel Melon hops. The Hallertau hops have a distinctive aroma with notes of passionfruit, gooseberry and pineapple. The Mandarina hops have a citrus character with notes of tangerine and mandarin orange. The Huel hops have a honeydew melon aroma with nuances of strawberry. These hops were chosen to complement the Traminette grape juice that was added during fermentation. This brew was named Tramonay Vineyard Saison and has 7.4 percent alcohol by volume. Having a small pilot brewery has allowed the brewery to experiment with unique ingredients not normally used in making beer.

The year 2013 represents the 125th anniversary of the brewery. It has changed its packaging, the first of which came out in April, to indicate the anniversary. A free sixteen-ounce can of Saranac Legacy IPA was placed in twelve-packs of Saranac bottles as a thank you to customers for their support over the year. The brewery had recently discovered an original IPA recipe created by F.X. Matt in 1914. This recipe was used to produce the Legacy IPA, allowing for changes in the brewing process since 1914.

In July, Saranac Pale Ale and Saranac Adirondack Lager were both awarded a gold medal at the United States Open Beer Championships. Judges came from Canada, England and the United States and evaluated more than 2,500 beers from around the world. Saranac Pale Ale won in the English Pale Ale category and Adirondack Lager won in the Marzen/Oktoberfest category.

Also in 2013, the brewery installed an anaerobic digester system, which pumps wastewater created throughout the brewing process into five thirty-two-foot-diameter digester tanks. This produces methane gas that powers the brewery generators. The system supplies about 40 percent of the brewery's energy needs and sends cleaner water to the sewer systems. The project cost around $5 million. The brewery is being helped financially in this endeavor by the New York State Energy Research and Development Authority (NYSERDA) and National Grid. Previously, when the various tanks in the brewery were cleaned, yeast, wort, beer residue and other solids ended up in the Oneida County Water Pollution Control Plant. This wastewater now goes into an onsite 200,000-gallon equalization tank. This tank normalizes the flow of the wastewater before it enters the 40,000-gallon digester units. The organics in the tanks are then treated by a mixture of anaerobic bacteria, including acidogenic and methanogenic organisms, which create a biogas composed of methane and carbon dioxide. The net effect from all of this is to clean up 80 percent of the brewery's wastewater. The brewery uses an average of 150,000 gallons of water per day, so this will take a big load off the municipal sewer system.

The digesters should be producing enough gas to run the four-hundred-kilowatt generator at full capacity. After that, enough excess energy will be produced to run 35 to 40 percent of the electrical operations at the brewery. The F.X. Matt Brewing Company has a history of recycling. It recaptures the carbon dioxide created when beer is made and reuses it in making soft drinks and in processing beer. It recycles 98.4 percent of all components used in its production and packaging, and it sells 100 percent of its spent grains to local farmers as feed.

Coming from a career at Procter & Gamble, Nick O. Matt's son, Nick R. Matt, joined the brewery in 2013 to manage branding and marketing. The brewery installed an exclusive new hop infusion process in 2013. This process maximizes the hop-to-beer exposure, which creates a fresher hop taste and a brighter hop aroma. This is just another example of the brewery's management dedication to investing back into the brewery to help produce a great product.

At the 2013 Great American Beer Festival held in Colorado, the brewery joined forces with home brewer Carl Woodward of Panther Lake, New York, who took home the Best in Show at the 2013 New York State Fair Home Brewer's competition. The brewery worked with Woodward to develop his Gose recipe into an exceptional entry in the ProAm competition. This entry was a German-style sour ale with 7.3 percent alcohol by volume. The brewery also submitted nine other entries for consideration. Unfortunately, it did not bring back any awards at this event in 2013, but the F.X. Matt Brewing Company has participated in this event since 1982 and has won numerous awards over the years.

New York governor Andrew Cuomo presented F.X. Matt Brewing Company chairman and CEO Nick Matt with the Pioneer in Industry Award for his leadership in growing the craft beer industry at a special Oktoberfest celebration at the Brooklyn Brewery on October 3. This was the first award of this kind. The goal of this event was to educate and engage buyers from the hospitality and tourism industries on the quality, diversity and accessibility of craft beer from New York State.

The brewery receives much of its supplies on the New York, Susquehanna and Western Railway, which runs down the center of Schuyler Street. The railway delivers covered hoppers of grains and gondolas for carrying glass for recycling. Insulated boxcars are used to carry the finish product to destinations around the country.

At this writing, the craft brewing industry is growing at a rate of 15 percent per year. The Matt brewery plans to stay ahead of this trend and is making plans to increase capacity. Currently, it brews about twenty times per week and is having trouble finding empty tanks in which to store the beer. It needs more space to ferment and age its beer and plans to add four to six tanks, each holding from 1,000 to 1,500 barrels of beer. Eventually, this expansion will force the brewery to add a second shift in the bottling department, which would add ten to fifteen jobs.

As plans stand at this writing, the brewery owns a building on Varick Street that currently houses a barbershop and also serves as the shipping facility for the gift shop. This building will be torn down and replaced by a new building that will house the new fermenting and ageing tanks. This area is the closest to the brew house of any available areas. The brewery has also purchased most of the properties located on the east side of Edwards Street across from the brewery's offices. These properties will be turned into a parking lot, which will give more parking for the brewery's offices and other neighboring businesses. Fencing will be added around the new addition, which will improve the appearance of the whole area. Fencing was added in 2013 to the new areas around the anaerobic digesters. The brewery plans to start the construction in the spring of 2014. The brewery bought all the property between the digesters and the main plant. This area will be made into a beer garden with trees, tables and terraces. This should be completed by the middle of 2014 and will expand the area used by the brewery for its Saranac Thursday events during the summer. First, a small building with benches and a green space will be constructed next to the anaerobic digesters. Then a deck will be connected to the tavern. Chris Talgo, owner of Nail Creek Pub and Brewery, believes that the expansion will boost his and will improve the looks of the entire Varick Street area. This will bring more people to this area for dining and various other events.

For these new projects, the brewery is seeking $100,000 in Excelsior tax credits and $90,000 in grants through the Market NY program for the estimated $395,000 project. The brewery was one of seventy-seven companies submitting projects for the Mohawk Valley Regional Economic Development Council to review. Those that will receive funds will be notified in December 2013.

The F.X. Matt Brewery is ranked as the eighth-largest craft brewing company in the United States based on volume. Over its history, the brewery has managed to change and modernize on a regular basis while producing quality brews that the public wants. Hopefully the brewery will continue to prosper, and we will be able to enjoy its products for many years to come.

# CHAPTER 24
# NAIL CREEK PUB AND BREWERY
## 2008–PRESENT

In 2003, Chris and Tracey Talgo bought an old apartment building on 720 Varick Street from the city of Utica. This building was located about one block from the Matt brewery. The building had been vacant since the early 1990s and was scheduled for demolition. They planned to open a pub and start brewing craft beer. Chris Talgo had traveled extensively while studying abroad and spent much time in the local pubs. It was from these travels that the idea for the Nail Creek Pub first emerged. Chris wanted to recreate an atmosphere where his customers could always feel comfortable.

The first thing they did was to put a new roof on the building, since you could see the sky from the basement when they bought it. They concentrated on fixing up the second floor so that they would have a place to live while renovating the rest of the building. Neither of them made much money, so the second-floor renovations happened little by little. After three years, approximately 95 percent of the second floor was complete. Chris then took a year off to write a business plan and obtain financing. During this time, Chris and Tracey worked at coming up with a name for their new place. Nail Creek once ran to the west of the Matt brewery but was eventually engineered to flow underground. Upon hearing about this creek, the Talgos thought it would make a great name for their establishment. Thus the Nail Creek Pub and Brewery was born.

The downstairs needed to be completely gutted. Chris and one of his friends spent much time gutting the interior. With the financing in place, he was able to hire contractors to start on the remaining work. The first thing

Nail Creek Brewery poster. *Author's collection.*

they did was to connect the barn in back to the house itself. This area was to be used for a game room, kitchen, brewery and office.

The first floor had a structural support wall right down the middle of the building that needed to be removed to open up the space. Talgo was able to integrate the wall into the bar design. The columns that appear to hold up the soffit above the bar are actually holding up the entire building.

They installed tile floors in the bathrooms, kitchen and bar. The rest of the floor was covered in cherry wood. Talgo used an old version of AutoCad to design the bar. A neighbor named Peanut offered to build the bar and do any other woodwork that needed to be done. The top of the bar was made of C-grade oak and covered with boat polyethelene.

The final step was to rebuild the porch, which was in bad shape. This was changed sometime later to increase the deck size and add an awning. The inspectors came out and passed the building, and that same day, their liquor license arrived.

Nail Creek Brewery coaster from the 2010s. *Author's collection.*

They opened the pub in 2008. At first, Chris could only afford four kegs and a couple bottles of liquor, but he was finally opened for business. The first beer that was served in the new pub was Utica Club Beer. He made it his goal to serve a wide range of different beers (eventually over 150).

Chris also had planned to open a brewery at the pub and figured that he could get it up and running in a couple months. He quickly discovered that this goal was way too ambitious. Chris Kogut, a veteran home brewer, passed by one day and saw the sign advertising that a brewery was opening soon and stopped by to talk to Talgo. Kogut offered his twenty years of brewing expertise and brought over several of his brewing creations for Talgo to try. Talgo really liked them, and the two formed a partnership with both men involved in the brewing process.

After much work, the brewery was finally in place and the first brews were made. The system can produce up to nine barrels (eighteem kegs) per month. The brewery produces mainly Belgian-style beers, which can take anywhere from four months to one year to produce.

On November 25, 2011, Talgo and Kogut unveiled the first two brews that they created: Belgium Double and Breakfast Stout. Both offerings were well received by patrons, and word quickly spread about these new beers. Since then, the brewery has also produced Belgium Strong, Saison! and Saint Patrick's Nitro Stout. The partners have indicated that they have received only positive feedback from the community and from their next-door neighbor, the Matt brewery.

# BIBLIOGRAPHY

## City Directories

*Boyd's Business Directory*
*Boyd's Rome Directory*
*Herkimer County Directory*
*Kimball's Oneida County Directory*
*Oneida County Gazetteer*
*Utica City Directory*

## Books

McKinney, James P. *The Mercantile and Manufacturing Progress of the City of Utica NY 1888*. Utica, NY: L.C. Childs & Sons, 1888.

Siebel, Dr. J.E. *One Hundred Years of Brewing*. Supplement to the *Western Brewer*. Chicago: H.S. Rich, 1903. Reprint, New York: Arno Press, 1974.

Walsh, John J. *Frontier Outpost to Modern City: A History of Utica 1784–1920*. Utica, NY: Dodge Graphics Press, Inc., 1982.

## Newspapers

*Amsterdam Evening Recorder*. 1884 to 1974.
*Binghamton Broome Republican*. 1828 to 1909.
*Binghamton Press*. 1904 to 1969.
*Hudson Evening Register*. 1867 to 1944.
*Little Falls Evening Times*. 1886 to 1960.
*Oswego Palladium Semi Weekly*. 1832 to 1989.
*Rome Daily Sentinel*. 1842 to 1920.
*Rome Semi-Weekly Citizen*. 1878 to 1903.
*Schenectady Gazette*. 1911 to 1970.
*Syracuse Daily Courier*. 1856 to 1898.
*Syracuse Daily Journal*. 1853 to 1882.
*Syracuse Evening Herald*. 1877 to 1897.
*Syracuse Evening Telegram*. 1898 to 1922.
*Syracuse Post Standard*. 1900 to 1921.
*Utica Daily Observer*. 1861 to 1882.
*Utica Daily Press*. 1882 to 1987.
*Utica Daily Union*. 1895 to 1897.
*Utica Herald Dispatch*. 1899 to 1921.
*Utica Morning Herald*. 1860 to 1897.
*Utica Morning Telegram*. 1919 to 1922.
*Utica Observer Dispatch*. 1925 to 2013.
*Utica Saturday Globe*. 1899 to 1919.
*Utica Sentinel*. 1825 to 1827.
*Utica Sunday Journal*. 1894 to 1902.
*Utica Sunday Tribune*. 1880 to 1910.
*Utica Weekly Herald*. 1863 to 1897.
*Waterville Times and Hop Reporter*. 1855 to 2007.

## Periodicals

*The American Brewers' Review*. 1907 through 1910.
*Beverage Industry*. November 1994.
*Brewers Digest*. 1952 through 1975.
*Brewers Journal*. 1933 through 1958.
*Capital District*. July/August 1985.

*Day & Night.* June/July 1981.
*New York Alive.* July/August 1983.
*Tap into Brew.* 1999 through 2001.
*The Upstate.* December 1942/January 1943.
*Utica Club Minutes.* 1961 through 1969.
*The Western Brewer.* 1898 through 1918.
*What's Brewing.* 1971 through 1988.

## INTERNET SOURCES

Old Fulton, New York Post Cards. Tom Tryinski. www.fultonhistory.com.
F.X. Matt Brewing Company. www.saranac.com.

# INDEX

## V



## W

# ABOUT THE AUTHOR

In college, Dan started collecting beer cans, which he used as piggy banks to store excess pennies. In his junior year (1972), he saw an article in a national magazine about a club that was formed for people who wanted to collect beer cans. He was amazed that other people collected beer cans. He joined the Beer Can Collectors of America (BCCA), and over the next forty-one years, he collected over thirty thousand different beer cans from over fifty different countries. Over those years, he also picked up other items dealing with various local breweries like bottles, signs, trays and tap knobs. From this, he became interested in local brewery history.

After college, he started working at Remington Arms Co., Inc. as an industrial engineer, a career that lasted until he decided it was time to retire in 2009. In the early 1990s, he became interested in writing a history book about local Utica breweries. The only time he had to do research was on weekends, and even this time was not always available. He started spending many hours at the Utica library going through microfilm of old newspapers one day at a time. This was a rather tedious task but needed to be done because he did not know when anything happened. He also spent much time at the local historical societies, which helped with his research.

Retirement gave him the time needed to finish the research to complete this book. This research has given the author a great appreciation for how rich the history of this area is. Future plans include other books on central New York breweries.